Young Man
from the Provinces

Young Man from the Provinces

A Gay Life before Stonewall

Alan Helms

University of Minnesota Press
Minneapolis • London

Excerpt from "Let's Get Together" by Chet Powers used by permission of Irving Music, Inc. Copyright 1963, renewed 1991, Irving Music, Inc. All rights reserved. International copyright secured.

Excerpt from "It Had to Be You" used by permission of Bantam Music and Gilbert Keyes Music Company. Words by Gus Kahn; music by Isham Jones.

The line from "Black Mountain" by Marge Piercy from *Available Light* that appears on the dedication page is reprinted with permission of Marge Piercy and Alfred A. Knopf, Inc. Copyright 1988 by Marge Piercy.

First University of Minnesota Press edition, 2003

Published by the University of Minnesota Press
111 Third Avenue South, Suite 290
Minneapolis, MN 55401-2520
http://www.upress.umn.edu

Library of Congress Cataloging-in-Publication Data

Helms, Alan.
    Young man from the provinces : a gay life before Stonewall / Alan Helms.—
1st University of Minnesota Press ed.
        p.   cm.
    Originally published: Faber and Faber, c1995.
    ISBN 0-8166-4268-0 (pbk.)
    1. Helms, Alan.   2. Gay men—New York (State)—New York—Biography.
3. Male models—New York (State)—New York—Biography.   4. Actors—
New York (State)—New York—Biography.   5. Gay communities—New
York (State)—New York—History—20th century.   I. Title.
    HQ75.8.H44A3 2003
    305.38'9664—dc21
                                                                    2002045402

Printed in the United States of America on acid-free paper

The University of Minnesota is an equal-opportunity educator and employer.

12 11 10 09 08 07 06 05 04 03   10 9 8 7 6 5 4 3 2 1

FOR

Lillian Helms
Luchino Visconti
Ira Barmak

"Memory is the simplest form of prayer"

—*Marge Piercy*

ACKNOWLEDGMENTS

I've changed a few names in this book to disguise the identities of men who, for various reasons, choose to hide their homosexuality. On the one hand, it's clearly the end of the twentieth century; on the other, it just as clearly isn't.

My heartfelt thanks to the following people for being generous with their help and encouragement: Deborah Barr, Bob Bent, Sara Bershtel, Vishaka Desai, David Eberly, Arthur Lambert, John Mitzel, John O'Brien, Howard Siegelman, and my persistent agent, Charlotte Sheedy. Valerie Cimino has been an exemplary editor, the eye in my storm. They say that gratitude is a short-lived feeling, but I'll remember mine for two special friends: Gordon Rogoff, who persuaded me the book was worth writing and then took time from the busiest life I've ever known to help me launch it; and Beth Hadas, who gave me my title, offered me unfailingly good advice, and cheered me on from first to last.

WHO IS NOW READING THIS?

May-be one is now reading this who knows some
    wrong-doing of my past life,
Or may-be a stranger is reading this who has secretly
    loved me.
Or may-be one who meets all my grand assumptions
    and egotisms with derision,
Or may-be one who is puzzled at me.

As if I were not puzzled at myself!
Or as if I never deride myself! (O conscience-struck!
    O self-convicted!)
Or as if I do not secretly love strangers! (O tenderly,
    a long time, and never avow it;)
Or as if I did not see, perfectly well, interior in
    myself, the stuff of wrong-doing,
Or as if it could cease transpiring from me until it
    must cease.

WALT WHITMAN
"Calamus" 16

PROLOGUE

Why would an anonymous man bother to write a memoir?

One way to explain is by saying that I grew up in an alcoholic home, which may be why the older I get, the less I seem to understand. In any case, people like me tend to have a lot of confusion in their heads, & this book is an attempt to unravel that confusion.

If it were only that, however, I wouldn't presume on your time. I also wanted to try to explain how that childhood fed into an especially glamorous life I lived in the gay worlds of New York & Europe from the late 1950s through the early 1970s—a dozen years of dinners with dukes, affairs with movie stars, things like that. I've occasionally begun someone else's book thinking "At last, a version of the life I lived when I was a golden boyman thirty years ago," but the book always went off in a different direction, so I've still never read a first-hand account of the life I myself once lived. Many have urged me to write of that life, thinking (I think) that it was some kind of picaresque adventure with the rich & famous. It was that, certainly, but it was much more besides.

My years of self-absorption as a gay celebrity went on in a world that's not only vanished; it's a world whose historians have been dying untimely deaths before they could tell their own stories of those times & places. Thus another reason for this book—to record my version for what it's worth. It would be wrong, however, to think of this book as a chapter of social & cultural history; it's more like a memoir containing some of the social & cultural history others might have written if they hadn't died of AIDS.

Finally, I suppose the heart of the matter is that I wanted to make a story out of my life, having felt for so long that it's composed of parts that fit poorly if at all. I hope I'm not guilty of more than the usual vanity, since we all spend a lot of time constructing narratives of our lives, stories we keep revising as we grow older—minimizing one episode, granting another its due, finding or creating the missing links that hold the disparate parts together in a fashion that makes sense for the present & tells us who we are. It's never given to us to finish our own stories, but there comes a time when they stand forth in enough relief to bear telling, even though they always lack certain cohesions & continuities.

So if you like, you can think of this book as one man's discovery that, having found his way to his late fifties & some self-acceptance & contentment, he's finally able to tell his strange story—a cautionary tale with a hopeful ending. We have few gifts of importance to give one another: our love & acceptance, our forgiveness, the stories of our lives. Learning to listen to other people's stories may be one of the few things that can help us survive these intolerant times.

Part One

· 1 ·

If in childhood I'd been only praised & told I was the best thing since zippers, I'd have grown up, encountered reality, become disappointed, & eventually recovered. If I'd been only abused & humiliated, I'd have grown up, been scarred for life, & probably killed myself. Since I got both, I got confused.

But that understanding is thanks to hindsight, & anyway confusion was endemic in my family, so let me begin with Mom, an illegitimate child born in Indianapolis in 1913. Her father visited her once in the hospital, sent Bernita, the mother, a check for five hundred dollars (a small fortune in those days), & moved to San Francisco where he was never heard from again, though he continued to live vividly in Mom's imagination. "He became a lawyer," she often told me. "I meant to have you look him up when you were out there, but I forgot, darn it. George Krebs—is that Jewish? They said he was Jewish & that was why him & Bernita didn't marry, but I don't know. I would've given anything to meet him. I always wanted to ask Bernita about him, but I was afraid she'd have killed me."

She well might have, for Bernita Gakstetter had a temper that could turn homicidal in an instant—like the morning her own mother walked in on her as she was climbing into her corset & saw that Bernita was seven months pregnant. "She laced herself real tight so no one would know, see, but that morning Grandma walked in before she got dressed. Well, Bernita got so mad she threw an iron at Grandma's head. She'd have killed her if she'd hit her."

Mom relishes these fragments of family mythology, but she tells them as if she's talking of someone else, & for good reason. "Grandpa wouldn't even look at me at first, but then he got so he was crazy about me." Not so Bernita, who a few months later sold Mom for ten dollars to a black

3

couple she knew from work. Mom's grandmother found out her where-abouts & bought her back, cash & carry.

Mom was installed in the Gakstetters' apartment one flight up from their shoe repair shop, & Bernita's brothers & sisters took care of her so Bernita could continue at her printing company job. Bernita was a "gath-erer," which meant that she sat at a revolving table assembling the pages of books as the table whirled past. Mindlessly absorbing work, & just right for a woman who, still young, already had a lot she didn't want to think about, none of which her parents would let her forget.

When Mom was three, Bernita married Earl Hunt, a man with a thick head of hair whom we called "Baldy," though I never knew why. Baldy was a pattern-maker who drank a lot & played the horses. I liked him for his risqué ways & mischievous humor, so I could never understand why he'd married the dour Bernita. People said she'd been a great beauty in her youth, in the wasp-waisted, pigeon-breasted fashion of the day, but by the time I got to know her she looked like a Mack truck upholstered in doilies.

"They fought something terrible, Bernita & Daddy did, sometimes with knives even. Boyohboy, *that* used to terrify me. One time they had an awful fight, Daddy locked Bernita out, & do you know she ran her hand through the glass to get back in—& then went after him with a butcher knife!" By the time Mom was ready for school, she must have been in a state of chronic shock, permanently scatterbrained—an espe-cially annoying form of confusion.

Since Bernita found every house she ever lived in too "grand" (mean-ing too expensive), she moved Mom & Baldy in & out of eight increas-ingly modest homes before Mom started high school—the only case I've ever known of planned downward mobility. By the time I was born in 1937, Bernita & Baldy were living in a converted garage just beyond the city limits—a dismal place without plumbing or indoor toilet or tele-phone or most other amenities of life. They got their water from a pump in the yard, their heat from a coke-burning stove, & their meals from cans. Bernita kept the garage obsessively tidy, even to the piles of ro-mance & crime magazines that were her only reading. Her only satisfac-tions were money & work, for they were sure things. It was feeling that frustrated Bernita, for feeling had led her to a man who'd sweet-talked her, made her pregnant, then abandoned her and her bastard. The first time in her adult life that Bernita had ventured into the world of feeling, she'd botched it, so she was careful never to venture there again. She was always one for the sure bet, the money in the bank—five hundred bucks

here, ten bucks there, it all added up to something she could count, &
count on.

Bernita was in fact such a miser that if stinginess were a religion, she
would have been a saint. Her favorite boast was that she'd never spent a
penny on a doctor or a dentist, & for years she locked Mom in a closet to
save money on a babysitter. She bought Mom one new dress a year (always on sale & often regardless of size), & put her to work at summer
jobs beginning at age seven.

"Did I ever tell you about my pet dog Babe?" Mom asked not long
ago. "Oh, how I loved that dog. She was a stray & a little bitty thing, but
she got out one night & mated with another dog, a big one I guess. When
it came time to give birth, she couldn't pass her pups. I heard her that
night whimpering out in the barn, & I begged them to take her to the vet.
Daddy was willing but Mom wouldn't hear of it. She hated spending
money on things like that. Next morning Babe was dead, & all the pups
too. It just tore my heart out. But you can't dwell on the past."

A good thing too, considering Mom's lacklove childhood, but Mom's
also ended up adopting a variation of Bernita's favorite remark. "Well,
now that's over," Bernita would observe with a sigh at the end of no matter what occasion—movie or spring cleaning, funeral or family picnic,
Christmas dinner or World War II: "Well, now that's over." It was Bernita's
motto, & it conveyed her sense that she'd maneuvered another step forward in the progress of a hazardous life. Or maybe she meant that nothing in itself was ever as remarkable to her as the fact that it always ended.
Bernita wasn't saying, except for "Thanks & goodbye" so she could get
home & go to bed in time to get up & go to work. Nothing but work &
more work & scrimp & save & stingy pleasures until that June morning
shortly after Baldy died when they found her in her front yard, flat on her
back in the uncut grass. "Well, now that's over."

It wasn't though, for a week later Mom called me in my dorm at
Columbia with the news that Bernita had left her almost a quarter of a
million dollars—a tidy sum in 1958, but not nearly enough to repair the
damage Bernita had done to Mom, & anyway it was the wrong currency.
Mom needed love, not money. While Mom was talking on the phone, I
could hear Bernita addressing her from the grave: "You always thought I
didn't love you? Well, there's a quarter of a million bucks: I guess that'll
show you!" She stands there in my memory, feet planted wide, hands on
hips & arms akimbo, while something mean & determined has its hand
in the small of her back & is pushing her forward against her will & better judgment, smackdab into life—a bitter business.

It's harder to tell you about Dad's childhood. We weren't close, & anyway Dad never talked about things of the heart. The men in my family talked about jobs & unions, politics & sports, but never about feelings. Midwestern German Protestants just . . . well, they just . . . don't. Thus, headaches & hemorrhoids, bad backs & bad dreams, & an especially vicious way with a quarrel. So the emotional texture of Dad's childhood is missing for me, but I can give you some facts & figures.

He too was a Hoosier, born in Indianapolis a week before World War I began. His father, Henry Helms, was a pattern-maker for the railroads; his mother, Beatrice or Bead, was the matriarch in his family, the major fact & figure of his childhood. Bead boasted a German baron for a paternal grandfather, & her father, Henry Albert von Sprekelsen, was a hugely impressive figure who cast a romantic aura over my childhood. Born in London in 1870, he was kidnapped by Gypsies when a year old & only rescued at the age of three. (Two whole years with Gypsies? What *happened*?) He ran away to sea at fourteen; by the age of twenty-one he'd sailed around the world eight times. Bead recalled him with more awe than affection, & she often wondered how he ended up in landlocked Indianapolis.

He prospered there as a contractor & architect, building some of the biggest buildings in a city renowned for its ugly architecture. Eventually rich & powerful, he counted among his closest friends a railroad lawyer named Charles Fairbanks, who later became Theodore Roosevelt's second vice-president. Imagine—for a child who saw his own life as unremittingly drab & dull to discover that he was descended from aristocracy via a man who hobnobbed with a vice-president of the United States! I studied my veins for signs of blue blood & thanked my lucky stars.

Bead sometimes mocked the pretensions of her upper-class background, but when she got dressed up in her furs & jewels & veiled hats & corsages, it was clear she cared about her glamorous past almost as much as I did. Marrying homely Henry Helms must have seemed a comedown, for Henry was so plain & self-effacing he sometimes didn't register. Bead wasn't one to complain though. "Are you keeping busy?" she always asked people in my family whenever they felt blue or out of sorts, "Are you sure?" Bead always kept busy. Even after the doctor told her she had a heart condition, she didn't slow down. "I should take it easy today," she'd say at 7:00 A.M.; then she'd wash all the woodwork in the house, cut the grass, & can twenty jars of Peach Delight before lunch; wallpaper the bathroom & head off to visit a sick friend & bowl in the afternoon; & after dinner, cut out a pattern for a new dress & work on her latest quilt. Her worst self-indictment was "I didn't earn my salt today."

I get the impression that Dad was a sensitive young man, at least in the beginning before he coarsened himself to suit America's benighted notions of masculinity. Bead saw to it that he & Mary Agnes (his older sister) took piano & singing lessons, & I can still can hear his beautiful, baritone renditions of "Oh Promise Me" & "The Old Rugged Cross" at weddings & funerals. At age ten or eleven, he talked Bead into drum lessons; soon after he was playing regularly in bands. "By the time I was twelve, I was making my own money for books & school supplies. Sometimes we made three dollars a dance, & a dollar an hour was big money in those days."

Unlike Mom, Dad did well in high school, skipping two grades & graduating at sixteen with a scholarship for college. Then the Great Depression hit, Henry was laid off, & like millions of other Americans, the Helmses were suddenly faced with losing their home. As they cast about for ways to survive, the bright promise of Dad's life began to fade—& thus the source of his confusion, his inability to figure out why life had borne him a grudge. He had to pass up his scholarship for a contracting job while Mary Agnes went to work at a downtown department store. Henry painted houses & did custom cabinetry, Bead worked in a clothing store & cleaned houses on weekends, & in her spare time she baked cakes & painted greeting cards. They cut each other's hair, Henry mended their shoes with worn belting he picked up on odd shop jobs, & each night after dinner they sewed beaded corsages & made parrots out of crepe paper stretched over wire frames that they sold to a local merchant for a quarter apiece. It was a time when people became distraught at losing a dime, elated at earning a dollar. "But no one complained," Dad says. "Most everybody was in the same boat, so people pitched in with a good will."

Partly no doubt because folks like the Helmses who were lucky enough to find work had faith that with scrupulous saving, they would pull through. None of the gnawing fears of permanent inflation in those days. Moreover, Bead had the kind of abiding religious belief that can make all the difference in hard times. For sixty-five years she taught Sunday school classes & women's groups at the Woodruff Place Baptist Church, & she performed what in fact if not name was a busy lay ministry. Members of the church came to her in their need & usually left consoled & fortified. Bead believed that hardships were God's way of testing the soul, & that things always worked out according to God's plan, &

that it was a waste of time fretting about the parts of God's plan that mortal minds couldn't fathom. So best get back down to work & stop worrying. She marched head-on into the parade of difficult days, spreading hope & cheer wherever she went.

A couple years into the Depression, Henry got a steady job as a pattern-maker with the New York Central Railroad in Elkhart, Indiana—up north by the Michigan border—two dollars a day, six days a week. It always amazes me to recall how hardworking the members of my family were, & none more so than Henry. Painfully shy, he was only comfortable on the job, or working in the yard or the garden, or in the shop he built as an addition to the garage where he used to disappear for weekends at a time—painting this, repairing that, making animal cutouts for yard decorations & toys for his grandchildren & Christmas candles & Easter crosses for the church. A meticulous worker who taught Dad the care of tools & the pleasures of manual craftsmanship, he was also a loving father & a henpecked husband who lost a lifetime of arguments to Bead, who hated to lose to anybody at anything. "Poor Henry," Bead would chuckle, as if Henry were a public joke. "Poor Henry," we laughed while Henry smiled at his shoes. "But he's the best man in the world," Bead always added, her sop to the vanquished. He was certainly one of the best but his virtues weren't showy, & I never got the sense Dad admired his father much.

I sometimes thought he hated his mother. Years later, after Henry died & Mom & Dad divorced, Dad went to live with Bead. Mom tells me that Bead sometimes showed up at family gatherings with ugly bruises on her face & arms, & Bead often hinted to me of dark goings-on. "But no one will ever know," she'd say, as if repeating a vow. I suppose I can understand some of Dad's resentment against Bead. So full of fundamentalist Bible wisdom & the success of her lay ministry, & imbued with the conviction that God was on her side, she could be judgmental & intolerant. She was a perfectionist too, & that's hell to live with. I can imagine that, from an early age, Dad must have harbored a deep longing to get in the car & drive away for good.

I, on the other hand, adored Bead, & she returned the compliment. As she explained to friend & stranger alike, I was her first grandchild, the spitting image of her illustrious father, & the best, the brightest, the most beautiful child God & Nature had ever produced. Finally, someone who understood me.

The biggest adventure of my childhood, starting at age four, was taking the train to Elkhart to visit Bead & Henry. Mom & Dad saw me off at Union Station in Indianapolis in the care of conductors who knew Henry & kept an eye on me throughout the trip. The trains had maroon horsehair seats, & if I sat bolt upright I could see through the window as the flat farmlands of Indiana rolled past. The trip took three hours, & we went through towns with strange, magical names: Kokomo, Peru, Gilead, Etna Green, Nappanee, Wakarusa . . . then pulling into the station in Elkhart, there were Bead & Henry on the platform waving me welcome.

They lived on a quiet, tree-lined street in a three-story house that was the grandest thing I'd ever seen: a screened-in front porch, bay windows on both sides, & a Mansard roof crowned by a weathervane rooster crowing over the tops of hundred-year-old elms. Flower beds in front & iron urns flanking the front steps, a big vegetable garden in back near the fish pond where in summer water lilies reared their lascivious heads. Inside the house, pots of amaryllis & African violets, two aquariums, piles of books & magazines & newspapers, a china closet full of crystal & silver, Henry's corner whatnots stacked with porcelain & ivory figurines, cedar chests full of lace tableclothes & embroidered linens—the house spoke to me of a world where all was abundant & generous, orderly & dependable, immense with possibility. Bead's gleeful laughter rang through the rooms as she went about her day cooking & cleaning, canning & crocheting, painting china & decorating the crosses & Christmas candles Henry made for the church. Hearty, big-boned women came to lunch: the Book Guild, the Bowling League, the Bridge Club, & members of the Eastern Star (Bead was a grand matron, whatever that was, but I knew it was extremely important). And now & then, in their confusion & grief, the friends from church.

Bead was my best friend, my surrogate parent, & my first teacher. In the big house in Elkhart, she taught me my ABCs & how to count in German. She read me stories from the Bible & a big picture book called *The Seven Wonders of the Ancient World*. She taught me the names of flowers & trees & birds, & how to recognize birds from their songs when we couldn't see them. She showed me how to take cuttings so they were sure to grow (you check with *The Farmer's Almanac*), & how to tell the distance of an approaching thunderstorm (seconds between lightning & thunder equal miles), & how to fix a new word in my memory (you write it down ten times without stopping). When she quilted at night, I got my first & best lessons in aesthetics. "This piece would be nice, don't you think? See how it picks up the color in the one beside it but makes a contrast in pattern? Yessiree, that'll do just fine."

In spring she took me into the woods around Elkhart to hunt for wild-flowers, & in autumn she called me into the yard at night to see shooting stars & the rare, magnificent northern lights. While we lingered, she named the constellations & told me their myths & how the heavens sometimes portended events on earth. She passed on to me her reverence for nature & her belief in the invisible powers that intervene in human affairs for good or ill, & she had notions of how to influence them—mostly through good behavior, prayer, & attendance at church, since the powers were somehow dimly related to the Baptist God.

And while she went about her busy day, she told me family stories that thrilled & filled me with wonder & pride. "He was quite grand, your great-grandfather was. Why, he owned his own flat-bottomed boat, didn't I ever tell you that? It held thirty-two people & he used it for outings on the water company canal. For special shindigs, he rented a railroad car & took his friends to Lebanon, where they'd have their lunch & all until they hooked up with a returning train. Oh, he knew everybody connected with the railroads & the banks, & the bishop used to come for dinner. Then when he retired to his farm down in Tennessee, he had railroad tracks laid up to the house so Vice-President Fairbanks could roll right up in our yard as big as you please." Thank God, thank God, I *really was special.*

Bead told me other stories as well: how after killing Abel, Cain fled to Africa where he sired the black race, & how Jews & especially Catholics would be sent to Hell at the Last Judgment, & how the Jehovah's Witnesses were really Satanists, which was why she chased them down the front walk with a broom whenever they came calling. Bead had seen flying saucers, & she knew from a book that the pyramids had been built with help from extraterrestials who raised the stones through sonic vibrations. It was depicted in the carvings in the tombs, along with the whole history of the human race, which included a disastrous prediction for our own times unless everybody woke up & started listening to God.

Bead got me listening to God. She explained that there were voices inside my head who knew what God wanted because He told them what to say, & she said I should listen to those voices very carefully whenever I was confused about anything at all.

Bead taught me to listen to those voices, & how to pray, & how to play bridge on Sunday nights when we gathered in the front parlor, the shades all drawn (good Baptists never played cards on Sunday), the radio tuned to Fred Allen, Henry sitting apart reading the paper. Or rather, she let me play at playing bridge, a game that consisted of our flinging the cards down until, the deck exhausted, she exclaimed "Hot diggedydam, you've done it again, you've won!" I was proud to be so good at bridge, for I knew it was an adult game & I wanted desperately to become an adult, to pass over my intolerable childhood & enter fullgrown into a world where I could get in the car & drive away for good. Bead encouraged me to feel adult. She took me with her wherever she went & showed me off to her friends ("He just learned 'perturbed,' didn't you, Albert Earl?"), & she instilled in me the belief that if I worked hard, did well in school, & said my prayers each night, I could revive the von Sprekelsen renown & maybe do other great things besides. I began to believe I could; I certainly wanted to, if only to please Bead.

"Hot diggedydam, you've done it again, you've won!" I couldn't lose with Bead. She gave me her undivided attention & unqualified love, she nourished my imagination, she explained how the world was put together, & she inspired in me a belief in the existence of beauty, justice, & truth. The beauty was mostly nature's, & it lay miraculous & inexhaustible all about us; the justice & truth were God's, & they issued alternately from Bead & the pulpit of the Woodruff Place Baptist Church. The truth & the justice were deeply biased, of course, but I didn't know that at the time, & anyway I needed something to ground me more firmly than the shakey home on Cruft Street.

My home always confused me because of the turmoil that went on inside it, & my relations confused me too: Bead & Henry didn't fit together right, while Bead & Bernita were a worse mismatch. And why were some of my cousins in mental institutions & prisons? As for Bead's ancestral glamor, where had it gone? How come some of my forebears had lived in a castle attended by servants while Mom & Dad & I lived such a meager kind of life? The family snapshots I perused in search of clues to unravel my confusions just confused me more. Here, for example, are Mom & Dad in their wedding picture, Dad looking illegally young & handsome, Mom elegant & darkly beautiful. They're twenty & twenty-one respectively, & by then they must have both been desperate to get away from home—Mom from cruel, unloving Bernita & Dad from strict, self-righteous Bead. Romance has shown them a way out. They look straight into the camera, two young people with open, trusting faces. They're setting out on their own at last & a hopeful future shines in their eyes.

And here they are again, standing in front of Bead & Henry's Indianapolis home in a picture taken a year later. Mom's clutching Dad's arm while his other arm searches for somewhere to rest. Dad's looking dapper in a bow tie & natty suspenders, his sleeves rolled up & his jacket tossed over his shoulders. Mom's wearing a hideous hat & she's buttoned up to the neck in a long wool coat. As if they're already living in different weathers.

And that's when I made my appearance, about the time Amelia Earhart started running out of gas.

· 2 ·

Let me say this straight out & as clearly as I can. There are many worse ways to grow up than the way I grew up, & many people reared in alcoholic homes have a much worse time of it than I did. But there's no competition in the world of suffering. Everyone runs the pain sweepstakes alone, & everyone in that race is a winner, which is to say a loser, which is enough confusion for anyone for a single lifetime.

We were poor, but poor wasn't degrading & hopeless in those days. One of my earliest memories of Mom has her at the kitchen table cutting coupons out of the newspaper, & she was constantly scheming to save a few pennies here & there. "Mame Buddenbaum always said she didn't know anybody who managed on as little as I did," she says with amazed pride. I remember one vacation with Mom & Dad & Bead & Henry—three days by car through the Smoky Mountains, Dad in a foul mood since he couldn't drink, & to this day I can't abide azaleas or rhododendrons. There was never any question of summer camp for me, & though it's now hard to believe, there wasn't even the extra dime I needed for admission to the swimming pool in the park nearby. We were the last people on our block to get a washing machine, so through most of grade school I came home on winter Mondays to find the house strung with wet laundry & Mom scrubbing clothes on a washboard in the kitchen sink. The last to get a TV too, & that miracle occurred only because Mom & Dad calculated that three years' savings from going without movies would pay for it. A bath was two pans of boiling water mixed with cold out of the tap, & most of my clothes were hand-me-downs, but I had toys & games, & a fifteen-volume set of *Childcraft* that I roamed in by the hour, & a musty encyclopedia with illustrations & maps, & free books from the lending library. We certainly weren't destitute, our neighbors were in the same boat, & anyway money isn't what matters most to children.

We lived in Bead & Henry's Indianapolis home at first; then around the time of my first birthday we moved to a five-room frame house in a working-class neighborhood on the south side of Indianapolis. Mom & Dad installed a coke-burning stove in the living room, wallpapered the living room & both bedrooms, put down a linoleum floor in the kitchen, & we were home.

From outside, the house always comes back to me as a face, its two front windows like hangdog eyes as if it were guilty or ashamed of what went on inside—all the yelling & screaming, the drunken violence & the beatings, Mom with bruises & black eyes & me with welts on my body from the razor strap (I'd vow not to scream no matter what, but he always beat me until I screamed), & everything in an uproar, an emotional chaos. I don't remember two consecutive days in that house without a quarrel or a violent fight between Mom & Dad. My earliest memory begins in my ears—the smack & thud of fist on flesh & Mom's rending pleas to Dad to stop. Then the sickening awareness that he wasn't going to stop, as if something inside him had taken over & wouldn't let him stop, & then the panic that sent me running to the neighbors to come quick & pull him off her. Those nights, Mom put me to bed & quieted my sobs with the assurance that "It won't happen again, I promise. Don't worry, don't cry, it'll never happen again." I believed her & hoped for that, & how fervently I prayed for it. But it always happened again, & then again, & then again & again until I came to hate the house on Cruft Street with the doleful face & the downcast eyes.

My earliest ambition was to become the richest man in the world so that I could buy all the taverns and burn them to the ground. My earliest dreams were recurrent nightmares. In one, sleeping alone in my parents' bed, I'm awakened by the sound of the window opening inch by slow inch. Through the window climbs a big black bear with an empty sack. He's staring at me with tiny, glittering, hateful eyes, & I know he's going to put me in the sack and take me away forever. I can save myself if I cry for help, for Mom & Dad will come rescue me, but I'm frozen with fear, & each time I try to call, nothing comes out but a strangled gasp of terror. In the other nightmare it's a holiday & the whole family is gathered in our living room after dinner. It's winter outside with snow on the ground, but inside everything is cozy & convivial. Suddenly I see a witch peering in at us through the window, then through the front door, then the window again, back & forth like that. I tell Mom & Dad but they laugh & shush me; there's nothing there, they say, I'm imagining things. But there *is* something there; it's real & I can see it, & it's intent on bringing us harm.

I saw right—we *were* threatened, by Dad's drinking & our own insane reactions to it. But to family & friends & the police who came in answer to the neighbors' calls, we always said everything was fine. The lie was a virus that spread through our lives, spawning other lies: he's all right, you're all right, we're all all right, everything's fine, now smile for the camera. Dad loved photography, & he made extra money taking pictures of weddings & graduations & Christmas card portraits & pinups of servicemen's wives during World War II. He took lots of pictures of us too—family portraits where we sit in a neat, catatonic row, our eyes dulled with sadness & laced with fear. What a sad, skittery lot we look in those old photographs as we try to smile for the camera.

There are other pictures in which the smiles look real, snapshots that show me with Mom & Dad being happy & affectionate together, but those are among the earliest pictures & I have no recollection of the times they record. Nor can I recall Mom's & Dad's smells, or Mom's pregnancies (Kent five years after me and Debbie eleven years after Kent), or what it felt like to be in the house of a birth, or any show of affection between Mom & Dad, any hugging or kissing or even holding of hands. For much of my life, the touch of another person, except in sex, was slightly repellent to me, like an invasion or violation of my body. Sometimes I scrubbed Mom's back in the bathtub while she held a washcloth to her breasts warning me not to look, or I scratched Dad's back through the sturdy cloth of his workshirts, but I felt no connection to their bodies, felt in fact uncomfortable touching them. Dad touched me mostly out of anger, Mom mostly out of a desire to compensate me for the bad times, & they touched impulsively & without warning. Whenever their hands came at me I flinched, & I learned early on to dodge & feint & run fast. I was there but I was gone; we were fine but we were awful; times were good but they were bad; they loved each other but they fought constantly; they loved me but I felt so lonely & somehow wrong & frightened that they couldn't have loved me in any way that mattered. Because of those happy photographs I know that my memory plays tricks on me, but the tricks sometimes tell, helping me sort through the lies.

When Dad was at work at the post office, things calmed down at home. Mom went about her housework while I did my chores or tended my gardens or sat on the front steps waiting for the Arabian prince on an elephant who would come & take me away. (Boy, would the neighbors be surprised when they found out who my father *really* was! And I wouldn't look back either.) During those weekdays, Mom's lusty alto rang through the house and into the yard as she sang "On The Road To Mandalay," holding onto the last note of each verse as if she were being paid by the second. Sometimes neighbor women dropped in for coffee & sat around the kitchen table gossiping & laughing, & I always found a pretext to play in the same room so I could be close to their happy voices. But however the day went, along about four o'clock the women dispersed & the singing stopped, Mom quickened her pace & became distracted, & a tension began mounting inside the house that was like a silent scream always asking the same frightened question: What will he be like when he gets home?

Sometimes he was in fine shape—good-humored & full of funny stories about the guys at work or the people on his parcel post route. Sometimes he was sullen & silent for reasons we could only guess at and knew to avoid. Sometimes he arrived home long after dinner had turned cold, so drunk that when he hit the back door he tripped over the step & passed out in his vomit. Sometimes he never came home at all, & we'd get a call from a stranger saying he'd been thrown out of a tavern & into jail, or from the police saying he'd been found passed out in his car on the side of a road somewhere. I came to prefer the nights he came home so drunk he passed out or the nights he didn't come home at all, for at least we had some peace & quiet then, though it was always laced with Mom's fretful worrying. Oddly, insanely I suppose, I came to prefer his bad moods, for his good moods gave me hope, but they were mercurial & could change to fury & violence in an instant. When he was drunk & in a bad mood, I knew what to expect.

So from mid-afternoon until 5:30 suppertime, the tension mounted in that house, climbing the walls in desperation, shrieking its silent scream. When we sat down to eat, we were always on edge. How I hated those suppers, for they were the only times when Mom & Dad couldn't avoid each other, even if they ate in silence with averted eyes.

When I was in grade school, Dad used to head off after Saturday night supper for the downtown YMCA where he was drummer & vocalist in "The Commanders," a dance band he owned with one of the guys from work. The Y dances were Dad's guaranteed night out every week, and after each gig he went out drinking with the guys in the band. Mom loved to dance more than anything else in the world, but Dad rarely invited her since her presence would have interfered with his drinking. Saturday night suppers thus had their own rending ritual.

Mom would begin, saying how much she'd love to go dancing, how long it had been since the last time, how she couldn't understand why Dad didn't invite her more often. "Sometimes it almost seems like you're ashamed of me." That was Dad's cue: Mom had gained weight, she didn't look good in her clothes any more, her clothes didn't look good, her hair was a mess. . . . Dad was bright & verbally deft & a master of the art of humiliation, so he always found ways to imply that he *was* ashamed of Mom, and that it was just as well she didn't know what the guys in the band said whenever she made one of her rare appearances.

She would be whimpering by now, he would threaten, she would start crying, he would yell or throw or break something or start to hit her, & then just as the kitchen began exploding, he was off to the dance looking handsome & dapper in his tuxedo while we sat back down to finish our supper: Mom weeping, Kent squalling in his high chair, & me wishing that Mr. Arabian prince would come soon because I didn't think I could stand much more.

I often awoke at three & four & five on summer Sunday mornings to the sound of the windows closing. Dad was finally home from the dance & raring for a fight; Mom was going through the house closing the windows so the neighbors wouldn't hear. I'd jump out of bed and run to get between them, to plead with them to stop, their hating words so tore me apart. But it never made any difference, except that sometimes I diverted Dad's attention so that—POW—a slap to the side of my head and—POW— a slap to the other side, my head snapping back & forth, Mom screaming "Not his head—please, Bud, oh dear God—*not his head!*" Mom would run for the neighbors while Dad chased me through the house to my closet where I held the door closed until he ripped it open & dragged me out & beat me until he was done with me, or until a look suddenly came over his face as if he'd just forgotten something, or remembered something difficult to understand. Then his eyes glazed over & he walked out of the room leaving behind Kent sitting up in bed screaming with fear & me sobbing, hating Dad, hating myself, hating life & God & the ground I walked on.

I never understood what was wrong, why Mom & Dad quarrelled & fought so much, or why Dad drank, or why we lived in such tension & sadness, or why there was never enough money, or why we laughed so little, or why we weren't like the other families on our block. I never understood why I felt such loneliness & such deep sadness. Surely the fault for these things was somehow mine, so I tried in every way I knew to make things better, fix things up, help us become a happy, loving family. I tried pleading with Mom & Dad to stop fighting, & they always promised but they never stopped. I tried in my prayers, asking God night after night to make Dad stop drinking, and for years I fell asleep confident that the next day things would be better, but they never were. I tried in my imagination by making vows that I would be a noble man when I grew up, and in my behavior by being the good boy I thought my parents wanted me to be, for that way they would be pleased with me & maybe *then* we would be happy, but my vows & good behavior never made any difference. I tried in kindergarten & then in grade school, doing my best & excelling other students, sure that my success would bring my parents pleasure & make them proud of me & happy we were together, but even those efforts, with real results, were like swimming against a riptide that kept pulling me out into a sea of sadness in which I feared I would drown. I turned to superstition & magic, avoiding cracks in the sidewalk with obsessive vigilance, reciting rhymed charms, making concoctions out of mud & grass & feathers & bones that I smeared under the front & back steps of our house while intoning a prayer that whoever crossed those thresholds would become instantly, permanently happy. I made a little cemetery beneath the lilac bush beside the garage where I buried every dead bird & turtle & mouse I could find, hopeful that the powers who watched over life & death would take note & reward me with a trans- formation in my family. But nothing ever woked, nothing ever changed. Everything always continued in the same sad, fearful, quarrelsome, vio- lent, tearful ways as before.

When I was four or five, Bead gave me a puzzle that showed a thatched cottage sheltered by an ancient oak, bright curtains at the windows, a stepping stone walk bordered by flowers, a Dutch door invitingly open. The puzzle looked like Hansel & Gretel's house, & it had a title— "Tranquillity." I worked it for weeks on end, confident that if I assem- bled the pieces in the right order, the completed puzzle would allow me to enter a world of love & peace & joy—a world of tranquillity. I worked that puzzle obsessively until the day I discovered a piece was missing, and then, after searching the house for hours like a crazed creature who re- turns time & again to look with growing desperation in the same empty places that he knows but can't admit are empty because of the remorse it would bring, I felt myself once again swept out into that cold, dark, infi- nite sea of sadness, certain I'd lost the only chance that remained to make things right, fix things up, discover the solution that would let us love each other and live a happy life together. And it was all my fault.

Surely if I'd tried harder, prayed more often, done better in school, been brighter or quicker or more clever or more tireless in my efforts to make things better, surely they would have gotten better. Surely the fault was somehow mine, the problem somehow me. Surely Mom's & Dad's sadness came from their disappointment in me, or perhaps it was God who was disappointed in me, or Mom & Dad & God too, all three of them found me wanting. So I worked harder in school & behaved better & prayed more often & longer & sought out more dead animals to bury in order to placate the powers that threatened my home. When I failed in any of these efforts—came in second in a spelling bee or misbehaved or forgot to pray or stepped on a crack in the sidewalk—my guilt showed me with a piercing clarity that, yes, the fault was mine, our failures as a family my own failed responsibility.

For years I lay in bed at night reviewing the events of the day & rehearsing the day to come, correcting lapses in my thoughts & actions to better prepare for the morrow, anticipating the coming day in its minutest details so I could be ready for whatever lay in wait, all the traps of a malevolent fate that was tireless in its ingenuity in making me fail. And when next day things didn't go according to the elaborate plan I'd rehearsed the night before & into the early hours of the morning, I was filled with rage & an inconsolable sense of loss & failure. I planned more carefully the next night, thought things through in greater detail, anticipated with greater caution, until I tossed & turned for hours & awoke the next morning exhausted, already sensing defeat in my fatigue, furious with myself for not being better prepared to resume my struggle with life.

Day by day, my sense of failure grew, & day by day, my sense of guilt, & slowly, day by day, the allure of self-punishment. What I saw of Christianity with its images of martyred saints & a bloody Christ showed me that suffering promised redemption. Maybe my sufferings weren't sufficient to make any difference to God. But I could suffer more, for I could learn to punish myself. I stood in the rain till I was soaked through & in the cold till I was numb. I pulled up my favorite flowers & left them to wither in the sun. I broke things, but only the things I loved, & refused things, but only the things I wanted. The voices told me what to do. And at night, when I asked in my prayers if I'd suffered enough, the voices said, "Almost, almost."

Yet surely this is exaggerated. I'm suspicious of the belief that I can somehow collect the shards of that past & assemble them into something not just coherent but true. After all, there are those early photographs, right?

Besides, I was often absent from my own life, regretfully mulling over the past or fearfully anticipating the future or escaping into a world of compensatory daydreams that alternated between heroic feats to save others & acts of homicidal rage. The present was often a blur, so maybe I didn't see it clearly. Maybe I'm not a good witness. Anyway, I survived, right?

I had Bead & my visits to Elkhart.

I had a host of invisible powers—genii & fairies & angels—bright familiars who whispered secrets & showed me things when no one was looking. They watched over & consoled me.

I had my imagination & I went there often, into a world of fortifying illusions in which I would grow up to be great or famous or powerful. Somehow or other, definitely great. My great-great-grandfather was a baron, & I had a small birth mark in the middle of my forehead like the caste mark of the chosen. I learned I had thirty-one teeth, a sure sign I represented a step upward on the evolutionary ladder. How could great things *not* come from a boy with thirty-one teeth? I would become the richest man in the world or president of the United States or the first man on the moon. I would make up for everything by becoming great. Alexander the Great . . . Frederick the Great . . . Albert Earl the Great. Failing all else, I would become a monk, but a great monk, a saint.

I had Susie—the absolutely-bar-none best dog in all of Indianapolis. "Heinz 57 varieties" we said when people asked her breed. Three dollars at the dog pound & the best bargain of my life. When Dad went for me, Susie went for him, though she learned to keep clear of the razor strap.

Thanks to Bead, I had the sense of a bountiful & nurturing Nature— the miracles of flowers & trees & birds & skies, snow & stars, bugs & butterflies, & a black locust tree down by Bean Creek that made a cave of bloom each spring where I crawled inside & looked out at the world through clusters of creamy, fragrant blossoms, feeling healed & whole, glad to be alive.

I had myself, & if Mr. Arabian prince didn't show up, well, I could learn how to raise myself with the help of Bead & other grownups. All I had to do was watch what they did & do the same. I practiced Mrs. Wallace's stern expressions in the bathroom mirror, & touched my napkin to the corners of my mouth the way Bead did at the end of a meal, & plucked the skin on my neck like Mrs. Teagarten. I learned some of Mom & Dad's expressions: "If you'd stop & think for a minute," "Why can't you realize," "Did it ever occur to you . . . ?" It worked. The photographs show a sobersided little adult by the age of six or seven.

I had the lies, & the lies helped enormously in their way.

Increasingly I had the voices. They were like companions who lived inside my head. They talked to me often, & when all else failed, they told me what to do. The voices were always dependably present.

And finally I had the growing conviction that even though I was wrong & guilty & unloved, I was also special, superior to all the other kids on the block. Bead said I was special, & Mom & Dad sometimes, & once I began school all my teachers said so. I got good grades & teachers favored me; therefore, I was special. More than special, the tests said: gifted; better than gifted, the voices said: unique. All the more reason then to assume that I could make the difference, solve the problem, find the missing piece of the puzzle. But no matter how hard I tried I couldn't, so my sense of inadequacy grew, & my sense of guilt, & my determination to punish myself still more, because no matter what anybody said, I wasn't special; I was a failure—incapable, insufficient, wrong, guilty, damned.

Yet surely Bead was right, & my teachers, & the recurring sense I had that no matter what, I really was extraordinary. But then why couldn't I make things right? A dozen times a week, back & forth, I conquered the world, it conquered me. It was all so profoundly, rendingly confusing: we're fine, we're weeping; he cares, he's leaving; we love you, go away. You're exceptional, gifted, your teachers say so & your tests prove it; you're destined for great things. There are no great things, only this waste of time, this fighting & screaming & running for the neighbors, & you can't be exceptional, no one can, you're nothing.

Whenever I blew the candles out on a birthday cake, I always made the same wish—to be granted three wishes. Let us be happy, let Mom & Dad love each other, grant me three more wishes. . . . Let us be happy, make Dad stop drinking, grant me three more wishes. . . . Let us be happy, make Mom stop crying, grant me three more wishes. . . . Let us be happy, stop all the screaming, grant me three more wishes. . . . Whole days at a stretch, whole nights tossing in bed.

"ShaZAM . . . SHAzum . . . SHAAA-ZAAM," I chanted standing in the rain ("Get in this house right this minute. What is the *matter* with you?"), inflecting the word as variously as possible, convinced that if I could discover the right pronunciation, I would be transformed into a Captain Marvel who could make things right. "Shuh-ZUM . . . SHIZum . . . Shuh-ZAM . . ." If only I could get it right.

Without any awareness that I was doing so, I began trying to absorb the tensions between Mom & Dad into my body, as if I might make them go away by taking them inside me. As suppertime approached each day, my body began to tense until, sitting down to eat, I was a mass of tics & twitches. ("What in the world is the *matter* with you?") When a tone of voice signalled the onset of a fight, I went to stand near them so I could perform my magical penance, feeling time & again like my skin was slowly turning inside out.

I got so I couldn't stand seeing anyone quarrel, even strangers, & always, always I *had to make it stop!* On an errand to the corner once, I saw a woman yelling at a drunk man who suddenly began hitting her. I ran between them, pleading for them to stop, then—ZAP! POW!—he turned on me. I hightailed it home & told Mom & Dad, who said I was wrong to do what I had done & I wasn't to do it again. But I had to fight hard not to, for I couldn't give up the belief that somehow or other I could make the difference, make the anger & violence stop & go away. I couldn't, but I couldn't stop trying, but every time I tried & failed I felt worse, but I couldn't stop trying.

I came to enjoy illness—its lure of lazy convalescence, its calm languors, the hovering ministrations. Aside from visits to Elkhart, the one unsullied week of my childhood was the time I had my tonsils out. Ooooh, that was nice: all that attention & ice cream & respite from the confusions of home & my abiding sense of responsibility for making things better between Mom & Dad. Like a vacation, illness was, & a consolation.

I won a chameleon at the State Fair when I was six or so. It mesmerized me; it was so mysteriously intricate & beautiful—living proof of Bead's contention that God revealed Himself in His creation. It was all of life given into my care, & I adored it. I lined its box with colored paper & fed it on flies & worms until one day it refused to eat. When I tried to coax it by pressing a fly against its mouth, it opened wide & bit my finger like quick scissors. The next instant it was dead, its jaws still holding tight to my finger.

I'd never known such sadness. It was dead & gigantic & I'd done it again—failed when it mattered most. Mom tried to solace me with talk of an animal heaven, but I was beyond consolation. And then began a process that grew into a habit that would persist for half a lifetime: remorse throughout that day, dwelling on the feeling as if unable to find my way out of it, & the same thing the next day, & then the next day, waking & thinking "I've forgotten something I need to remember. What is it?

Because I have to get it back." Then, "Oh yes, that horrible sadness . . ." Then reviving it & nursing it through another day, unable to let it go, as if it were something to be cherished, something that nourished me.

But again I come back to the troubling sense that there's something distorted or partial or just plain wrong here. Surely there were happy times & tranquil times, times when the promises were kept & the plans worked out. The old photographs keep telling me that. It couldn't have been as bad as I recall because, again, after all, I survived, right? I must simply have a distorted or a partial view.

Then let me put it this way: Yes, Mom & Dad loved me & I loved them. Yes, there were good times when we were able to relax & laugh & enjoy each other. But even during the good times, we were always waiting for the mood to change, the shoe to drop, the windows to close, the screaming to start, the sirens to come wailing up the street. Every time a door opened unexpectedly, I never knew whether it was love on a platter or violence foaming at the mouth. "Never a dull moment," Mom used to say.

One afternoon Mom was busy out in the garage, then returned to the house humming & looking smugly pleased. She winked at me, but she wouldn't say what she was up to, so I figured she had planned a surprise for me, ohboyohboy. When Dad got home he lingered in the garage, usually a sign he was having a swig or two. Suddenly he let loose with a bellow that carried for blocks, for it turned out that Mom had found his latest sequestered bottle of cheap wine, poured some out, peed in it until it was full again, then recorked the bottle & returned it to its hiding place. That one day alone, the booze took up from about four o'clock, when Mom hatched her plan, until past midnight, when Dad got in the car & drove away. The booze took up days, weekends, vacations, whole years of our lives.

Cinder paths, vacant lots, trash heaps, abandoned cars, tag-ends of rotting clotheslines, rusting cans & broken toys . . . sometimes even the earth looked soiled & tarnished. Sometimes even the time left over from the booze seemed exhausted & defeated.

Then one bright day I had school, starting with a storefront kindergarten down at the corner of Cruft & Shelby. Not so easy, let me tell you. You couldn't whisper to your neighbors during rest period, you had to keep strict time marching to the Golliwog's Cakewalk, & you had to draw a horse before anyone had explained the laws of perspective. The horse stumped me at first (what do you do with four legs & no perspective?), but once I put my thinking cap on I arrived at the solution: you draw it in profile to show two of its legs, then you make the other two sprout out of its back. That way, you get a gold star & your drawing goes up on the bulletin board.

Once I got the horse right, I *loved* kindergarten. It was a revelation for me—a kind of institutionalized Bead, all orderly & dependable & full of discovery & adventure. And like Bead, my teachers gave me the loving attention & praise that were in short supply at home. Starting with kindergarten, school became a consolation for home as well as an escape from it. Finally, everything was going to be all right.

On to P.S. Seventy-two. I was bright & quick, I worked hard for my teachers, & I thrived. I got the best grades & won the spelling bees & knew the answers to the hard questions & was soon reading beyond my level. My teachers extolled my virutes. I suppose it's therefore no surprise that the other guys in my class did what most normal American boys would do under the circumstances: they called me names & beat me up.

Mom & Dad gave me a pair of boxing gloves & Dad went about teaching me to defend myself. I dreaded being taught anything by Dad, for even when he wasn't drinking he was impatient & critical. Whatever it was—riding a bike, punting a football, shooting baskets—he explained succinctly & only once, then stood back & waited. I always failed the first time (why else did I need to be taught?), whereupon the inevitable yell of disappointment: "Not *that* way, dammit! Here, gimme that." But I had to learn to defend myself, so on with the lessons.

They didn't go well, for I hated violence of any sort, having seen a god's plenty by the time I was seven, & I never understood Dad's enthusiasm for boxing. The smack of fist on flesh was the ugliest sound I knew. And how you were supposed to think straight about jabs versus feints when some lunatic was coming at you determined to remove your head from your body was beyond me. I got through the lessons as best I could, though I wasn't what you'd call a natural talent.

The next time the guys attacked, I stood my ground. That gave me the advantage of a surprise lasting roughly point five seconds, whereupon I got beat up again. Dad had taught me the Art of Boxing; the second-grade bullies knew only the Mechanics of the Slugfest. In that little world where might made right, the bullies' verdict held: I was a brown-nosed teacher's pet.

"You're too sensitive," Mom & Dad told me when I complained about the kids at school, but Mom nevertheless invited my whole class home for a surprise birthday party, thinking (I think) that a party for my class-mates might blunt the edge of their dislike. One Friday after I'd lied yet again in Show & Tell, claiming that Henry's animal cutouts dotting our front yard were in fact live animals, my own personal menagerie, the whole class began tagging along as I set out for home. What in the world . . . ? "I wanna see the flamingo . . . I wanna hear the parrot talk . . . the monkey, the monkey, I'm gonna play with the monkey." My heart divided into two parts, one rising to my throat, the other sinking to my stomach. I must have bluffed my way through it somehow ("Did it ever occur to you I was just kidding?"), but it was a devastating humiliation. And Mom was confused & hurt that I didn't enjoy my party.

I was now a brown-nosed teacher's pet liar. A short time later, after Mrs. Wallace discovered I couldn't read the blackboard from the last row, I became a four-eyed brown-nosed, teacher's pet liar. Could things get any worse?

It turned out they could, for with a dawning sense of horror, I began to realize that I was the worst thing any American boy can be—I was (I can hardly bring myself to write the word) a *sissy*. "Why aren't you outside playing with the other boys?" Dad would ask, arriving home to find me reading or drawing in my bedroom or arranging the latest trophies in my butterfly collection. (Always the same litany of disparagement: "Why aren't you, why don't you, why can't you?") What was I supposed to say? "I'm not outside playing with the other boys because basically they frighten me since, being an abused child & growing up in this existential mess, I'm frightened of everything except Mom & Bead & nature & books & playing with girls, or better yet alone"? I just said "I dunno" & dutifully marched outside to join the gang in another edifying round of "Shoot the Birds" or "Torture the Cats."

I understood the real meaning to Dad's question, & to Mom & Dad's repeated observation that I was "too sensitive," & to the remarks I sometimes overheard to the effect that I was a "delicate" child. My parents had wanted a little boy; they'd wound up with a neurasthenic aesthete. "I know," Mom enthused, inventing another scheme for Dad & me to spend time together, "You can both go fishing this weekend! Won't that be fun!" We went fishing. I caught a sunfish that was a miracle of opalescent beauty. How could anyone kill such a thing? Couldn't I throw it back in the river? "Ya don't go fishing just to throw the goddam fish back in the water, fer chrissakes."

Yes, I did prefer playing with girls, for boys were loud & insensitive, unmoved by beauty & pain, rough & unimaginative. And I failed at so many things that mattered to boys. I couldn't dribble right or spit well or hack up a goober or belch loudly or produce one of those earsplitting whistles with two fingers in the mouth that carry for blocks. I was acutely embarrassed by such inadequacies, & I never felt wholly compensated by my ability to fart at will. With girls I didn't feel any sense of competition, & they were quieter & gentler & altogether more interesting than boys. Judy Delameter had shown me her private parts & Phyllis Cox had initiated me into the miracle of peanut butter on bananas. So what if girls couldn't dribble right or tell the difference between a Phillip's screwdriver & a jitney wrench? I couldn't either. And the girls' parts in the backyard musicals we put on for our parents were much more fun than the boys' parts. But most fun of all for me at that age was working in my gardens— my wildflower garden in the strip of shade between our house & the Clarkes', & my flower garden out back beside the garage. Now I ask you—a seven-year-old son for whom the acme of life's pleasures consists of coaxing a hybrid rose into bloom? Sorry, Dad.

But it was worse even than Dad or anybody else knew. Whenever Dad & Mom went away for a few hours & left me alone in the house, I dressed up in Mom's clothes in the closest I could come to Arab prince drag: scarves for turbans, lots of jewelry, a little makeup, you get the picture. I put a dab of rouge on the birthmark in the middle of my forehead, & staring at my transformation in the mirror, I kissed my reflection while murmuring the most exotic words I knew—"Cathay . . . Ali Baba . . . Samarkand . . . Scheherazade . . ."

So I was a four-eyed, brown-nosed, teacher's pet liar sissy of a particularly suspicious sort. My intelligence, which was supposed to have made everything all right, had become a liability with the kids at school. And things at home were worse than ever. Dad was drinking more & he & Mom were fighting more, & when their fights were violent, which was more often the case, they unhinged me for days at a time. Given what was by now my highly developed ability to nurse sadness & grievance, I was never over the last fight before the next one began. Now the sensation of drowning in sadness was almost always with me.

Meanwhile, World War II was dominating the life of the nation. We followed the war on the radio & in the newspapers & the newsreels, & it appeared prominently in my comic books, which now featured monocled German sadists & Japanese torturers with foot-long fingernails. Bead collected hundreds of dollars for the War Chest Drive, rolled bandages for the Red Cross, & went to Chicago every couple of months to give blood. Mom & I went once a week to a nearby school to redeem food stamps for meat & sugar, & I remember when pennies changed from copper to zinc & you couldn't get a decent rubber ball. The war even showed up on our supper table: "Not dried beef & gravy *again!*" Every now & then, the sight of a new gold star in a neighbor's window, & at night the burning candle, hushed us & brought the worst reality of the war to our street.

One April afternoon in Elkhart I was playing in the backyard when Mrs. Minix came out of her house & began hanging up her wash. Bead & Mrs. Minix hadn't spoken in years (some antediluvian quarrel about the property line), so imagine my astonishment when Bead came running out the door & across the yard where she fell weeping into Mrs. Minix's arms. "He's dead, Minnie. It just came over the radio. Roosevelt's dead." I knew that Roosevelt was the president of the United States, but I had no idea he was important enough to get Bead & Mrs. Minix speaking again after all those years.

A few weeks later, Aunt Ida & I were at the Garfield Cinema one Friday night watching Dan Dailey propose to Betty Grable when suddenly the screen went dark, the lights came on, & a voice over the PA said, "Ladies & Gentlemen, Germany has just surrendered." Instantly the crowd was on its feet, everyone shouting & cheering, all the sorrows & deprivations of those years suddenly released in a huge celebration of victory. People literally screamed with joy & some knelt in the aisles to pray. Then one by one we fell silent as the voice of Kate Smith came over the loudspeakers, & one by one we took up the song—"America the Beautiful"—until we were singing so loudly I thought the ceiling would come crashing down. When the song ended, the audience erupted all over again. The man beside me picked me up, hugged me, & passed me to someone in the next row; on & on, row after row, people hugged me & tossed me in the air as they wept & cheered.

At the Garfield Cinema a few months later, we watched in awed silence as a gigantic cloud shaped itself into a hideous bloom high above the earth, its stem seeming to suck the earth up into the sky. I couldn't comprehend it, or the figures of the dead whose numbers were greater than the population of Indianapolis, or the scenes of the devastation & the soundlessly weeping survivors moving slowly through the ruins.

With the end of the war, gasoline was no longer rationed, so we drove up to Elkhart now & then to visit Bead & Henry. I always wanted to go to Elkhart, but three hours each way in a confined space with Mom & Dad were unmitigated hell on wheels. I passed the time counting telephone poles & red-winged blackbirds & keeping on the lookout for Burma-Shave signs:

AT CROSSROADS DON'T
JUST TRUST TO LUCK—
THE OTHER CAR
MAY BE A TRUCK.

DON'T TAKE A CURVE
AT SIXTY PER—
WE HATE TO LOSE
A CUSTOMER.

The landscape of northern Indiana filled me with foreboding, it was so relentlessly flat & spare. It seemed to proclaim the vanity of human wishes, saying that life is hard & mean & unyielding, unlovely & without grace, & all those things forever. I could never find an echo of myself anywhere I looked. Now & then there were some Amish or Mennonite children playing at recess beside a one-room brick schoolhouse, the boys in black, the girls in gray dresses & bonnets. Here & there was a barn & a clump of trees, then a house where a light was turned on at dusk. It looked like the land could swallow you up if you ever had the misfortune to enter it. Every so often, we read in the newspaper of a woman who had been found somewhere in that part of the state chained to the foot of a bed by a Mennonite father still furious with her for having ridden in a car with a boyfriend twenty years before. She would be thirty-five or so & stark, raving mad. "I can do that to you," the landscape said. "Don't go in there," the voices said.

Back in Indianapolis, I spent whole days daydreaming of the time when I would leave home & enter the world where Einstein & Eleanor Roosevelt & Albert Schweitzer performed their noble deeds. The image of Schweitzer playing his homemade organ in the African jungle took up permanent residence in my imagination, accompanied by a procession of humanists & philanthropists who gave millions to found libraries & schools. One day I would join the company of such people; I too would become a "benefactor," doing good & making the world a better place.

Until then, I had no choice but to continue with my busy little life, which meant forays with Susie down to Bean Creek to catch minnows & crawdads, & afternoons roaming the fields with my butterfly net, & the backyard theatricals we put on for the delectation of our parents. Summer nights while the neighbors sat on their porches talking quietly, the lights out to save money on electricity, we tossed hats in the air for hours, trying to catch the bats that swooped around the street lamp. When the Second Church of Christ the Redeemer a few doors down had its week-long revival meeting, we stood across the street & watched through the open doors of the church while they went into loud trances in which they spoke glossolalia or what they called "tongue talk," their sign of salvation. On rainy days, Phyllis Cox & I racked our brains & then we cooked:

fried fish with molasses, mushrooms boiled in ice cream, pickles baked in orange juice. (Phyllis's mother caught us one afternoon & was about to make us eat what we'd just made until she discovered we'd stuffed the hamburgers with Ex-Lax.)

I played with my erector set, & built cardboard castles, & created an entire cardboard village (Elizabethan) in which all the roofs were marked with the names of famous books, & sold lemonade sweetened with saccharin from a jerrybuilt stand in front of the house that sported a sign saying "No Saccharin." One summer, Bead & Henry took me to Sault Ste. Marie up north on the Canadian border to see the locks. I was so intrigued to learn that "Sault" was pronounced "so" that when I returned home, I got a French grammar out of the library & spent the rest of the summer studying French. (Whatever possessed me? Who did I think I was going to talk to?)

Spring & summer, I worked in my gardens. In my wildflower garden I grew trillium & Dutchman's breeches, Solomon's seal & blue-eyed-Mary, woodland phlox & fringed gentian, wood geranium & touch-me-not. I even had a jack-in-the-pulpit!

In the back yard by the garage, a small plot of land with a syringa bush in the corner had served as our Victory Garden during World War II, but after the war I got to do with it as I pleased once I ceded room for a few rows of vegetables. In that little world maybe twelve feet square, I made a version of the garden in the "Tranquillity" puzzle. I laid a path of slate stepping stones that wound among beds of nasturtiums & columbine. In the shade of the syringa, I sank an aluminum pan that served for a fish pond. The ugly metal fence along the alley I disguised with blue morning glories & purple sweet peas. In the center of the garden, I placed a bird bath; surrounding it, yellow & cream-colored roses. (Not red, never red; red roses were ordinary, banal.) When the ragman jingled down the alley in his horsedrawn cart, I followed behind with a dust pan to collect the droppings for my roses. While the other kids were fishing down at Bean Creek or swimming at the pool in Garfield Park, I weeded & hoed, transplanted & pruned, fertilized & watered my garden. It was all perfectly clear, & one of the few verities of my life: I would be the George Washington Carver of my generation. ("Now his hero's a nigger.")

But if it was amazing what happened when you put seeds in the ground & watered them, it was beyond comprehension what grew out of books—the adventures of medieval knights & Saracens, the history of the Aztecs & the Incas, the lives of the Founding Fathers, the voyages of the Vikings, & the travels of Richard Halliburton in whose footsteps I would one day follow. There wasn't anything you couldn't get out of a book. It astonished me how many different kinds of people there were in the world & how many different ways they had invented to live their lives. Even the words on the page turned out to be little adventures. "The dictionary says that 'mantis' comes from a Greek word meaning prophet," Bead explained. "So then a praying mantis is a . . . ? A praying prophet, good for you!" I loved roaming in the dictionary & the encyclopedia (Were there really elephant graveyards & petrified forests? When would I get to see them?) & was thrilled by how things connected when you followed the words on the page. In a world that seemed constantly on the verge of falling apart, it was miraculous how the world of a book held together. Every two weeks I went off to the Garfield Library & returned home with the maximum eight books I was allowed to check out at my age. Eight books every two weeks from the ages of seven to fourteen equalled well over a thousand books in which wrongs were righted, patience paid off, & the good prevailed. I especially loved books about people who had overcome great odds in accomplishing extraordinary things. If Edmond Dantès could escape from the dungeon of the Château d'If, uncover the treasure of Monte Cristo, & plot his vast revenge, I could surely escape from 1214 Cruft Street. And just think: Pizarro, an ignorant swineherd, had conquered the Incan empire! It was all in a book.

"You shouldn't read unless your teachers tell you to, & that type's too small, you'll ruin your eyes." But praise the Lord, they let me read.

They also determined that I should have a hobby, something more substantial than my butterfly collection & my cardboard castles. It was a day & age in which people talked of the need for "inner resources" & the importance of the hobby in promoting the well-rounded person. The obvious hobby for me was photography since Dad had all the equipment & had turned the utility room into a darkroom. *Childcraft* promised that "Taking photographs is a hobby which you will find not only interesting but entertaining." Want to bet? Long weekend sessions cooped up with Dad while he developed & printed were even more boring for me than baseball, so I failed photography. Next, Mom & Dad bought me a secondhand upright piano & I began lessons with Mrs. Kilgore, a cheerful, blowsy matron who'd played for the silent movies. Mrs. Kilgore was especially adept at tremolo fortissimo, rendering everything from Bach to Chopin as if it had been composed to accompany a Mack Sennett chase scene. I practiced my scales, did my Czerny exercises, learned to sight-read, & before long I had a repertory of funeral marches that I banged out as loudly & lugubriously as possible.

Back at school, I began playing the piano for assemblies, and taking the leads in school plays, and getting pimples, and thinking I couldn't stand being unpopular any more. And Brylcream wasn't living up to its promise. The other kids said I was a nerd & a prissy, smartass teacher's pet. I was too. I'd have done anything for my teachers' approval, & did do all the obvious things like stay after school to clean the blackboards & erasers—an offer compounded of equal parts of desire to linger in the company of my teachers, fear of the bullies waiting in the alley, & reluctance to return home.

There *had* to be some way out of my life. If only I were popular . . . if only, if only . . .

Then Kent was nearly killed just after his fifth birthday. It was Thanksgiving, Bernita & Baldy had stopped by for a visit, & Baldy had sent me to the corner to buy a racing form. Whether because Kent liked to tag along or because Mom created as many occasions as possible for us to be together, there he was tagging along, another of my crosses.

I was looking in the windows of Klein's Dry Goods Store when from behind I suddenly heard screeching brakes & a dull thud. I turned to look, but there was nothing—no car, no Kent, nothing. Down by the light a woman screamed & that's when I saw him: lying in a heap, one leg twisted up under his back. Speeding to make the light, a driver had hit him so hard he'd been shot forward fifty feet before landing in the middle of the intersection.

I ran screaming all the way home, then I was back down at the corner with Mom and Dad where a crowd had gathered around his body. Kent was lying in a pool of blood now, his leg still hideously twisted. An ambulance came & Mom & Dad went with him to the hospital where the doctors expressed doubt that he would live.

A week later, however, he was brought home encased in plaster, & for the first time ever, calm reigned in our house. We spoke in whispers & turned the radio down & tiptoed whenever Kent was sleeping. I practiced the piano as softly as possible. And—praise the Lord—Mom & Dad didn't fight. I began to hope that maybe, just maybe, some lasting good might come from the fact that my brother had nearly been killed.

But Kent wasn't off the crutches before it began all over again—the screaming & fighting, night after night, until I thought I would lose my mind. After the pleasures of that month-long lull & the hope they'd inspired, Mom & Dad's fighting seemed worse than ever, & in fact the most horrible image I have of their failed marriage comes from that time.

Dad would knock Mom to the floor & stand over her with his arm raised, threatening to hit her again if she spoke. Mom would rise to her knees, then sink back down, shielding her head & choking back her sobs. An eerie silence would descend, punctuated by Mom's whimpering & Susie's growling. It was an image of the degradation of one person subjected to the tyranny of another, & whenever I recall it, as now, it still has the power to fill me with rage & sorrow.

"I hate you, I hate you," I screamed at him. "The day you die will be the happiest day of my life." Over & over again, day after day, screaming as loudly as I could.

In bed at night, I made plans to run away. A couple of times I packed a bag & made it a few miles from home, but I always chickened out—a four-eyed, brown-nosed, teacher's pet liar sissy coward.

I even began to feel anger at Mom. I'd always taken her side, & it was seeing her abused & humiliated that unhinged me the most. For years we'd plotted together: "Quick, Albert Earl—go get his license plate," she urged each time he drove off after a fight, so off I went running down the alley to read the numbers through my tears. (I was over forty before it occurred to me that she could have memorized the numbers or written them down to save me those sad sprints.) But I began to tire of the hope she kept inspiring in me that she would divorce Dad & *then* everything would be all right. Why wouldn't she divorce him? I knew it was shameful for a woman to divorce, & I understood that we'd have a hard life without Dad's salary, but I would *do* something. She always backed down. She was increasingly distracted & tired, gained more weight & gave up wearing makeup, wore housecoats to holiday dinners. She was increasingly defeated, & I didn't want to be allied to anyone who was defeated. How many times, I wondered, could she ask, beg, implore Dad not to belittle her, hit her, get in the car & drive away? Her capacity seemed endless. I sometimes think Mom's forty years with Dad were living proof of the Spanish proverb that says the three worst things in life are to lie in bed unable to sleep, to wait for someone who never comes, to try to give pleasure but fail.

For the first time in my life, Bead was no help. She & Henry had moved back to Indianapolis by now (1949), so she could see at close hand how awful things were on Cruft Street. But she just advised me to pray some more (like she was doing, she said), & she told me that in a few years I would be grown up & could begin a life of my own. A few *years*? Such a span of time stretched in my imagination beyond the boundaries of eternity. A few years was at least forever, and I needed help now. Didn't Bead understand? Didn't anyone understand that we were all trapped in that house with the despairing face & that there was no way for us to escape? *Wasn't anybody paying attention?*

Batman was listening, because every time those evil men tied me to a tree & threatened my life, he came in the nick of time to vanquish them & save me from a fate worse than death. Then he untied me, gently stroked my hair & caressed me, & that's when I came. Night after night, even though it would soon make me lose my mind.

"Stop that in there," they yelled from the living room—except for the night Dad walked in on me unannounced & walked to my bed & lifted the covers & said "Jeeeee-zuss Christ!" I'd been so taken by surprise that I'd not had time to remove the pencil from my ass, so I lay there on my stomach pretending to be asleep, pretending that sleeping with a pencil up my ass was the most natural thing in the world. He never mentioned it.

And then that Christmas, Mom & Dad gave me a present . . . a game set of some kind based on a comic book hero. There was a board, & some cards & dice, & there may have been a mask & a cape. It was fine for a child of five or six but I was twelve; twelve years old & invisible to my parents. For what seemed the millionth time, I was overwhelmed with the sensation of drowning in sadness.

"You're too sensitive," Mom & Dad told me yet again about I can't remember what, just the general mess & desperation of my life, I suppose. "Don't let things bother you so much." That actually sounded like good advice, but how could I do that? Where could I go to learn the lesson of How Not To Let Things Bother You So Much?

To the movies, as it turned out.

Before the TV made its ominous appearance, we went to the Garfield Cinema every Friday night. For fifty cents for adults & a quarter for children, you got to see two & sometimes three main features, two or three cartoons, a newsreel, six previews of coming attractions, & sometimes a travelog for good measure. When we staggered out around eleven at night after four or five hours of the silver screen, the world always looked badly lit & appallingly decorated, like the great scene designer in the sky had made a huge mistake. Back home, I became wholly absorbed by the characters in the movies I'd just seen, & I daydreamed for days on end, imagining myself as the strong, capable hero who was admired by everyone because he caught the crook or shot the Indians or rescued his friend from behind enemy lines. Just as often I identified with the woman, sometimes as strong & capable in her own way, more often a victim who

needed to be rescued. I especially liked characters who sacrificed themselves on behalf of a noble ideal.

One Friday night we saw *The Heiress* with Olivia de Havilland &
Montgomery Clift. If I'd known then that I would one day meet Montgomery Clift, perhaps that would have reconciled me to the long duress
that in the meantime was my life.

In any case, & in case you never saw the film, it takes place in
New York City circa 1870. The wallflower heiress to a large fortune
(de Havilland) is courted by a handsome fortune hunter (Clift) who con-
vinces her to elope, then abandons her at the appointed hour, having
learned her father will disinherit her if she marries him. Our heiress sobs
her way through the night, emerging the next day a disillusioned woman
who suddenly looks a lot less dowdy. When her father dies a short time
later, she refuses to attend his bedside, having realized that he loves her
no more than her false suitor. Ten years pass. Our heiress now lives a
largely reclusive life, which is a shame since by now she's quite beautiful
& very rich. Fortune hunter unexpectedly returns, ragged about the
edges & with a flimsy excuse for his actions that rainy night so long ago.
Can't they be friends? Can't they, now that he thinks of it, elope this very
night just as they planned to do all those years ago? She agrees, but we
see the glint of vengeance in her eyes. When suitor returns to collect her,
she tells her maid to bolt the door. "Can you be so cruel?" her pandering
aunt asks. "Yes, I can be very cruel," she replies. "I have been taught by
masters." She douses the lights. On the other side of the door suitor sees
them going out & panics. Carrying a single candle to light her way &
looking magnificent & irresistably beautiful, she climbs the stairs to the
accompaniment of suitor's frenzied knocking.

Boy was that movie ever up my alley: hateful father, innocence betrayed,
cruel abandonment, then the long, slow wait until one day—vengeance
triumphant! I was thrilled to see how, once she learned the trick, the
heiress was so cool & controlled in her feelings, & how she turned her
suffering into a work of art, emerging at the end as a radiantly beautiful,
wholly self-possessed woman. The heiress had clearly figured out How
Not To Let Things Bother You So Much.

I mulled the movie over for days & then I made a vow. I would never
again let my parents into the secret places of my mind & heart, never let
the sadness or pain of that home enter me, never again experience such
turbulent feelings. I would keep them out at all costs, would never, so far
as I was able, permit the humiliations & the violence to affect me. I
would feel nothing rather than risk those riptides of sadness & despair.

That was how I could stop the pain, & that would be my final vengeance on that home & that life. In my imagination I was saying to Mom & Dad, "I'll never let you get to me again. Whether you ignore me or beat me, from now on I'll be impervious to you. Moreover, I will become as different from you as possible, & my difference will be the sign of my repudiation of you & all you stand for." In reality I was vowing never again to show pain, or accept, or forgive, or give satisfaction, or feel deeply, or love. I would henceforth count on no one & nothing but myself. And so, on a hint from Hollywood & in flight from my pain & confusion, I buried my treasure & decimated the powers that people the city of the heart. In closing myself off to protect myself, I damaged myself in ways I couldn't foresee at the time, but my vow helped me survive, & thank God I made it. My vow was the deepest & most enduring of my self-punishments. "Good for you," the voices said.

· *3* ·

Thank God for my enduringly damaging vow. At long last, relief from my feelings of confusion & pain. Nothing changed at home so the feelings of course continued, but in an unacknowledged, subterranean way, so deeply buried that I was largely unaware of them. As before, they sometimes emerged in the form of nightmares or insomnia or odd tensions in my body, or in flashes of violent daydreams in which I bludgeoned Dad to death with a sledgehammer or machine-gunned pedestrians down at the corner. But for the most part I felt blessedly free of the turbulent emotions that had tormented me for so long. There were now even times when I could hunker down with a book or a *Burpee Seed Catalogue* & read through one of Mom & Dad's quarrels without paying any attention, as if their bickerings were no more than a nasty buzz in the background, like a power transformer or a plague of flies. No more fear of drowning. "Very good," the voices said.

"You read too much," Mom & Dad said. "Come watch TV." I was glad we'd finally gotten a TV, even though its arrival meant that the flimsy structure of our family life collapsed even more. Now Mom made supper & left it on the stove so we could arrange our meals around our favorite programs. But that was good, for now we had a new means of avoiding each other.

We watched TV almost every night, & especially the nights Dad played in the band or got in his car after a fight & drove off. Mom & Kent & I were like mourners gathered in front of the console—aptly named since it served us as consolation. Yet even from the first, television made me nervous. I liked the comedy shows & variety hours, & I always stayed up late on Saturday nights to watch the wrestling matches since they usually provided me with a good-looking, well-built man I could take to bed to fantasize about. But no matter what I watched, when the set went off I experienced a sinking sensation at the return to my small, flat, gray little life. On TV, life appeared larger, more coherent & tidy, more fun & far more glamorous than anything I knew from my own experience. From the start, I hated the guaranteed disappointment I felt whenever we turned off the set.

Back to the books, & school, & the ordeal of being the most unpopular kid in school. At twelve, I hadn't read George Saville, the Marquis of Halifax's dictum: "Popularity is a crime from the moment it is sought; it is only a virtue where men have it whether they will or no." Popularity thrust upon one, willy-nilly & whether or no? Such an idea wouldn't have made sense to me. All I knew was that I didn't have it & I had to have it, because at twelve nothing mattered more. For an American adolescent in the '50s, to be unpopular was to be an outcast, a reject, a social leper. So how could I become popular?

With my head finally above water thanks to my recent vow, I could think more clearly about my plight. I pondered the problem & soon came up with a simple plan that amazed me with its success. I figured that the trick was to worm my way into the good graces of the guys, for where the guys led, the girls would follow. I therefore played to the guys. I stopped staying after school to help out, started sassing my teachers in minor ways, & broke enough rules to get sent to the principal's office now & then. I put an end to all piano playing at home & abroad, & became an accomplished raconteur of dirty jokes about niggers & kikes & hillbillies that I learned from Dad. In my new incarnation, it wasn't hard to get the kids to start calling me "Al" instead of "Albert," for it was obvious to me that no one with the name "Albert" or "Albert Earl" had even the slightest chance of becoming popular. I also dressed the part whenever I could, sneaking into the filling station at the corner on my way to school to change from Mom's sales-bought clothes (two-tone Buck Rogers T-shirts, etc.) into things more presentable. Then fate lent a helping hand in the form of a pornographic photograph I found one day while rummaging through Dad's drawers: three Asians, a naked woman & two men in short black socks, all wholly abstracted. I copied the drawing on tracing paper & took it to school where I charged the guys a dime an ogle, thereby increasing my popularity & netting almost five dollars before I got caught.

My teachers were confounded—their model student purveying porn? They called home, but I don't recall that anything happened beyond whatever embarrassment Dad felt at having his pornographic photograph discussed at school. My report cards began to speak of "bad behavior"

& "slipping from the high standards Albert has previously maintained," but Mom & Dad didn't seem to care, & I sure didn't, for my plan was working. It took a year all told, but I was nevertheless amazed at how easy it was, although in retrospect my success wasn't that surprising since if you're willing to devote yourself to something, work obsessively at it, & sacrifice anything that gets in your way, there's almost nothing you can't achieve.

It worked, it worked, I was popular at last! The phone began to ring for me, though I was careful not to invite anyone home. "Ets-lay oh-gay oo-tay ee-they ark-pay," we said to one another, & when our parents figured out Pig Latin, we invented Negative Talk, in which we said the reverse of what we meant. That really drove them crazy.

My success at school must have emboldened me at home. Whether because of that, or my vow, or a surge of pubescent hormones, I began to assert myself.

One evening I was working at the typewriter when Dad arrived home in a crabby mood; shortly after, Mom began going through the house closing the windows with Dad close on her heels. Seconds between lightning & thunder were fast approaching zero. When they entered my room, I announced with Olympian calm that unless they stopped fighting within five minutes, I would throw the typewriter through the window. I doubt they heard a word I said, but they certainly heard the crash of glass as the typewriter sailed through the window & landed with a thud & a clatter of keys in the front yard. Ah, silence—the rare bliss of it. Of course, I had just destroyed my typewriter, but it took a lot to get through to them.

Freshman year in high school, I went out for track. The popularity stakes were now much higher, & it was imperative for my success that I have a sport. Years of running from bullies had made me a good sprinter.

I often came home with ribbons that I arranged on Dad's plate at the supper table to greet him when he got home from work, a way of saying "See, Dad—although I don't give a damn what you think about me, I really am a worthy son." One evening I lined up three blue ribbons in his plate: the 220, the 440, & the mile relay. Even my grudging father was bound to be pleased at that.

He hit the back door half-soused & cussing a blue streak. Swept up into his mood, Mom became so distracted that as we sat down to eat, she dolloped a ladle of Franco-American spaghetti into Dad's plate & all over my ribbons. Neither of them noticed; then a minute later Dad was yelling & Mom was crying & Kent was looking shell-shocked (which was how Kent usually looked at the supper table), & the familiar, deep tug began pulling at me. I pushed it away; then with a detachment I can still recall, I went into my bedroom, got my baseball bat out of the closet, returned to the kitchen, took up a position behind Dad, & hit him in the head. Odd as it may sound, I didn't want to hurt him, just stop the stream of filth & abuse coming out of his mouth. I hadn't thought forward enough to imagine an aftermath; I just figured I'd knock him out & we'd get on with supper.

But I hadn't knocked him out. He felt the back of his head & stared at the blood on his hand; then he turned slowly & looked up at me, his face twisted with fury & hatred. "Don't you *ever* turn your back on me again," he threatened in a low, quavering voice. But he remained seated, & I knew I had won.

My popularity campaign went well during freshman year in high school. Aside from my success in track, I ate parts of a dissected frog in biology class, & brought my sperm to school in a bottle, & threw pie over my head in the cafeteria so it landed on the tables of unpopular girls, some-times on the girls themselves. That Al Helms was one helluva guy, lemme tell ya.

Sometimes I got caught, but nothing ventured, nothing gained. Toward the end of my freshman year, the faculty sponsor of the Student Council stopped me during a class break to say that although I'd been nominated for the council & my grades were quite good, my behavior disqualified me from running. We were standing on the stairs & I was looking down at her. Just over her shoulder I could see the eleven by fourteen inch hand-tinted photographs in a glass case of me and the other candidates for the school's annual popularity contest. A boy & a girl from each class, eight students chosen out of two thousand. As Mrs. Howe explained why I couldn't run for Student Council, just over her shoulder I could see what really mattered to me. Finally, finally, I was winning!

By my sophomore year, I was one of a dozen guys who were the social leaders of the school. We travelled in a pack, & formed clubs called the Barons & the Satans, & hung out at drive-ins on weekends, & went to sock hops & roller rinks & homes where parents were away for the week-end & we could drink revolting things like raspberry brandy & orange-flavored gin.

We drank a lot at the Stengel brothers' place. That's where I first got drunk &, on a dare plus quarter bets, ate two moths, a grasshopper, a beetle, & something none of us could identify. The guys were vastly amused & admiring, but I spent the rest of the party beside the toilet in a fit of dry heaves. The guys said it was the bugs but I knew it was the booze.

A quiet story circulated in high school that Chuck Stengel liked to give blow jobs. Guys in the know talked about it, but in an amused, non-judgmental way, as if they were talking about an eccentric but harmless appetite, like the Habsburgs' for dwarfs. So the Stengels' parties were always laced with the possibility of the sexually forbidden, & in fact we all got so drunk that whenever Chuck disappeared with someone behind a locked door, it was hard to say next morning whether that had happened or we had imagined it.

I went to the next Stengel party with a plan to make Bob Wolfe. Captain of the basketball & football teams in grade school, Bob was a good-natured jock with a handsome open face & the perfectly proportioned body of your average Hoosier godling. He palled around with a goofy guy we called Bonzo, & the previous summer the three of us had jerked off a couple times under the footbridge down at Bean Creek. No touching—just absorbed, silent looking while we beat our puds to see who could come first.

Well into the party that night, I took Bob aside & told him I knew a trick I could show him upstairs. Once inside a closet, I whispered that I knew how we could get our peters in each other's mouth at the same time, & he whispered back "Yeah?" in a tone that said, "Proceed with caution." I got him in a sixty-nine (my own invention, mind you), but the floor was covered with metal toys, so after a few painful minutes of novice fellatio, we stopped. By then I was in love, or at least in an advanced stage of lust. When I woke next morning I knew for sure what had happened, & boy, was I glad.

Though nothing sexual ever again transpired between Bob & me, I mooned over him for months, but I never once thought I was . . . well, you know. I knew—everyone knew—that boys went through a "phase" with other boys. What was a little cocksucking between high school buddies?

The more adventurous members of our gang began hanging out with Virgil, a man about twenty-five years old with a Cadillac & a membership at the Elk's Club downtown where for some reason minors could drink illegally in public, or at least Virgil's minors could. I knew that those forays always ended up back at Virgil's in hard-on contests, with Virgil blowing each guy in turn throughout the night, but I'd never been invited. One more social hurdle to clear.

The invitation came. I went, got so drunk I was afraid to go home, &

called Mom to say I was spending the night at a friend's. While the rites of tumescence got going in the living room, I passed out in Virgil's bed. Some time later, I woke with a searing pain in my ass & found to my horror that Virgil was fucking me. I made him stop & I passed out again, whereupon he fucked me awake a second time. By then I was too frightened to sleep & it was too late to go home without creating suspicion in Mom & Dad. I lay in bed beside Virgil listening to the sounds of the house, no one now but the two of us, the other guys all gone home, & I tried with all my might not to feel anything.

Virgil drove me home next morning, but I made him stop before we got to my house since I didn't want to be seen with him. Walking the rest of the way home, I tried to make sense of what had happened the night before, but I was so confused. What Virgil had done to me was painful & it made me feel deeply ashamed, but I'd known those feelings from Dad's beatings. In fact, though the shape of the night was new to me, its emotional texture was familiar. All I could think was that I shouldn't tell anyone about what had happened since, the way I saw it, it was my own fault. I shouldn't have been hanging out with those guys, shouldn't have gone out with Virgil that night, shouldn't have drunk so much, shouldn't have stayed over, shouldn't have let Virgil put me in his bed, shouldn't have trusted him when he said he wouldn't do it again. I did what I'd always done for years with so many other painful experiences—I blamed myself, then buried the shame so deeply that in some fundamental way it ceased to exist for me.

Thirty years later on a terrace in Tuscany, a friend asked about my adolescent sexuality, so I told him about jerking off with Bob & Bonzo, & about sixty-nining with Bob, & about the older man who was hot for my teenage ass & who fucked me twice in my sleep. "In other words," my friend said, "you were raped." Me, raped? I was dumbfounded. For thirty years I'd had all the facts but never been able to explain them with the right word.

Time to hunker down in high school. Mom & Dad explained that if I wanted to go to college, I'd have to do it on my own since they couldn't help out. I wasn't surprised or resentful because the few other kids I knew who were going to college were doing it on their own, so fine—no problem & no complaints. But I was sobered.

"They're hiring out at GE. Mame says that Gritton boy got hisself a job making two fifteen an hour, can you beat that? And with benefits too.

I hear him & that girlfriend of his are getting married. Why does college matter so much to you?"

Because it was my guaranteed escape from home, that was why, & because the prospect of a life like the Gritton boy's made my gonads shrivel. But since my only chance at college was a scholarship, & since they didn't give scholarships for eating bugs & throwing pie, it was clearly time to mend my ways.

I'll spare you the saga of how hard I worked in high school my last two years, how much I succeeded, how many prizes & awards I won, how many offices I was elected to, how many speeches I gave & plays I starred in & school records I established, & how deftly I managed during it all to increase my popularity. I will say that I loved every immortal moment of my successes, & that they were wonderfully garnished with the growing sense I got from girls that I was now considered attractive, or as they put it, "cute." Was it Elizabeth Taylor who said, "There is no deodorant like success"? No aphrodisiac either. But being "cute," I discovered, brought new responsibilities. I had to learn to jitterbug & maintain a tan during the summer (which meant sweating through blazing hot days on a sheet in the back yard slathered all over with baby oil mixed with iodine) & pay more attention to my wardrobe (I had an all-white outfit with white shoes & another that was pink & charcoal gray with gray shoes), & I had to learn to maneuver in public without my glasses. I also had to date, though I hated it—all that slack, wet-mouthed kissing in the back seat of a friend's car with a girl mushy as Jell-O. Ugh! Give me muscles, preferably Bob Wolfe's.

I'd worked at part-time jobs from the age of six, when I had a paper route & cut the neighbors' grass. A few years later I got a job as a stock clerk at the corner grocery store where it was a peculiar ecstasy each night after work to throw damaged eggs at the concrete wall of the garage out back. Now I got summer jobs as a laborer through a von Sprekelsen contractor cousin, & I squirreled away my earnings except for the money I spent on a set of weights & subscriptions to weightlifting magazines. After an equatorially hot day of working on a road gang, I would get out my weights & huff & puff myself into a second sweat. After each workout, I checked my progress with a tape measure in the floor-length mirror in the living room. "Why do you do that?" Mom asked with worry, for she sensed something odd. "Just because," I answered with the airy vagueness allowed the American teenager. But I too thought my behavior was odd since I knew that none of the other guys lifted weights or pored over muscle magazines like I did. And I knew to lie when I went three nights in a row to the Garfield Cinema to see *Faviola*, an Italian film starring Massimo Girotti as a Roman slave wearing a skimpy loincloth that was shocking even by Roman slave standards. It was beginning to wear on my nerves, this "phase" of mine. I'd sure be glad when it ended.

During senior year, articles about me appeared in the Indianapolis newspapers—not, thank God, because I was arrested for stealing from the pharmaceutical supply store where I worked after school, but because I'd been elected president of the Indianapolis Federation of Student Councils, a group composed of Student Council officers from the dozen high schools in the county. No doubt it was a season of little news. There were other articles about still more honors & prizes & awards. One article, reporting that an Indiana businessmen's group had named me its "Teen of the Year," led off by saying "Al Helms is what every parent hopes his son will turn out to be—poised, self-confident, personable, and intelligent"—& terrified of losing out on a scholarship. But by then, I had such a class act going that none of the chinks showed, as you just read.

The SAT's were a breeze. I enjoyed tests, and I was used to highly stressful situations. Everything was working out my way, thus reinforcing the woeful delusion that with enough premeditation & perseverance, I could make life do whatever I wanted it to.

I wanted life to get me a scholarship to Wabash College in Indiana or Columbia University in New York City. Life got me a scholarship to both, which confused the hell out of me. Why couldn't life have spared me the decision? I flew to New York for a couple of days to check out Columbia, sitting in on a French class and strolling around the campus (thoroughly disappointing by midwestern standards). I spent the rest of my time sightseeing: the Empire State Building, the Statue of Liberty, the United Nations. What an electrifyingly exciting city New York was! I became gaga at the prospect of living in such a place—a place that, incidently was eight hundred miles from home, whereas Wabash College was a mere thirty. Distance from home plus the excitement of Manhattan plus the cachet of an Ivy League school settled the matter.

At graduation I gave the commencement speech (based on Robert Frost's "The Road Not Taken"), all snazzed out in a fresh burr haircut & a navy blue suit with a one button roll & fifteen-inch pegged pants. Bead & Mom & my teachers were immensely proud of me, especially Mrs. Howe, the Student Council sponsor who'd helped save me from becoming a delinquent. Dad didn't seem displeased, which was the best I ever got from Dad.

That last summer I worked again as a laborer—nine hours a day, six days a week, one fifteen an hour—on a large National Homes project in a huge dustbowl that never got the breeze, lugging three-hundred-pound road forms under a sweltering sky. Hard work, but the money would help out in college, & I gained the benefit of learning to tell time by the sun.

On a tip from a Columbia sophomore, I read *The Iliad* to prepare myself for the fall. Aside from the part about Achilles & Patroclus, I disliked it immensely. The catalogs were interminable, Agamemnon was stubborner than Bernita, Hector shouldn't have been killed, & it was first to last full of boastful, bloodthirsty men who enjoyed nothing more than killing & plundering. Even at eighteen I understood that masculinity wasn't worth dying for. If that was the sort of thing they liked at Columbia, what was I getting myself into?

Toward summer's end, Paul Clarkin came to visit. I'd met Paul the summer before at a national Student Council conference in the Rockies. Each state (there were then forty-eight) sent one boy & one girl; I was the boy from Indiana, Paul the boy from Colorado. Going & returning (my first trip in an airplane!), I'd stayed with Paul's family in Denver, & Paul & I had struck up an ardent friendship. We'd corresponded ever since, & the feeling I had for Paul was something I'd never known before, something compounded of love, admiration, & tenderness, something like the feeling between Achilles & Patroclus. Now Paul was visiting me for a few days before going to Dartmouth in the fall.

Without telling Mom & Dad, I'd arranged with Bead that Paul & I would stay with her & Henry, & thank God for my foresight. Paul's family lived in a large, comfortable home in a rich neighborhood. They ate dinner in a dining room, together, & they spoke civilly to one another during meals. They'd put me up in a guest room overlooking a swimming pool. That night during supper on Cruft Street, I saw more clearly than ever how poor & small & cheap my home was, & I hated it more than ever. I hated eating off a plastic tablecloth under an overhead light in a kitchen with an ugly linoleum floor. I hated Mom's uninspired cooking & Mom & Dad's unpracticed attempts at being gracious. I couldn't wait to get out of there.

When I steered Paul to the car after dinner, Mom & Dad were taken by surprise. They followed us out protesting—"But we fixed up the bedroom. We thought you were staying here. . . ." Stay in that house with someone I admired, who had been elected president of the national conference & was going to Dartmouth in the fall? Someone who came from a nice home where people didn't yell & belittle each other morning, noon, & night? Were they kidding? I'd never invited a friend home for more than an hour at a stretch, & I certainly wasn't about to risk the most important friendship of my life by staying a whole weekend in that house where who knew what might happen.

As Paul & I got in the car, I looked back to wave goodbye. Aside from the Thanksgiving when Kent was nearly killed, it's the only time from those eighteen years that I can summon an image of Mom & Dad being close. They stood on the front porch bewildered & hurt with the realization that I was ashamed of them but unable to do anything about it. Then Dad put his arm around Mom & hugged her as she fought to hold back her tears. At long last & without even trying, I had brought them together. They were so vulnerable & hurt that the sight of them nearly broke my heart, but I couldn't risk it.

A few weeks later I piled my bags in a Columbia student's car, said goodbye to Mom & Dad, hugged Kent & my two-year-old sister Debbie goodbye, & drove away from the house with the sad, frightened face where I had lived so many years in such confusion & pain, the house that for my entire life I had wanted to escape. Finally I was leaving all that sadness behind me. Thank God, thank God, forever, Amen.

· 4 ·

I arrived at Columbia in the fall of 1955, bright & curious, naive in the ways of the world, closed off from feeling & the capacity to love, adept at ingratiating myself with others, ambitious & energetic & apparently "cute," highly motivated by fear. I was giddy with relief at escaping my family but full of apprehension at what life would be like in this strange new world. I was also immensely impressed with myself—a fact the voices took note of as I unpacked in a dormitory on Amsterdam Avenue: "Look at you, boyohboy have you done well, the best scholarship Columbia gives & far better than you had any right to expect, though it could be that you're in over your head, there's so much you don't know, & you hated *The Iliad* which apparently they dote on here, yet your smarts have never failed you before, except this is an entirely different league, this is the Ivy League, the big time, & those prep school boys are much better prepared than you are, so you might not make it, though maybe with enough hard work & luck . . ."

Founded as King's College by royal charter of Charles II, Columbia had celebrated its bicentennial the year before, granting honorary degrees to Churchill, Nehru, Einstein, & Queen Mother Elizabeth of England. The college had produced more Nobel Prize–winning scientists than any other school in the country; six Nobel laureates taught in its Physics Department. Among its alumni were Alexander Hamilton & Theodore & Franklin Roosevelt; its last president (Eisenhower) was now president of the United States. The faculty included Lionel Trilling, Meyer Schapiro, Margaret Mead, I. I. Rabi, Jacques Barzun, Moses Hadas, C. Wright Mills, Polykarp Kusch, Gilbert Highet, Mark Van Doren—names that meant no more to me than those marching in solemn procession around the frieze of Butler Library: Socrates, Plato, Aristotle, Homer, Dante, Copernicus, Newton. . . . Clearly, I needed an education.

But later, later, for now I was off to Times Square with my new room-mates. What fine fellows we were, gawking at the lights & the locals as we found our way to the bar in the Astor Hotel, where we raised many a glass to newfound friendship & the fact that the drinking age in New York was eighteen. Sloshed on grasshoppers, I performed cartwheels all the way to the subway. Publically & legally drunk for the first time in my life with no worries about returning home to a fretful, inquisitive Mom & a judgmental, punitive Dad—what bliss that first, wild taste of adulthood was, how unsullied the fun & freewheeling freedom of it, with no one to answer to but myself, & myself not asking any questions. Columbia was going to be great.

Light blue beanies in place, we were shepherded through Freshman Orientation Week. I joined the Glee Club & went off to Camp Columbia in Connecticut for a long rehearsal weekend: three days of standard rep, three nights of vodka punch. The last night, I wound up skinnydipping in a freezing lake with a big blond senior premed from Sweden. Columbia was better than great; Columbia was the best.

A few weeks into the semester & Columbia was hell. Nothing made sense to me: the Greeks' code of honor, Plato's politics, irregular verbs in French, Giotto's jammed perspectives. I couldn't remember the details of the classical orders, or see the beauty of the Doric, or understand who the Dorians were. As for the Celts, the Visigoths, & the Ostrogoths, weren't they all vandals? "No, Mr. Helms. Who can tell Mr. Helms who the Vandals were?" Someone always could & did. High school hadn't prepared me for anything like this. All I knew for sure was that I understood nothing whatsoever, & as the days passed & I worked harder, there was always more I didn't understand. My sense of ignorance grew, & with it my fear of failure.

The voices never slept. "All well & good, that charade of success at a second-rate high school back in Indian-no-place, but now that you're competing in the big time, you can't make it, eh? People are finally seeing through to the real you, not dumb exactly, just not smart. . . ."

I studied every night until three or four in the morning, drag-assed up at seven for the breakfast provided by my prepaid meal plan, & trudged off six days a week to Michel Riffaterre's 8:00 A.M. first year French class. Riffaterre had a military crew cut & a mutilated ear—shot off, rumor had it, during his second escape from a Nazi detention camp during World War II. His class was like a detention camp: we conversed only in French, spoke only when called on, & got dressed down whenever we made a mistake. When Riffaterre called on me to "Lisez phrase sixième,

Monsieur Helms," I obeyed, pleased to discover that the accent I had worked to perfect years before on the front porch of Cruft Street was in fact quite adequate. Then the barked command to "Traduisez, Monsieur Helms." Punchdrunk with fatigue & crazed with fear, I thought I was hearing a garbled version of "Whadja say, Monsieur Helms?" I repeated what I'd just read, whereupon Riffaterre yelled at me & my mind went blank. After weeks of this torment, a classmate whispered that "Traduisez" meant "translate," so translate I did. I then learned that students with a final grade of B- or better were allowed unlimited cuts, & that there was something at Columbia called "the gentleman's C," grades handed out to lackluster students with no shame attached. Better absent than yelled at. The worst that could happen was that I would fail the course, & I was doing that already.

I was even more miserable in my other courses. French was a fairly straightforward matter of practice & memorization, but Homer and Plato? Oedipus and Job? The words swam on the page, melding into a blur through which I occasionally glimpsed traces of meaning, but nothing solid that I could take for my own & connect to anything else. It seemed that all of knowledge was a world of floating islands and I was swimming in a deep sea, now & then glimpsing a distant land called "metaphysics" or "epistemology" that came briefly into view before receding from sight. Studying was like reading while drifting off to sleep: most of the words made sense when I looked at them, but once I read past them, they floated off beyond the reach of comprehension.

In grade school & high school I'd been spoon-fed knowledge, & I'd learned how to guess at what my teachers had wanted of me & provide it. At Columbia, my teachers wanted me to think, but I didn't know how to think. A professor would direct us to an idea in our reading, then line it up alongside another idea from another book, then ask us what we thought. I'd strain hard to guess which idea was right, then cast my silent vote & wait to see what happened. It kept turning out that neither idea was right or wrong—instead, there was right & wrong in each. That was a bewildering way to go about thinking in my view (how could you ever figure anything out for sure?), & a much harder way, since it meant you had to understand & analyze more things, & compare & contrast more things, & remember more things, including doubts about all the things. It was exhausting, this business of thinking, & it seemed like a perverse game in which everyone knew the rules but me.

I'd rarely been challenged intellectually in high school, but now, all was challenge & incomprehension & this peculiar activity called thinking. The other students didn't seem fazed. Many of them prep school boys & college-bound from the cradle, they seemed to be thriving. They bandied unfamiliar names about, quoted from memory, & argued in genial, impassioned ways about readings I hadn't understood while I sat mute & terrified, isolated in my sense of intellectual inferiority.

One morning during my Contemporary Civilization class, I made a list of everyone cited or quoted by the other students. Of twenty-one names, I recognized three: Eisenhower, Einstein, & Christ. I took my list to the professor & explained my plight. Perhaps Columbia had made a mistake? Perhaps I should go back to Indiana? Professor Webb got out my record (What did it say? Who had written it?) and said he thought things would probably improve if I gave it more time. Could I hang on until Thanksgiving? Yes, I thought I could, though I didn't tell him I was so miserable I was crying myself to sleep every night. Very well then: I would persevere, & if by Thanksgiving I wasn't climbing aboard, we would then discuss my withdrawing.

But the hanging on was a new hell for me. From as far back as I could remember, I had invested most of my pride & self-worth in being bright & right, & that had never failed me. All gone now. And because for the first time in my life I felt stupid, I also felt awkward, & humorless, & dull, & unattractive, & generally abhorrent & pointless. Bad enough that I was an intellectual failure; I was a social flop too, a hick away from home, hopelessly Hoosier. At a tea to welcome midwestern freshmen, a faculty wife asked, "Lemon or cream?" "Both," I said, & I can still hear her appalled "Ah-haaaa" as she turned to mix the concoction. The first time I showed up at a fraternity rush party in a Billy Eckstein rolled-collar shirt & my one-button commencement suit with the pegged pants, I felt like I'd been caught spitting in the Christ child's eye. I couldn't even talk right. I said "melk," the other guys said "milk." I said "ruff," they said "roof." I said "crik" for "creek" & "al-u-*min*-i-um" for "a-*lum*-in-um" & "*gen*-u-*ine*" for "*gen*-u-un" & "*q*-pon" for "*coo*-pon" & "*in*-jun" for "*en*-gine." Back home, we had always "warshed" our hands & "rinshed" them, but not at Columbia. In the dining hall during dinner & supper (now "lunch" & "dinner"), the guys baited me into talking Hoosier for their amusement. Wouldn't it be "neat," I suggested one day, to see that production of Gilbert & Sullivan's "*Mik*-a-doo" advertised in the school "*nooze*paper"? "Ter*rif*ic" the guys said, howling with laughter.

I was failing in every way that mattered to me. My smarts? All gone. My high school popularity? Of no account. And if I couldn't succeed at

Columbia, I was doomed to a miserable little life in a factory or a shoe-store back in Indianapolis. The Gritton boy began to haunt my dreams.

But through the gift of desperate determination, I did hang on, & Dick, the Swedish swimmer, helped with his assurances that Professor Webb was probably right, I'd probably see the light before long. I certainly saw it whenever Dick & I were together. Dick was the one bright spot in that murk of doubt & fear pervading my life, & soon we were spending all our free time together. He was tall & blond & had a swimmer's taut body that came from summers lifeguarding & a mile a day in the Columbia pool. Flushed with health & sun, he looked like a giant, friendly peach. Late at night we sat on a stairwell in his dorm discussing the *Symposium,* heady reading for a sexually naive young man who had long felt secret yearnings for other men, & now for this one man in particular.

One Saturday night when the dorms had emptied out, Dick challenged me to a wrestling match. Over & over he pinned me, & over & over I came back for more, just happy to be with him. Who cared who was winning? We were both winning, right? Sweaty & tired, we stripped & showered, then sat wrapped in towels on the side of his bed. When he reached toward me, I knew that, yes, yes, this was what I wanted more than anything else in the world. We made love, & in the next few weeks, oh God, what joy! I was in love for the first time in my life, & wholly loved, & finally safe.

If Dick was my reward for an unhappy childhood, all the years in that miserable home had been worth it. Every pain & sorrow I'd ever known not only didn't matter, they vanished, as if there had never been a world but the new one I was now entering, circumscribed by the embrace of Dick's strong, gentle, loving arms. I was so happy that if God had appeared & said "It's time to die," I think I could have died with a sense that my life had been blessed.

Suddenly, miraculously, my studies began to make sense—Aristotle *was* saying something in the *Ethics* I could understand, & I *could* discern the imperial designs of the *Aeneid* & conjugate irregular French verbs with ease. Shortly after Thanksgiving, I was able to report to a pleased Professor Webb that I was doing much better than I'd hoped.

Thank God, thank God: I was free, I was living in New York City, I was attending Columbia, I was learning to talk right, I was in love, & I could understand Aristotle! Suddenly everything made sense & life was glorious beyond my wildest expectations. Life was altogether neat, no matter how you pronounced it.

Except that I had to go home for Christmas. I'd avoided a Thanksgiving trip by pleading work, but there was no way around a Christmas visit. Oh, how I hated that house upon my return, everything smaller & poorer & meaner than I'd remembered. Bead was a disappointment too; she seemed pretentious & provincial, & I saw for the first time what a bigot she was. When I spoke of Columbia classmates like Harvey Silverstein & Joel Goldfarb, she arched an eyebrow & said "Jews." It hadn't even occurred to me. "Are there many Jews at Columbia?" she asked, as the school visibly sank in her estimation.

But I got back at them. I flaunted my new learning, laced my conversation with French, & tormented Mom & Dad with Stravinsky's *Oedipus Rex*. "Do you *have* to play that again?" Mom protested. "For heaven's sakes, Albert Earl!" I didn't like it either, but that wasn't the point. "The point," said Bernita, "is that someone's gotten too big for his britches." We parted with relief all around.

With Dick's love & Professor Webb's support & a new ability to read with concentration & pay attention in class, I finished that first semester well. Grades were posted on a wall of the gym with names attached for all to see. The Wailing Wall, we called it. Fine by me, let them look; I'd done extremely well.

Second semester, Dick & I roomed together. Freshmen weren't supposed to room with seniors, but Dick knew somebody in an office who pulled some strings. Now you would think I'd have been in seventh heaven, right?—living with the man I loved wholly, wildly, even in my sleep? But I wasn't. Or rather, I was but I wasn't. It was bliss, but it was torment. "Terrific," the voices said. "However . . ." What a huge relief not having to sneak around the dorms at odd hours for a hug & a kiss, & knowing that behind our locked door we could do whatever we wanted without fear of detection. No more driving up to Bear Mountain on weekends so we could be alone together in a motel room. We now had a perfectly normal reason for spending so much time together & for sleeping in the same room every night. And sleeping wrapped in each other's arms was ecstasy, granted.

On the other hand, although I wasn't positive, I didn't think this relationship that buoyed me sky-high a dozen times a day was just another way station on the journey through my interminable "phase." For years I'd calmed my mind with the belief that my attraction to men would soon give way to the standard heterosexual longings of my friends in high school. After that first night in Dick's arms, I wasn't so sure any more. As best I could tell, what went on in our bed every night after we locked the door was an expression of my fullblown, adult, here-to-stay sexuality. But what did that make me? A latter-day Damon or Pythias? A queer & a homosexual? I was thrilled when one day in Humanities (we were discussing some ancient Greek or other), the professor said "Of course, gentlemen, we're all aware that men sometimes experience erotic attraction for other men," but I knew from the murmurs & shifting chairs that the other guys were acutely uncomfortable with such an idea. Never mind: Aristophanes knew better than they, & Aristophanes was right: Dick & I were halves of a former self now made whole by our rediscovery of each other at long last. Yet the other guys didn't live in a world where Aristophanes' theory of sexuality held sway. For them, a man who desired other men was unnatural, pathetic, disgusting, sick, in a word (that awful word again), "queer."

Could they be right? I knew there were men who wore makeup & carried purses, and I too thought they were unnatural & pathetic, completely "queer." But I wasn't that kind of man, nor was Dick. As far as I knew at the time (& it would take two years before I knew otherwise), Dick & I were the only two men in the world the way we were—masculine men who loved men. Dick knew differently but he never told me, thinking perhaps that my ignorance of the gay world would somehow keep me "pure" & "innocent," or maybe thinking that my ignorance would keep me exclusively his, as indeed it did. But it made me desperate too, for I thought that if I ever lost Dick, I would lose everything that mattered to me, & I would then be completely alone. So I brought a backburner panic to our relationship that laced many of our best times together with tension & fear.

Compounding my confusion about whatever it was I was (a pervert? a Patroclus?) was the nutty notion that a good life (and surely I was now living a good life) would be diametrically opposed to the life I'd known on Cruft Street. Therefore, I reasoned, a good life would be not just devoid of screaming & humiliation & violence, but also of all misunderstandings, disagreements, & difficulties of any kind. It would, in a word, be perfect. Yet that model didn't correspond to the life I was living with Dick. Sometimes he was tired & distracted, or stumped by Kant, or busy with a friend. Sometimes we disagreed about which movie to see or which grocery store to rob for our dinner. We even began to argue about the nature of love. "You can't love anyone till you love yourself," Dick maintained, which drove me crazy because it sounded so selfish & self-centered. But instead of revising my notions, I concluded that there must be something wrong with our relationship. And if there were, well, it must somehow or other be my fault, & I'd better attend to it, better *do* something. Our least disagreement simultaneously confirmed my sense that there was something missing in our love & filled me with alarm at the prospect of being alone in the world.

Loving Dick sometimes even felt dangerous since my previous experiences of trusting had often brought me violation & humiliation. I thus found myself trying to be open out of a closed self, trying to live a perfect life in an imperfect world, & trying to love in a relationship hedged with anxieties & fears of my own invention. I don't know if I was an easy man to love, but I certainly couldn't have been an easy lover.

As much as I'd always hated the scenes of quarrelling & fighting between my parents, Dick & I began to quarrel & fight. I learned early on that Dick had a heart murmur, so one day after an argument cut short when he stormed off to class, I plotted a simple revenge. I left a suicide note on his desk, figuring it would give his heart a corrective jolt, & went off to a movie. When I returned, his immense relief soon gave way to immense fury at my deception. He raised his fist to hit me, then smashed it through a panel in the closet door. We wept & kissed & hugged & made up & calmed down & settled in at our desks, me with a book, Dick with tweezers picking the splinters out of his knuckles. An hour later, done with his surgery, he stood up &, from behind, bashed me in the head. I didn't black out, but for days I felt woozy & had inexplicable, piercing headaches. At the infirmary, a doctor told me I had a mild concussion & should take it easy for a few weeks.

One night during another argument, one of us (I don't remember who) threw a mug through the open window & out onto Amsterdam Avenue. It didn't hit a passing car, thank God, but it did create enough fuss to bring an assistant dean to our room next day to ask some questions. The dean appeared to buy our lame excuses, but during my senior year I learned that damaging suspicions had been entered in a secret record of my life in the dorms. Three years' worth of suspicions, as it turned out.

But I've misrepresented this love affair. Much of the time, Dick & I got along well; much of the time, in fact, I was so deliriously happy that my joy could find expression only in—what else?—poetry, reams of it; execrable stuff in which "flamingoes stately plied their wedding barks" & other equally preposterous things transpired. With a love like mine (unique, unparalleled), I wanted to be, had to be, was *born* to be a poet. I scribbled in class & at the movies, on subways & in the gym, on the backs of envelopes & on toilet paper when the Muse inspired me in the john. For even with its anxieties, the love affair with Dick deserved to be immortalized. No matter what worries came my way—a difficult exam, bad news from home (was there any other kind?)—there was always Dick, & with Dick I could survive anything. Dick was the bedrock on which I was constructing a new life, & the confidence he gave me, along with the joy & freedom from usual frets, sometimes led me to the transcendent.

One afternoon, fresh from a reading of Hegel, I paused on the steps of Low Library beside the statue of Athena (the Columbia Alma Mater) to watch the hundreds of people going to & fro in the plaza below. Suddenly I became aware of the multitude of personal particulars that composed the lives of everyone I saw—all the tastes & desires, the hopes & fears, the geraniums on the windowsills & the mail waiting in the hallways, the photographs on mantels & desks & bureaus, the drafts of papers & the plans stretching far into the future, all the possessions, ideas, ambitions of the day & night, the address books & the pocket change, the friendships & loves & hatreds, each fact specific to each person. It wasn't that I felt I'd come to know any of the people below, but that I was suddenly aware of the dense texture of humanity. The atmosphere took on mass & weight & I seemed to rise in the air, to see as from a great height above my body. I saw the fabric of life, woven of innumerable strands of suffering & hope, fear & joy, each strand interconnected & strummed into being by a vast, incomprehensible spirit. It was a feeling of great power & humility, reverence & awe, for Life itself was walking in the plaza below, & I had to clutch a fold of Athena's bronze robe to keep from swooning.

Though born in Sweden, Dick had grown up in Brooklyn. Since he was a lifeguard every summer at Rockaway Beach, why, he wondered, didn't I get a job at the beach that summer & live with him & his family in Brooklyn? What a great idea, except I couldn't swim. But a week later I could, & a month later, thanks to Dick's rigorous training, I was swimming a mile a day. I next enrolled in the lifesaving course that was requisite to getting a job at a New York City beach. So much depended on my passing the course that every Saturday morning when I arrived at the municipal pool on East Fifty-fourth Street, my stomach was churning with fear. I changed into my trunks, stopped in the john to vomit, & proceeded to the pool where I learned how to save people from drowning. During the last class, we had to swim half a mile in a competitive time, & everything depended on that final test. Dick knelt at one end of the pool; each time I lapped he yelled "Faster—C'mon, Al, FASTER!" I passed the test & got the job, which meant that Dick & I would be together for the whole summer.

My first day as a lifeguard was the first time I'd ever seen the ocean. A storm was passing as I got out of the subway in Far Rockaway, & I heard a dull, thundering noise that grew as I walked toward the beach. When I climbed the boardwalk, I couldn't believe my eyes: beneath a Manichean sky was a heaving universe of roaring water, mountainous slabs of it crashing together & sending spray thirty feet into the air, then slamming on the sand with a force that shook the boardwalk. I couldn't swim in that, let alone save anybody.

But by summer's end I'd saved thirty people except for the two who died on me—an old man & a boy of fourteen, both cold & white as fish when I brought them out of the water. What a distance the Naptown sissy had travelled—from fleeing the grade school bullies to sitting high on his lifeguard tower, remote behind Ray-Bans, bronzed & bossy, telling those kids to stop roughhousing it, whistling to warn that man not to go beyond the jettyhead, reveling in the glances from girls who strolled past a dozen times an hour for closer looks. Better still were the stormy days when we closed the beach & I wrapped a tarpaulin around the base of my tower & crawled inside to read *Anna Karenina, The Charterhouse of Parma, The Brothers Karamazov & The Idiot, Madame Bovary, Portrait of a Lady,* & the other novels recommended as summer reading by my Humanities professor, Charles Van Doren, who would soon become a national celebrity as the star of the TV quiz show "Twenty-One." (I'd stolen all the books, handsome Heritage Club editions, from the college library.)

Best of all was making love with Dick in the guard house at the end of the day after the other guards had gone home & the beach was deserted—the walls of the guard house washed with purple & gold from the setting sun, the smell of the sea & our sweat, the salt taste of Dick's body. It was perfect, like living in a movie, the way life was supposed to be.

Living with Dick's family in Brooklyn, however, was far from perfect. Imagine spending an entire summer with your lover in his parents' home, terrified of being discovered, hiding & editing & downright lying, sneaking a squeeze as you pass on the stairs, meeting in the bathroom to hug & kiss (checking first to make sure the door is locked), touching hands or feet under the dinner table with a thrill of dread. Why didn't we go crazy? Why did we ever think that would be fun? More likely we thought that being apart would be intolerable. This was intolerable too, but fun.

At summer's end, Dick began medical school at Bellevue & I moved back into the same dorm room with a music major who was also assistant director of the Glee Club. Professor Webb, now Bob to me, had become my Columbia mentor. No doubt recognizing me for the country bumpkin I was, Bob took it upon himself to introduce me to the world of high culture. Wow, *Culture!* I knew I didn't have any & I wanted as much as I could get.

First, Bob invited me to an evening of the Little Orchestra conducted by Pierre Monteux. The closest I'd ever come to live classical music was Dad's rendition of "Oh Promise Me" at weddings & an occasional aria by an overblown Met diva on the Ed Sullivan show. At home, "music" meant Dad's band music, or the country & western songs that glutted the Hoosier airways, or the pop schlock of TV variety shows. Mrs. Kilgore had worked me through the "Moonlight Sonata," but then I'd abandoned the piano in deference to my popularity campaign. Now, however, I was rooming with a guy who read music so well he preferred the flawless performances inside his head to the mortal efforts at Carnegie Hall, & one of my classmates was John Corigliano, whose father was concertmaster of the New York Philharmonic. John had an autographed photograph of Toscanini on his desk in the dorms. That was culture, & that's what I wanted.

I arrived at City Center that night full of anticipation. Then as the lights dimmed & the audience quieted down & Monteux led the orchestra into the opening bars of who now knows what, I was seized with an overwhelming desire to sleep. The music was so beautiful, so transcendent, so why was I sleepy? I listened harder, wondering what exactly I was supposed to be experiencing, but only became more sleepy. "Please, dear God, please don't let me fall asleep; I have to stay awake." I dug my fingernails into my palms, sat bolt upright, fixed my eyes on Monteux's stubby figure, & was swept away with fatigue. I pinched my skin & pulled the hairs on my wrists & twisted my legs into contorted positions, but no matter what, every few minutes I drifted off into a delicious haze until I jerked spasmodically awake, horrified with embarrassment. Head in hand & elbow propped on the arm of my seat, I feigned soulful absorption in the music, but my elbow slipped & my head bobbed, revealing my ruse. I became terrified I might snore; I couldn't sit still or not sit still; my legs began to spasm. If this was culture, you could have it. Far as I was concerned, it was unmitigated torture.

Bob's second invitation came a short time later. With Patty, his girlfriend, we would go to the ballet. Now surely I was cursed. If classical music, which at least had a large audience, had quelled me, how much more thorough my defeat by the recherché ballet. I'd only seen snippets of ballet on TV, and when Dad derided it for being sissy, it was one of the few times we ever saw eye to eye.

City Center again, for Balanchine's New York City Ballet. The curtain rose, revealing a V-shaped formation of women in calf-length tutus with Melissa Hayden at the apex, right arms raised in visible anticipation. Then, Tchaikovsky's Serenade in C Major for String Orchestra, the opening measures descending with the dancers' arms in a wedding of music & body so complete, so perfect, I swooned with sensuous joy. The combination of the aesthetic & the erotic so overwhelmed me that within thirty seconds I was a dedicated balletomane for life.

Thanks to Bob, then, my cultural life was well-launched just as my emotional life began to go haywire. Something was wrong but I didn't know what—only that Dick seemed increasingly distracted & distant. We now met only on weekends, & even then he sometimes postponed or cancelled a meeting. When he discovered me under a blanket in his Bellevue dorm bed, wrapped head to toe in red ribbon as a birthday present (not an easy operation, I assure you: tying the ribbon was an almost impossible feat), he hadn't been pleased. He'd pulled back the blanket, taken a long, silent look, & said "What the hell is this?" After my twentieth birthday dinner, instead of spending the night with me as I'd hoped, he drove me back to Columbia & dropped me off on Broadway. I was walking across the campus as the bells began to toll the hour I was born. "Ten o'clock," the bells rang. "Alone, alone, alone . . ."

Despite the signs of trouble in our relationship, Dick and I had planned to spend another summer together, but his mother's growing suspicions scotched that scheme. Instead, we would meet in New York at the end of August & spend a week's vacation in New England. I needed that guaranteed payoff to get me through a summer back home.

My family was now living in a new house Dad & Henry had built south of the city—a rectangular, three-bedroom affair of cinderblock trimmed in curlicues of wrought iron. But the floorplan made sense, the rooms were full of light, & the house was set amid magnificent oaks & maples & walnut trees on half an acre of land.

Though the house was supposed to give Mom & Dad a new lease on life (as Kent was supposed to have done, & Debbie in her turn), it was clear that their life together had reached a new level of disintegration. They still ate their meals separately, but at least there were no quarrels about which TV shows to watch. Mom had taken to picking through the neighbors' trash ("It's a crying shame what people throw out. Would you wear that?" she'd ask, holding up a raspberry & lime green plaid sweater vest), & she'd retrieved two abandoned television sets & had them repaired, so there were now three sets going every evening. Dad was still working at the post office, though he'd been arrested for being drunk on the job & been given a stiff warning. He was still pissing away a substantial portion of his salary on booze, still crabbing & complaining his way through his furious days. He & Mom now slept in separate rooms & avoided each other as much as possible, coming together only for hateful quarrels that were never resolved & thus provided ammunition for the next round. In the old days they had offered each other the repeated if dimming hope that things might improve between them, but now that hope was gone. Their normal conversation had degenerated into a continual exchange of snide remarks—as if they'd gotten so used to their mutual rancor they could no longer hear how awful they sounded. But at least Dad hadn't hit Mom in my presence since my baseball bat attack years before. Kent & Debbie intimated awful goings-on, but whenever I quizzed Mom she shrugged me off & changed the subject.

Mom's conversation was by now little more than a series of subject changes: "Remind me to get more tomato preserves from Bead, you love them so, & maybe I'll make tapioca. Boy, Mame sure loves tapioca. Did I tell you her oldest girl got married to that boy you worked with at the grocery store when you were little? I want to remember to have them stop by so they can see you. Oh, that time we went to Brown County with Mame's chapter, I wet my pants going & coming, we laughed so hard. Mame sure is the spitting image of Flo, & did I tell you Mary's moving to Florida? It's a great life, ain't it?"

It was pathetic to see that Kent & Debbie were now showing the results of their lunatic upbringing. Kent still looked mildly shell-shocked when awake; asleep, he was impossible to rouse. "Kent, it's time to get up. Kent, do you hear me?—you've overslept again. Kent, Kent?" Mom & Dad had made the mistake of sending Kent to my grade school, where he was constantly reminded of an estimable older brother whose example was still fresh in the minds of his teachers. He'd begun to acquire the habits of the diffident: the shuffling manner, the averted eyes, the sheepish smile, the muted voice. "The spitting image of Henry," as Mom said repeatedly.

At age four, Debbie had been given full rein over her diet. For breakfast she ate Oreos & drank Pepsi; for lunch, Oreos & Pepsi & ice cream.

"Mom, her *diet!*" "I know, I know. Don't get me rattled." A couple times we were all out driving when, in the innocent way children have of creating trouble, Debbie said, "Me & Daddy went there" & pointed to a bar along the highway. He never took her inside the bar, of course—just locked her in the car so she'd be safe. Since his drinking wasn't seasonal, he sometimes left her in the car for two & three hours in the dead of winter. "Aren't you ashamed of yourself?" Mom would say, shooting him a disgusted look, then, "Look—Guernseys, I just love Guernseys!"

Poor Kent & Debbie. I didn't feel close to them—siblings are rarely close in alcoholic families, & the difference in our ages didn't help—but still they were my brother & sister & I would have liked to help them. Yet the effort seemed doomed. I felt like a man who has spent his last ounce of energy escaping a sinking ship & who now sits on the shore watching others drown. To help Kent and Debbie I would have had to reach beyond my own pain, & I wasn't able to do that. Feeling impotent, guilty, depressed, exhausted, I shifted to remote control & let things take their destructive course.

That summer I got another job as a laborer on another National Homes project through another von Sprekelsen cousin, & weekends I lifeguarded at a pool near the new house. Spare moments on the job & at the pool, I did push-ups; at home I did pull-ups from a beam in the garage. At summer's end, I would have a better body for Dick.

One evening Mom & I were talking in the living room when she looked out the window & exclaimed "Oh my God." Skunk drunk, Dad had missed the driveway & his car was perched over the drainage ditch, one wheel whirling in air. Wearing his best fix-'em demeanor, he was pulling weeds from the ground a full foot below the wheel.

"Quick, before the neighbors see him," Mom said, as if there were a neighbor within a mile who didn't know of Dad's dipsomania. But out we ran to drag him protesting into the house, whereupon a huge ruckus ensued, for after twenty years Mom still hadn't tired of arguing with Dad when he was drunk. When I tried to intervene, he called me a "homosexual" & then, while I was absorbed in the shock of that new turn in our relationship, he started hitting Mom. I jumped between them, Dad & I grappled on the floor, then it was over & he had a broken arm. Mom called Bead & Henry, who came right away, & we settled into a long quarrel. "If it weren't for you," Bead kept saying to Mom, hinting at Mom's responsibility for Dad's drinking while Dad muttered in drunken agreement. But something central was being edited. Bead's accusations suggested something beyond what she was saying. I insisted on knowing what it was until Mom, weeping now, turned to me & said, "I slept with a man before I married your father. She's never let me forget it." Mom's face was contorted with shame & a plea for me, someone, *anyone* to tell her she wasn't the reason Dad drank.

Twenty years of emotional tyranny hurtled into view. For twenty years, Bead had been using that ammunition on Mom, parcelling it out in poisonous doses to suit her warped vision of her son. Dad had obviously told Bead of Mom's peccadillo way back at the beginning, & Mom had suffered all those years from guilt & shame & the abiding sense that maybe she really was the reason Dad drank.

I nearly lost my mind with rage. "I don't ever want to see or speak to you again," I screamed at Bead, the heroine & savior of my childhood.

Bead & Henry took their alcoholic son away soon after, but they made him wait until next morning when the booze was off his breath before taking him to their doctor to have his arm set.

So all in all, just another average, run-of-the-mill summer at home. I got through it by vowing I'd never return, & by crossing off the days on the calendar so I could see the steady approach of my reunion with Dick. Forty-nine-and-a-half hours of hard labor a week plus sixteen hours at the pool on weekends, plus all those push-ups & pull-ups, plus the continual drain exacted by being with my family didn't leave much time or energy for reading, so I used the thought of Dick to get me by. I did more push-ups for Dick, & more pull-ups for Dick, & wrote more letters to Dick, longer & better letters, & I bought a new suit out of my earnings, a proper Ivy League suit because I knew Dick would like it. Every time I thought I'd drop from fatigue on the construction job, or when Mom & Dad's quarrels made me feel like my heart was careening out of my body, I thought of Dick. He always got me through. There was a kid of peerless body & unparalleled sexiness on the construction job who suggested we go swimming some night after work, but I was saving myself for Dick. One of the weekend lifeguards, a high school gymnast Phidias would have swooned for, stayed to help me close up the pool each night, then joined me in the shower where he had a habit of turning the conversation to matters sexual, but my love for Dick was a pure thing, a torch, an emblem, a grail, a sacred vow. And anyway, though I had thought that maybe there were other men like Dick & me, surely there weren't. I must have been imagining things.

Toward the end of August, Dick called one weekend to say he couldn't get free for our New England trip. He was sorry, but something had come up. He'd meet me at Grand Central Station & explain. I felt an anticipatory dread but I managed to suppress it.

A few thousand push-ups & pull-ups later it was time for release from the prison of home. Mom & Dad saw me off at Union Station. I was mouthing goodbyes to Dad through the window when the train began to move. Immediately we were in a tunnel that turned the window into a mirror in which I saw the phoniest, emptiest smile I'd ever seen. The history of my father & me was written all over my face, a revolting sight.

I was careful to put my new suit pants aside so they'd have a clean crease when I met Dick. Eighteen hours later, the conductor called "Grand Central Station." I changed into my pants, & my body was tan & I had some new muscles & a new suit, & then I was walking through the gate lugging my bag down the ramp & into the Grand Concourse, a gigantic Roman amphitheater pierced by a shaft of sunlight in which Dick stood, tanned in a T-shirt, smiling. For three months I'd waited for this moment. At last, there he was.

I went toward him, my heart bursting with love, but he didn't say "Hello" or "What a nice suit" or "Dig that crease" or "Welcome back, I love you." He said "It's over between us. I'm going straight."

I can't retrieve the feeling of that moment, but I know I lived the next week in an abyss of despair. I wandered around Manhattan crazed with grief & sorrow, oblivious to my whereabouts. It caused me pain whenever people looked at me, I felt so ashamed & so disgustingly queer. I drank away the nights in bars until closing time, then returned to Dick's dorm at Bellevue where I slept on a borrowed mattress at the foot of his bed, because he felt it was best we not sleep together. Thinking he didn't want to touch me, I became even more repellent to myself.

Dick's rejection & the sense that I had somehow brought it on myself went to the marrow of my bones. After a childhood of feeling wrong & unloved & years of closing myself up to keep away the hurt, I had managed to open myself to Dick. Now the thing I'd feared most had happened. If Dick had said "It's all over between us," there might have been hope, but "I'm going straight" meant that it didn't matter Dick was the only other man in the world like me, because now he wasn't. Dick's love for me had been an aberration, a real "phase" in his life, but I knew I didn't have it in me to change as he was doing. I believed I was loathsome, & I knew I was alone.

I'd never seen anyone grieve, so instead, I drank & nursed my pain, treating it like a companion. There was always the sense of a heavy sadness in my life that, awful as it was, was mine, was deserved, was all I had, & so was to be nurtured & then revived whenever it showed signs of fading.

The school year began, I moved into a single room in the dorms, & I tried to immerse myself in my studies. But every waking moment I was miserable with the thought of being abandoned by Dick. I wrote poetry about the death of our love—half the poems ending with "He is gone" & half with "I am alone." I decided I would know I was over my pain when I could read one of the poems out loud without crying. That happened one night in early November, but instead of feeling the relief I'd hoped for, I felt more miserably alone than ever.

For weeks on end I saw no one. I didn't want to see Dick, & because we'd been so exclusively involved during my two years at Columbia I'd made no friends, except for Bob & Patti & another English major, a bright, chipper guy named Jay. I'll never forget Jay—not our passionate discussions of literature over lunch & dinner, or our sorties to the Thalia movie theater with Jay's Barnard girlfriend, or the football games we attended at Baker's Field, or how one evening, hoping to break out of my isolation, I worked up my courage & told Jay I was . . . that way. And I'll never forget how calmly Jay received my news, & how, just as calmly, he told me we could no longer be friends.

There were Bob & Patti, but by then I couldn't risk another rejection. I went through those autumn days dulled by sadness & loneliness & the abiding sense that it was all my fault. Having felt more than whole when I fell in love with Dick, I now felt less than half without him. And from having been inspired to a transcendent glimpse of a world full of the thick, rich quiddity of life, I'd now entered a world where all the people & objects & even my own feelings were flat & featureless. The only urgency I felt came from the voices, which now were riotous & relentless.

It's half-an-hour before the library closes & I'm trying to make sense of my reading, trying to absorb & relate & deduce & condense & get it once & for all, but the voices keep saying "This is hard & you're probably not going to get it because you're probably not really bright despite the grades & pretty soon they'll find you out," if only I could be like the other guys & understand this stuff, but whoa & what if it isn't that guy from the pool again, God he's so sexy & eyeing me in the showers like that I wish he'd speak to me or come to my room some night & take off his clothes & climb in beside me with his "lithe sheer of waist" is how Whitman puts it, I'll bet it would be great making love with him but he probably isn't, probably just my imagination except why does he stare at me like that? "And did it ever occur to you that some people just stare a lot?" oh why don't you shut up, go on, *shut up,* & where was I anyway, okay now, so the late medieval world begins to fall apart when what happens? economic expansion & the dissolution of . . . ? why don't they give examples, say straight out that Francesca got tired of doing all the weaving herself & hired twenty women & opened a shop on the Via Whatever, whereupon *Boom,* no more medieval world, "You are *not paying attention,* & everyone else in your class will have read this material in half-an-hour but you need an hour & more," so maybe I should underline instead of take notes, or underline but take notes too, but fewer notes, but then why am I tired if swimming is good for the brain & wakes you up except it tires me too although I'm sure alert for Mr. Sexy Stares over there, so maybe I'll start saying hello & see what happens, he has such a great body & the way he moves & that face, I love those slanted eyes like wolf eyes that see through you to secrets you didn't know you have, "lupine" is the word like the flowers Bead used to pick on the highway, arriving on Cruft Street with huge bunches in her arms singing "Hello there, look what *I've* got" except she's such a bigot, & there he is again looking back, good, I'll bet he does one more time, I hope he does, if he does I'll say hello next time at the pool no matter what, I promise I will but in a noncommital way so if he isn't it won't matter unless . . . dammit, I was *sure* he would, so I'm probably imagining things except why does he stare like that? oh well, nothing makes sense any more, so So Long for now Mr. Lupine Eyes, "You see? you see?" oh will you for *Chrissakes shut up* because I have got to get this show on the road so I better start back at the beginning to pick up the argument but "This time pay attention, *pay close attention!*" for "At this juncture, the Thomists, realizing that a break with the crown would jeopardize their mission to Rome . . ."

The voices were so clamorous & persistent that few things ever silenced them, although stealing more books from the college library helped. I'd stolen books ever since my freshman year, from the library & the bookstore too, using a strategy that worked quite well. You have to be brazen about stealing. Inexperienced thieves skulk & hide, making their guilt obvious. Don't do that—be bold & brassy, as if the volume of Molière's plays you've just dog-eared & written your name in has been yours for years, & you'll rarely be apprehended. (The "rarely" is the rub.) This, however, was a new, more intense chapter in my career as a petty thief. Within a couple of months I had pilfered a few dozen books—three volumes of Gide's *Journals* with drawings by Cocteau; a nineteenth-century edition of *Tom Jones;* sixteen volumes of eighteenth-century drama (gold-tooled, leatherbound books with engravings); a fifteenth-century Latin text bound in parchment. God only knows how, but I even managed to get Baugh's three-inch-thick *History of English Literature* under my belt & out the door. I spent hours in my dorm room rearranging the books. They were a gift from life to compensate me for the recent past, & having them around me created the illusion that I somehow possessed their contents & thus partook of the world where people lived who owned & read such things.

Then one Saturday morning I got a call from a guy named Ronnie who said he'd met Dick, & that Dick had talked of me & mentioned that I came from Indianapolis. "Yes?" I said, bewildered but pleased that someone, anyone, had called me. "Well, me too; I'm from Indianapolis too," Ronnie said cheerfully, as if total strangers who'd grown up in the same city normally made contact whenever possible, like Shriners or terrorists. "So I wondered if you'd like to work out at my gym this afternoon." "Yes, sure . . ." Yes, *anything* to end my isolation. We made plans & hung up.

Immediately I felt uneasy, but I didn't know why. Something just seemed strange. I called back with a lie, saying I had to babysit for a professor, but since I had an extra ticket for the ballet that night, maybe he would like to join me? The extra ticket was a lie too, but I figured everybody's booked on Saturday night.

"I'd love to," Ronnie said. "And a friend of mine is having a cocktail party, so we can stop in for a drink on our way to the ballet."

We made new plans & I spent the next couple of hours conning a ticket from a classmate in the dorm. Given my childhood, lying came easily to me, but like most habitual liars I always went too far. I said that an uncle, my father's favorite brother & a man who had always been kind to me & even footed some of my Columbia bills out of a meager income, had suddenly turned up in New York, sick with a mysterious malady doubtless aggravated by grief at the recent death of his wife, my favorite aunt & a saint of a woman who, etc., etc., etc. I got my ticket & went off to the East Sixties to meet Ronnie, hoping he looked remotely like a Hoosier uncle.

Not by a long shot. In his mid-twenties, he was trim & fit & dressed to the nines in a dark three-piece suit with a tab collar shirt & French cuffs & shoes shined to a dazzle. Everything about him was polished & preened, pressed & groomed, tailored to a T. What a bumpkin I felt in my baggy tweeds & flattop haircut. Ronnie was immaculate, his apartment was immaculate, his psychoanalyst roommate was immaculate in an identical three-piece suit.

After some aimless chat about the agonies & ecstasies of growing up in Indianapolis, we left for the cocktail party. Then into a cab for a three-block ride to a posh building with two doormen and an elevator with an elevator man; then down a long, carpeted hallway, through a door leading into a marble foyer beyond which was a huge living room with maybe fifty men of various ages dressed like Ronnie & his roommate. Without any preparation or the slightest hint of what was about to happen, I had just walked into a world of men like me, & I simultaneously experienced two overwhelming, diametrically opposed responses: "My moral universe has just been turned upside down," & "Thank God, I'm no longer alone." The dread of a new fear, the euphoria of an immense relief.

Part Two

· 5 ·

Before Ronnie & I left the party that night, a movie producer had offered me a job in France the following summer on a film being made near his villa in St. Tropez, where a guest room was at my disposal. Come again? Well, I was taking a French conversation course, wasn't I? But my French wasn't fluent, I told him. Oh, I could learn more, I could manage somehow.

Though barely half an hour into that new world, I understood perfectly well that Mr. Hollywood St. Tropez had something in mind besides my linguistic skills. But my relief in discovering that I was no longer alone was far greater than the trepidation I felt at what this new world portended. If you had told me every man in that room was also a Nazi sympathizer, it wouldn't have bothered me, not much anyway. All I cared about was that I would never be alone again, and that when I went wherever those men gathered, I would never be despised & rejected for what I was.

What a rollercoaster joyride those next few weeks were as Ronnie paraded me through a bewildering succession of gay parties & bars & brunches & dinners & more parties & restaurants & clubs & dance palaces & still more parties. I was amazed at how many gay men there were in New York, & at how rich & famous some of them were, & at how warmly they welcomed me into their world. Wherever I went, I was flattered & fussed over & made to feel extremely special.

One day Ronnie was on the phone when I heard him describe me as a "U.T." Later I asked, "What's a U.T.?"

"A Universal Type, someone everybody wants."

So that's what I was—not a Damon or a Pythias, not a fruit or a queer, not thank God that most loathsome of all things human, a "homoSEKshual,"—but a Universal Type. That sounded great to me, & as more time passed, I saw that what Ronnie said was true: everywhere we went, I was someone everybody wanted.

At one or another of the innumerable parties we attended, a curator offered me a personal tour next time I stopped by his museum, a famous playwright invited me to his new hit on Broadway, a German prince gave me his card & hoped I would visit next time I was in Munich &/or Marrakesh, & there was a famous designer, & a beautiful ballet dancer, & about the time I began reeling from it all, I found myself sitting on a couch talking to one of the most beautiful men in America. He was a model whose face was just then smiling from sea to shining sea in posters promising that if you too smoked Newports, you might become as peerlessly handsome with similar power to stop traffic in public. He was extraordinary—one of those physically perfect people who seems a creature of another species—& I was astounded to realize he was coming on to me, saying he'd like to "get together, maybe tomorrow night when my lover'll be out for the evening." I could hardly register what he was saying, it so flustered me to look at him. I half expected to be struck blind, & I kept thinking, "This can't be happening, it's something out of a dream."

Then, in a maneuver that would soon become habitual, a part of me stepped outside myself & saw that everyone in the room was observing us. Conversation had paused & people on the fringes were pressing closer for a better look as Mr. Drop Dead Gorgeous went about making his pass. I sensed a vicarious thrill pulse through the audience as we exchanged telephone numbers, & I thought, "This must be what it feels like to be a star."

The denouement the following night was a fiasco, thanks to my paralyzing self-consciousness at being with a man of such supernal good looks & with a body to match. He was nice about it, and he tried to get me to relax, but each time I calmed down enough to think I might actually be capable of enjoying myself, he would admire my face, or my arms, or my hands, or have me turn over on my stomach so he could admire my ass, & again I became paralyzed. Eros retired in defeat & I headed back to the dorms feeling disappointed & bewildered.

Confusing, this coming out business—at least the way I was doing it. I liked being desired, especially by men who were beautiful or famous or rich, but it made me feel dishonest since I didn't imagine myself the way they did. I craved the flattery, yet it came so easily & automatically that it didn't seem genuine. I loved it every time some glassy-eyed man murmured "You're *soooo* beautiful," yet the words made me painfully self-conscious. I couldn't get enough of the compliments & praise but couldn't change the subject fast enough each time the conversation focussed on me. I soon learned what to expect from the interminable round of parties & brunches & dinners & dances & bars, but I couldn't refuse a single invitation. Along with the pleasures of casual sex, I came to know its frustrations, yet sex was my irrefutable proof that all the fuss & bother over me were based on something others considered real. Without even the dimmest knowledge of what was happening, I was becoming a bulimic of male homosexuality, gorging & vomiting several times in the course of a week.

The voices sealed my confusion. "Since you now have what so many others crave—acceptance & admiration, your pick of parties & people, first choices for sex, approbation of your every word & deed—since you have what so many are miserable at *not* having, surely it's good, & good to have, so nothing can be wrong."

Fair enough, but then why was I so confused?

In my dorm room, I studied my face in the mirror. I was good-looking, yes, but there were guys at Columbia better looking than I was. With Dick I'd never thought much about looks. He was a nice-enough-looking man, but what had mattered to me with Dick was the sense of emotional completion I'd felt with him. I'd fallen in love with him because he was caring & had an oddball sense of humor & endearingly stubborn ways, & because he kept alive in his imagination the finest version of me that could possibly exist. Yet in this new world, looks seemed immensely important. Everywhere I went, I kept hearing not just that I was handsome or attractive or beautiful, but *incredibly* handsome, *extremely* attractive, *very* beautiful. That's heady stuff, & you have to work hard to resist it. I didn't even try, just studied my face in the mirror to see if I couldn't find what those men saw in me. I saw how flustered they got when we met & I saw the intensity in their eyes. I saw their eagerness & desire, but I couldn't see what inspired them.

I began to feel like a fraud, so I tried harder to please, & succeeded more, & became more confused, & felt more like a fraud.

Somewhere early on in that endless round of gay goings-on, I met a photographer's agent & a plastic surgeon who both asked if I'd ever thought of becoming a model. Was there a single attractive young gay man in all of America in those days who hadn't thought of becoming a model? It was glamorous & lucrative work, & being paid for your looks was the ultimate confirmation that you were attractive, right? Besides, I was now sleeping with some of New York's top male models, so yes, I'd thought of becoming a model.

The agent arranged for test shots & we met to study the results. No doubt about it, they said, I could be a successful model. I needed to let my hair grow, & buy the basic wardrobe of course, & I also needed a nose job—nothing major, no no no—just a very slight alteration to accentuate my nostrils by way of creating more definition for the camera. The plastic surgeon would perform the operation, which would be described as correcting a deviated septum so that Dad's post office insurance would pay, and I could recuperate at the surgeon's apartment where he would keep an eye on me, along with his mouth as it turned out.

A nose job seemed a small price to pay for the chance to appear on the covers of *Esquire* and *GQ,* & anyway, I wasn't paying, so on with the operation. Once the bandages were off & the swelling went down, I was relieved to see that the change was indeed minor. I was also glad I was finally beginning to see what all the fuss was about. No one at Columbia remarked on any difference in my face, & my absence & black eyes were explained by the official lie: surgery for a deviated septum.

I told that lie to Bob & Patti, which was the first sign I had of how much I was moving away from my life at Columbia. My deception of them was so acute that I might well have stopped seeing them, but that wasn't possible. Bob had arranged with the dean to teach me a year of British constitutional history tutorially, so once a week I went to his high-rise apartment overlooking Harlem for a couple hours of conversation about the books I'd read & the essay I'd written. (What an extraordinary privilege—in four years at Columbia, I never heard of the like—& how blasé I was about it at the time.) Now & then, Bob & Patti invited me to dinner or the ballet, but increasingly I was uncomfortable in their company, for I felt I had to conceal my new life & was constantly afraid I might give myself away.

There were awkward moments. Once they surprised me by showing up at Grand Central Station to wish me bon voyage on a trip home to Indianapolis, & they perforce met a misty-eyed Ronnie who suddenly looked screamingly gay to me. One evening I lied to get out of a dinner at Bob's because an invitation had come for a party I absolutely had to attend. I was suddenly very sick, I said, could barely talk, should get back to bed immediately. Imagine Bob's & my astonishment when, all showered & duded up for a gay night out on the town, I answered the knock on my door to find Bob standing there on a mercy errand, proffering the dessert I'd missed by being taken so suddenly, critically ill. There he stood, the man who'd made the crucial difference in my college career, who'd been unfailingly generous with his time & support, the only per-

son I knew in New York with a strong, disinterested affection for me, &
he was the last person in the world I wanted to see. And poor, frightened
thing that I was, all I could think was, "I must learn to lie better."

I couldn't tell Bob about my new life, or at least I thought I couldn't. It
seemed far too risky to come out at Columbia. Arthur MacArthur was
the only student I recall who was in any sense of the word "out," which
is to say that Arthur was conspicuously nelly—a living affront to his
father, the General, which was surely the point. Until I met Arthur I'd
never known French contained so many sibilants, but I admired him for
not caring or seeming to care what people thought about him. We all
cared so much about what people thought of us in those days, & wanted
so much to be accepted & (please God!) popular, & tried so hard to con-
form & never offend or under any circumstances appear foolish. Arthur
didn't give a damn & I liked him for that; also for his hatred of his father,
which created a bond. When the country went into mourning at the General's death, I watched the New York obsequies on television. Following
the horsedrawn caisson down Fifth Avenue came the two black-clad
figures for whom America was opening the wellsprings of her deepest
sympathy: a veiled Mrs. MacArthur dabbing her eyes, & dear, sweet
Arthur grinning from ear to ear.

But Arthur was the exception at Columbia, so I was careful to edit &
dissemble & keep my new life as hidden as possible. Gay men began to
call me in the dorms (calls were tapped & more entries made on my
secret record), & occasionally I invited a trick back to my room for sex
(notice was taken, more entries added); otherwise, I kept the two lives
strictly separate. I went to my classes, did my work, & continued to get
good grades. I even won the John Jacob Coss Memorial Prize, awarded
to a member of the junior class "in recognition of qualities which give
promise of future distinction." I was in fact about to distinguish myself,
but not in any way John Jacob Coss had ever imagined.

Increasingly I lived for the times off campus: the glamor parties &
opening nights & famous people & fabulous fucks. People said "I've
heard so much about you" & "You're even better looking than I was
told." There were so many men saying so many things that I couldn't
keep them straight—the men, that is, not the things. I began to feel like a
finalist in a gay popularity contest, & it looked like I just might win.

The summer after my junior year in 1958, I remained in New York doing
test shots & putting together a modelling portfolio; otherwise, I spent my
time exploring the gay world. It was such a different world, & now such

a vanished one, that it's not easy to explain. Intensely secretive & hidden, it went on mostly at night behind the unmarked doors of bars & in apartments where the shades were always drawn. The 415 Bar on Amsterdam Avenue was typical: you walked in, saw a few locals talking with the bartender, & figured you'd made a mistake. But through an unmarked door in the back & down a flight of stairs, you entered a cavernous basement teeming with hundreds of gay men who were dancing & laughing & cruising & kissing & drinking & passing out in the johns. No wonder that during my two years with Dick I'd not had the slightest suspicion such a world existed. It was determined to remain as hidden as possible.

The men were too. Everyone I knew was more or less closeted & spent a lot of time in the workaday world passing for straight. Save for a few artists & hairdressers & decorators & dancers, we were all terrified of being found out. Gay men regularly married for the sake of appearances or inheritances & just as regularly committed suicide. If you heard that a gay man was seeing a shrink, it meant only one thing: he was trying desperately to "go straight," which sounded more like a road sign than a way of life. Parents routinely disowned & disinherited their gay sons or had them committed to mental hospitals where they were subjected to shock treatments & lobotomies & a popular therapy of the day called "aversion therapy": "by means of hypnotic suggestion and conditioning, the author has been able . . . to create deep aversions in the male homosexual to the male body." How do you do that? "Suggestions of filth associated with the male genitalia of their partners were implanted in their subconscious and reinforced periodically during the hypnotic trance." Psychiatrists published abominations like that with pride & impunity. In their view, which was mainstream America's view made professional & scientifically unassailable, homosexuality was an abnormality to be corrected at all costs; the most barbarous treatments were justified in the name of destroying such pernicious tendencies. There were gay men walking the streets of Manhattan in those days who had been rendered incapable of sex or had their memories obliterated by electricity. For some, it would take years to put their minds back together again; for others, the effort was hopeless. Of all the enemies we had, psychiatrists were among the most dangerous. And our parents, of course. I never met anyone who was out to his parents; you had to be crazy to do such a thing.

There was no place in public where it felt safe to be gay. Even inside the gay world you weren't secure, since bars & parties were raided all the time. You'd be having a beer & a chat with someone in a bar when suddenly the police would appear at the door screaming "Stay where you are, this is a raid!" Fear would sweep over the place, followed by a stampede for the back door, people falling over each other & jamming the exit in their panic to get out. During one of my own terrified escapes, I was fleeing out the back when I saw a fat man I knew wedged in the bathroom window leading to the alley. The next day, his name appeared in the papers along with the names of the other men arrested in the raid—a couple of dozen all told, an average take. He was fired of course, & evicted from his apartment, & there was nothing he could do about it. There were no legal aid societies or political action groups for gays in those days, no gay weeklies or bimonthlies to publish his plight & raise money for his defense. What defense? Firings, evictions, arrests, entrapments, blackmail, muggings, murders—they happened all the time, they came with the territory.

At parties, you knew the instant the police had arrived. The room would fall silent & without even turning to look, you knew a couple of New York's finest were at the front door, "Fuckin' Faggots" scrawled all over their faces. Sometimes they told us to keep it down & they went away; other times they told us to break it up & then stood at the door as we filed out between them like guilty things caught in a shameful act. I never once heard anyone protest or ask why we had to break it up. We just did as we were told.

Except for the drag queens, bless their sassy, revolutionary hearts. But they always got beaten up & arrested & thrown in jail, over & over again. "Such masochists," we said. "They're really sick."

Whenever our world came into conflict with the straight world, group loyalties crumbled. Threatened with arrest or blackmail, thrown out of a party, chased down a midnight street by a gang of fagbashers, it was each gay man for himself, running for fear, lost in a panic to save his own skin. We didn't have much political awareness, partly no doubt because our enemies were so often invisible: cultural opinion, legal precedent, psychiatric theory, social convention, religious stricture—nothing you could insult or demean or punch in the face in return. The most pernicious enemy of all, & the most invisible, was our own self-hatred.

Almost all of us bought into the straight notion that there really was something wrong with us, something abnormal & perverted & ultimately pathetic. It still astounds me to think how many derogatory names the straight world has invented to designate gay men: fags, faggots, pansies, perverts, inverts, aunties, flits, queers, queens, cocksuckers, nellies, sickos, homos, sodomites, pederasts, sissies, swishes, fairies, fruits, & the list goes on. The reverberations of that lexicon sounded even in our dreams, inducing a kind of concentration camp mentality. We were disposable, the scum of the earth, living crimes against nature (thank you, Thomas Aquinas), & we knew that socially, religiously, legally, psychoanalytically, & in every other way that mattered, we were beyond the pale of what was considered acceptably human. I don't remember that we talked about the sense of shame the straight world bred in us, but it was pervasive in our lives, & I don't know anyone of my gay generation who's ever been able to shake it. I certainly haven't. You can still see it in the timid gestures toward self-exposure of a John Ashbery or a Jasper Johns, & in the furtive, guilty cruising of gay men in their fifties & sixties.

With so much fear & danger hedging our lives, it's no wonder we were a wildly romantic bunch. Mainstream America was too, of course. My parents had grown up in a world fed by Hollywood fantasies of romantic love, & the lyrics of popular songs urged a desperate, eternal monogamy: "Once you have found him / Never let him go," & then the repeat in case you weren't paying attention the first time. In 1957, 96 percent of adult Americans were married, if you can imagine such a statistic. Heterosexual marriage was the only model of adult life that existed at the time, so gay America was busy coupling in imitation of its masters.

Since romance thrives on obstacles (Tristan & Isolde, Romeo & Juliet, Cupid & Psyche, Antony & Cleopatra), there was no more fertile ground for romance in those days than the gay world. I don't think I ever made love with a man without first convincing myself he was a potential long-term lover, & if the first date went well, which invariably meant the first night of sex, I was ready next morning to shop for monogrammed towels. All the frenetic cruising & partying & sexing had as its goal the paragon lover, a gay knight on a charger who would sweep us off our feet & make everything all right, compensate us for the oppresssion we had to put up with & for the pervasive sense there was something lacking in us that only the right man could supply. We fell in love a lot, & conducted our mostly brief affairs with operatic drama—passionate avowals of eternal devotion, fits of jealous rage, wrenching breakups replete with nervous breakdowns & threats of suicide. The few of us liberated enough to resist the notion that gay men were incapable of sustained affection managed successful relationships, but most of us got "married" & settled down for a brief while, then broke up & broke down, then grieved & cruised until we met the next candidate for our troubled affections, & thus the same round all over again.

There was almost always an element of the frantic & the excessive about our pleasures. Parties & pimples, tricks & true loves, suicides &

sales—everything was "fabulous" or "horrible," "terrific" or "terrible," with nothing in between, no "all right" or "fine" or "okay." It was all very hectic, extreme, loud, & mildly hysterical. Yet very conventional too in that gay men's relationships aped straight marriages with their clearly assigned roles of "butch" & "femme," "top" & "bottom," "husband" & "wife."

I didn't know anyone who didn't have a camp name. Two giant weight-lifter friends were dubbed "Martha" & "Hilda," & I once lived with a gorgeous Neapolitan-Sicilian we called "Gina," by which time I was "Hanya" & "Celeste." I didn't know anyone who didn't have a sun-lamp or take a long time in the bathroom or wear clothes too small for comfort. I didn't know anyone who didn't belong to a gym, unless he was hopeless material, or anyone who didn't care a lot about bodies. I didn't know anyone who didn't have a type ("He'd be gorgeous if he weren't blond") or a limited repertory of sexual practices ("What do you do?" we always asked to make sure our desires could cooperate). I didn't know anyone who didn't drink a lot. A typical evening began with drinks at someone's apartment, then wine during dinner followed by a brandy or two, then more drinks at a bar afterward. I often staggered home at three & four & five A.M. with vodka & wine & brandy & beer sloshing around in my disconsolate stomach.

You can find the feel & flavor of that world in Frank O'Hara's poetry. He was on the scene a lot & he wrote about it, though usually in guarded ways that require deciphering. But he clearly conveys the sense of lots of romantic, glamorous, frenetic living & high hilarity, & beneath it all, some sadness laced with a little shame & a little self-hatred.

But this is all after the fact. I didn't analyze my experience at the time, I just lived it. "You kept from thinking and it was all marvelous," as Harry says in "The Snows of Kilimanjaro." If I bothered to think anything at the time, it was probably "Lucky me, fiddledeedee," nothing more profound than that. I was too flustered for thought, too dazzled by the sexual & social opportunities that existed for me in that world.

The sex was everywhere. The parties & bars & dances & dinners yielded a lot, but gyms were even better sources, for in a gym you could see what a man had to offer physically. A goodly portion of attractive gay Manhattan worked out at the West Side Y, & I never went to the Y without the expectation I might go home with someone afterward. At the least I usually got a telephone number or two for future reference. Sex was out in public too, walking down the street at all hours of the day & night. Noon or midnight, three in the afternoon or ten in the morning, before lunch or after the theater, on your way to the post office or in the subway—it was abundantly there for the having. I knew guys who had sex three & four times a day, & if they couldn't, they masturbated three or four times a day. Usually they got what they wanted. Some of my most exciting times happened when I connected with an attractive man in the supermarket or on the street, & fifteen minutes later we'd be curling each other's toes in one of our apartments. But you had to be careful about the sexual opportunities you encountered in public if you wanted to avoid the homophobia & violence that existed everywhere & were so easily aroused.

As for the social opportunities, I wouldn't believe them if I hadn't lived them. In the next four years, I met Noel Coward & John Gielgud, Laurence Olivier & the Lunts, Bette Davis & Gloria Swanson, the *West Side Story* crowd (Bernstein, Robbins, Laurents, & Sondheim), Katharine Hepburn, Lena Horne, Rock Hudson, James Baldwin, Judy Garland, Rex Harrison, Nat King Cole, Dali & Margaret Rockefeller (the Marquesa de Cuevas), Robert Redford & Jane Fonda, Ava Gardner & Jack Dempsey, Williams & Albee & Inge, Gore Vidal & Eleanor Roosevelt, Marlene Dietrich & Adlai Stevenson, Jackie Kennedy & the Dalai Lama. (I'm namedropping, yes, but how else can I make the point so neatly?) In the ensuing years, I met many more such prominent people. Some I met by chance or through common friends, but some became close friends & a few became lovers. If you were a presentable young gay man with manners & a good suit, there wasn't anywhere you couldn't go in the worlds of art & entertainment, & those worlds easily opened up other vistas. Because I was gay, I had much more social mobility than if I'd been straight. As for the gay world, it was much smaller & more concentrated then than now, so instead of being a small fish in a big pond, which would have been my lot as a young man coming out these days, I was vice versa. Today you can live a gay male life as a leather queen in Chicago or Houston or Des Moines without traversing the boundaries of other subworlds, but in those days, the gay world was concentrated in New York & its members inhabited several subworlds simultantously. A Manhattan leather queen circa 1958 might well be a member of the opera queen set, which included people from the gym queen set, some of whose members were writers & painters & playwrights from the arts queen set, which spilled over into the international queen set, which boasted some tearoom queens & trade queens, & so on throughout that whole, elaborate, secret world. The result was that you knew people throughout the only concentrated gay world in America. And they knew or had heard about you—or at least about me.

Since a good body counted for so much in gay New York, that summer of '58 I joined the West Side Y. I had a perfectly good body to start with—well-proportioned thanks to Mother Nature, developed & toned from construction work & my daily mile in the Columbia pool. But always willing to find myself wanting, & now inhabiting a world where bodies counted for a lot, I had to have a better body, the best body on the beach, a body that would make people swoon.

Four times a week at the West Side Y, I lugged & hoisted & pushed & pulled & pumped & strained until I got what I wanted—a body like the Doryphorus of Polyclitus but with no Venus girdle (i.e., no love handles, only the taut line of muscle from waist to hip, a "lithe sheer of waist"). Pleased at how quickly my body responded to exercise, I turned my visits to the gym into a fetish. If I had a date or a party or any kind of evening out, I needed a thorough workout beforehand as a prop for my wobbly self-esteem. So I'd pump up the muscles, squeeze into some Levi's, & off I'd go into the night.

People did in fact say that the sight of me walking on the beach made them swoon; one man claimed he'd had to leave the beach to recover. But compliments about my body were easy for me to accept. I might doubt my looks, but never my body. From the time I became addicted to the gym, I knew that my body was superb. And luckily I was saved from the grotesque models of male bodybuilding that exist these days. Steve Reeves was the Mr. Universe of the late '50s—a handsome man of classic features with a body of classical proportions like you see on Greek statues of older gods & heroes, the mature Zeus & Poseidon for example. Nothing like Arnold Schwarzenegger has ever existed in the world of art.

Not yet a year into my gay life & already it bewildered me whenever someone didn't want me. That sexy Slavic waiter in the restaurant on Bleecker Street, with wavy blond hair & dark eyebrows & lupine eyes & an ectomorphic body all shoulders & wrists & cowboy legs showing through his tight pants, he certainly wanted me. Desire was written all over his beautiful, brooding face, so it was easy to make a date with him to come back to my place when he got off work around one in the morning.

In fact, he'd wanted me so much I wasn't worried when it got to be 1:10 & even 1:20. It was only around 1:30 that I began to pace the apartment & look out the window to see if he was coming up the street, then 1:45 when I ran downstairs to check the doorbell, first disconnecting the phone in case he called during my absence, then back upstairs fast to reconnect the phone & look out the window again & check myself in the mirror to reestablish the fact that yes, I was attractive, I was so attractive I hadn't met anyone who didn't want me, so he'd be along soon, there was some explanation, he was held after work or something until it was 2:30 & then 3:00 & 4:00 & 5:00 with the dawn coming up but still the frantic hope he would come despite the growing, horrible realization that I was being stood up for the first time in my life, was being abandoned & was thus what I feared in my worst thoughts: worthless because not really that attractive & therefore someone others would stand up, which was to say, abandon. What was happening to me simply *could not happen,* so even at 6:00 & 7:00, sitting in the window watching early risers on their way to coffee shops, I still nursed the dying hope that the phone would ring. There *had* to be a different ending from the one I was living through, for it was intolerable, a kind of hell, & so back to the window to search the street now filling with people on their way to work, & me alone, not really that attractive after all, a fraud the Slavic waiter had seen through just as everyone else would soon see through me. I was unattractive & worthless: it all showed in the mirror.

It would take me more than twenty years to work my way through that confusion. During that time, legions of men offered me their company & their affection, their bodies & their secrets, but it was usually the ones who turned me down or stood me up or didn't call or somehow rejected me who made the most lasting impressions. Given my childhood, rejection always felt like abandonment, & whenever it happened it was devastating. I'd been out maybe nine months & established an extraordinary record of social & sexual triumphs, but all of that counted for nothing the night the Slavic waiter didn't show.

"Never mind, my dear," said Sam Sloman, "for*get* that Slavic slut. You are di*vine,* do you *hear? Absolutely di*vine! Now pay attention to your mother!"

Sam Slomon—*aka* Sally Slomon, your Aunt Sally, your mother, & the Sobo heiress (his father invented Sobo Glue)—was the Elsa Maxwell of New York gay society in the '50s & '60s. Every few weeks Sam gave a party in his over-decorated Village apartment for sixty or seventy of New York's most beautiful gay men, along with a sprinkling of the older rich &/or famous. Most attractive gay men about town eventually found their way to one of Sam's loud, jampacked, giddy, trick-fix drunkfests. The first time I went, I was in the bathroom when Sam barged in to change for his drag number. He stripped & got in the bathtub as I started to piss. "Over here, my dear. Go ahead, your Aunt Sally's a golden shower queen. Oh come *on,* for heaven's sakes, just a little bit, don't be such a tight-assed

WASP. Right here on my leg. Come on now, do what your mother says."
I did what my mother said. "Ohhh, I may just *faint* with joy. Well, *that*
was certainly refreshing. What a *kind* young man you are, every bit as
sweet as you are *beautiful*." A short time later, Sam emerged from the john
to entertain us in a hula skirt, with breasts & wig of shaving cream. When
he wasn't falling down drunk, Sam's drag numbers could be hilarious.

Sound sort of pathetic? Not really. "Humani nil a me alienum puto,"
says Terence ("Nothing human is alien to me"), & besides, considering
Sam's story it was a miracle he could function at all. When he was sixteen
& living with his family in Brooklyn, he sneaked out one night to attend
a drag ball in Manhattan. Returning home drunk & wobbly in high
heels, he saw a man cruising him in a car, so he flounced & teased the
man all the way home. When he turned up his front walk, the driver
pulled in behind him. Sam's father had been cruising his son, having mistaken him for a woman, & a loose one at that—one of the more startling
ways to discover that your namesake & heir is gay. A week later, according to Sam, his father tried to push him into a two-thousand-gallon
churning vat of Sobo glue.

Sam had grown up in a world even more benighted about gaydomry
than the world of the 1950s. In the '20s & '30s, there wasn't even a
Giovanni's Room or *The City and the Pillar* to read as a young man.
Sam's early passions were for drag & trade, & he remained faithful to both
his whole life long. He told me that his first sex occurred when Harpo
Marx seduced him as a boy vacationing with his parents at Grossinger's.
Sam boasted of the experience as a grown man, but if in fact it happened,
it must have been unnerving for a boy of twelve. Though a real mensch &
full of street smarts, he'd often been beaten up cruising the docks for
trade. It had to be harder for Sam to be gay in the 1930s & '40s than it
was for us in the '50s. Constantly fortified by booze & pills & a succession of unsuccessful shrinks, he was one of the people who helped pave
the way for gay men of later generations. But everyone's heard about
prophets in their own countries.

I met Sam when he was forty-five, & he was then an interior decora-
tor who'd done some well-known New York restaurants. (Why do so
many gay men become decorators? It's a way to design alternative
worlds, or at least to improve on the existing one.) Short, stocky, balding,
an inveterate camp & very butch, Sam was like most gay men I knew
then, & many I know now, in that he thought he was missing a piece, a
part, a something that could only be supplied by the right man, which in
Sam's case meant the right straight stud—a sailor or Marine or carpenter

or bricklayer or telephone line repairman or . . . well, you get the type. The illusion kept him cruising so constantly that I often thought he must have cruised in his dreams. Sam would walk up to a stud in broad daylight & exclaim "You are the *most* gorgeous & sexy man I have *ever* seen in my *entire life!* Do you *realize* how *gorgeous* you are?" A Santa Claus laugh in here, then "My dear, a man like *you* deserves the *best* blow job of his *life,* & that's the *least* I'm offering you." More often than not, he got the guy—through flattery or jokes or promises to pander or persistence or money. Sam's life was a continual demonstration that where there's a will, & sometimes money, there usually is a way.

I saw a lot of Sam that first summer of being out in gay New York. He adored me, but he didn't lust after me. He paid my way & pandered for me. He made sure I met all the attractive young men he knew, & he served as a go-between for older men too shy to approach me on their own.

"Remember Joe Hastings, the advertising queen? Tall, skinny, nervous, looks like a dachshund? Matter of fact, she *has* a dachshund. Well, you've done it again, my dear. She's *mad* for you, says she'll do *anything,* I can't get her off the phone. Would you consider dinner? the theater? a trip to Europe? adoption? I can't remember it all, but I *do* remember a firm offer of a thousand dollars if you'll spend the night with him."

A thousand dollars for a single night of sex (equivalent to roughly five thousand dollars today)? That was the offer, & the best proposition I've ever heard of. I turned Joe down for the simple reason that I didn't find him attractive, but by way of compensation I let him buy me a custom-tailored sport jacket from Dunhill & take me to a few opening nights. Also a few parties—the most closeted parties of all, attended by diplomats & politicians, heads of corporations, top military brass, the gay men most terrified of exposure. Aside from occasional remarks about attractive men, those gatherings could have passed for stag parties, the men were so resolutely masculine. Their dates were West Point cadets, college athletes, Olympic medalists—impeccably butch young men beyond a hint of suspicion; young men like me.

Surely one reason for Joe's munificent offer was the fact that in a world of so many effeminate men, I was masculine. I enjoyed the camping of others but wasn't good at it, & I wasn't about to do anything in public I didn't excel at. I could pass for straight except when some hawk-eyed homophobe found me slavering at high noon over an Italian demigod. With little to lose, I was more out than most (away from Columbia anyway), which meant that though I felt shame at being gay, I didn't show it. And a lifetime of learning how to please plus the knack of altering myself to suit the moods & needs of others meant that I was well prepared for success in that world.

Since society is essentially a form of theater (something the French have always understood), people devoted to social success need to be adept actors or they'll end up with bit parts. I was ready for most leading roles in that world of sexual fantasy. I couldn't satisfy anyone's need for a leather or S&M type or your average slackjawed sheet-metal worker, but otherwise I had several roles in my repertory:

Ivy League student intellectual? Down pat.

College athlete lifeguard with body of death? No problem.

All-American boy next door oozing with Hoosier? The Norman Rockwell boyman type which was then the reigning image of the attractive American male? That's exactly what I looked like.

Soulful aesthete who swooned at Balanchine, haunted museums, & could quote reams of poetry from memory? I put my heart & soul into that one.

Withdrawn, tormented, meditative young man? Right up my alley.

Spoiled, self-centered, unavailable brat star of the gay world? Watch me do my stuff.

In short, there was the face for the face queens, the body for the body queens, the mind for the mind queens, the brat for the brat queens, & a deeply confused, worthwhile young man for those who wanted to rescue someone. Also the carefree young man who didn't seem ashamed of being gay (an impression greatly aided by the eight hundred miles between me & home). I was able to serve as a multipurpose screen on which men could project their different desires, & I served eagerly, with a desperate neediness, for the more people wanted me, the more I mattered, right? "That's right," the voices said.

I didn't think of it this way at the time; I just thought, "Wow, everybody wants me, I really *am* unique." I was aware however that the life I was living was a lot of work & took a lot of time, but I figured that, as the French say, "Il faut souffrir pour être beau"—One must suffer to be beautiful. I had to show up at a lot of social events, & endure a lot of flattery, & spend a lot of time at the gym, & make sure the clothes fit right, & balance a bewildering number of demands on my time. Just going to a party could consume half the day. The preparations included going to the Y for a thorough workout, concluding with a two mile run & a mile swim, after which I had a sunlamp treatment. Then home for a nap before showering & shaving & dressing & preening. At last I was ready, except for a glass of milk & a tablespoon of olive oil to coat my stomach as a guard against hangovers. And that was just a single party.

The payoff for all this effort? I was becoming the most celebrated young man in all of gay New York.

I was taken on for a tryout period by the Hartford Model Agency (owned by the A&P heir Huntington Hartford, who soon sold it to Eileen & Jerry Ford). Odd that I would persist in modelling since I hated being photographed, worried as I was that the fuss over my looks was mistaken & convinced that the other male models were better looking than me. But the money was so good & the strokes for my ego so gratifying that I swallowed my diffidence & showed up for bookings.

Clearly, I thought, I needed to know more about my looks, the better to tend them, the better to nurture my fledgling career. I don't know how it is for other models, but for me it wasn't possible to think about my looks & body & hair & skin & teeth only from nine to five Monday through Friday. I came to think about them around the clock. I developed an extraordinarily acute sense of my physical self that I lost only when drunk or asleep or in the throes of sex. I studied myself until I knew every square millimeter of my body, from the beauty mark on my left cheek to the shape of my toenails. The really beautiful, I thought, are flawless— the ones like gods, that is. Whenever I arrived at a party or restaurant or anywhere I knew people would be ogling me, I headed straight for the john to check myself out in the mirror to make sure the gift of the look was in prime working order. Always my comb, never my glasses. I learned which was my better side & positioned myself so that side faced whomever I wanted to impress. Whenever there was no one to impress, I had a boring evening.

The modelling jobs began coming in on a regular basis. They sometimes interfered with my classes at Columbia, but no great matter. It was enviable to be a model & my career was taking off, hip hip hurrah. One more thing I'd wanted a lot & managed to get.

My advisor at Columbia was Andrew Chiappe, a brilliant polymath who was legendary on campus for his incisive mind & immense knowledge. Lionel Trilling & Meyer Schapiro used to drop into his office to have him decipher a phrase of Hegel, or translate some medieval Latin, or explain the essentials of Rajput painting. I found him so intimidating that his innocuous "How are you, Mr. Helms?" used to render me speechless.

When Professor Chiappe suggested I apply for a Rhodes Scholarship, I therefore took it as a sign from on high. I applied, & after a couple of preliminary rounds I became one of the midwestern finalists, which meant a trip to Indianapolis for the interview that would winnow a field of eighteen or so to the two who would go to Oxford in the fall. Chiappe's recommendation augured well. I had a custom-tailored three-piece suit (a gift from an admirer), & I could count on a first-rate education to support me in the interview. I headed for Indianapolis, nervous but hopeful.

The morning interview was exciting—questions about structural relations between Bach's music & mathematics & other such ingenuities posed by a genial group of a dozen former Rhodes scholars seated on the far side of a large table. Clearly I performed well, clearly they liked me.

After lunch, three of us were called back for a final interview. When my turn came, the examiners began with questions that seemed somehow odd.

"If you were to go to Oxford, Mr. Helms, would you miss the world of Broadway theater?"

"Probably not. If I did, I could take a train to London."

"Have you ever been in the homes of any of your professors?"

"I've often been in the home of Professor Webb, and I once attended a wedding reception at Professor Hofstadter's."

"When you lived in the dormitory, you sometimes had guests?"

Their drift became clear & I began to panic.

"Now & then, yes."

"Where do you go when you go to Greenwich Village?"

"No place in particular . . . that is, movies mostly, & the Amato Opera Company. It's not expensive. The operas aren't very good, I mean the performances, but I go there and . . . sometimes a restaurant . . . nowhere in particular. Mostly I just walk around."

"You live off campus?"

"Yes."

"And you have a roommate?"

"Yes."

"Would you tell us about him, please?"

How in God's name had they found out about my roommate? If they knew about him, they knew everything.

"He's . . . a dancer. I like ballet and . . . it's a temporary arrangement. I thought it would be good experience to live off campus my last year. He was looking for a place at the same time, & . . . anyway it's temporary, so . . ."

I blushed & stammered, forgot my place, repeated myself & stopped in mid-sentence, trapped & defeated, the Rhodes lost.

"Thank you, Mr. Helms, that will be all."

A few minutes later, or an eternity later, I couldn't tell which, the examiners called us together & announced the winners—the other two students who'd been called back after lunch. Then a receiving line, a gauntlet for me, to shake hands with the examiners. I wanted to scream insults, weep, run out of the room, but I went down the line & minded my manners. There was one man, however, a college dean, who detained me to say that if he could ever be of help, he hoped I would contact him. There was that at least, which at the time seemed like small pickings but now seems magnanimously humane under the circumstances.

The Rhodes was the first big thing I'd ever wanted in life that I hadn't got. (Oh sure, there was Dad's drinking, but I mean the first *possible* thing.) And to think I'd lost it because I was gay, & had been spied on & set up like a clay pigeon, & then, full of hope & trust, shot down by that company of urbane, genial humanists. But I didn't despise them for what they'd done to me, or the culture that told them it was a necessary & right & moral thing to do; I despised myself for the fact that in constructing a gay life in a straight world, I'd been heedless, had left clues to my sexuality lying about for the straight world to find & use against me.

It was clear I would pay dearly in the straight world for being gay. I'd lost Jay, my only friend at Columbia, & some of Dad's feeble love as a result of our last fight when he'd finally confronted me with my homosexuality. My relations with Bob & Patti were strained because of the duplicity I practiced with them. I'd been spied on in the dorms & now lost the Rhodes. Maybe it was better to cut out of the straight world completely, leave it as far behind as possible—which meant leaving behind a world I identified with my intelligence & academic accomplishment, although that didn't occur to me at the time. I just wanted to get away from being despised & humiliated. I would be safe from all of that in the gay world, & safe in modelling, a world where in those days half the male models & photographers were gay & no one was punished for his sexual proclivities.

The morning of my commencement I was admitted to the Columbia infirmary, & as the ceremonies were beginning I underwent an emergency appendectomy. "Barely in time," the surgeon said. "Five minutes more might have been too late." Mom & Dad & Bead & Henry came later that day to say how proud they were; the first in our family to graduate from college, I was Phi Beta Kappa, magna cum laude, & winner of the Alexander Moncrief Proudfit Fellowship in Letters, which gave me two years of graduate study at Columbia or Yale, take my pick. My pick was to postpone the fellowship for a year, pleading some lie or other (my family was in financial trouble, I think that was it), & to put the world of academe behind me.

Before I do, a nod to Columbia, for it gave me a superb education & permanently altered my life for the better. It was a formal place, with many students attending class in three-piece suits & all of us addressed as Mr. Family-Name-Only. But we were taught in small classes by full-time members of a first-rate faculty, & the curriculum gave us such a solid liberal arts education that from that day to this, I rarely draw a blank in general conversation. Our requirements included a year of great books, two years of political & social philosophy (Plato to the present), a semester of fine arts & another of classical music, one year each of two sciences, two years of a foreign language & three years of gym. That's right, three whole years of gym. Columbia took seriously the Greek ideal of a sound mind in a sound body. You couldn't graduate until you'd swum three lengths of the pool in the buff, though indulgent gym instructors were known to look the other way when the athletically-challenged got towed back & forth by a friend with a pole.

Our education was in many ways racist, sexist, & elitist. There may have been black students at Columbia during my four years there but I don't recall any, nor do I remember reading the works of any black writers or many women writers. Ivy League schools were exclusively male, & women were barred from entering our dorms—a policy we protested with an occasional panty raid at Barnard on the other side of Broadway. But in 1955 who, except Allen Ginsberg, was calling for social revolution, & he was crazy for all we knew. We were members of the Silent Generation—"the tranquillized Fifties" is Robert Lowell's apt phrase for the period—& we weren't given to political protest or questioning the status quo or the wisdom of our elders. Fewer than 10 percent of American high school graduates went on to college in those days, & we weren't just attending college; we were attending an Ivy League school, with an arrogance founded partly on the confidence that our futures were secure. There was no doubt in our minds that the world had reserved a place for us; it only remained for us to choose. When the Columbia College newspaper boasted about "the natural superiority of the Ivy League man," many of us swallowed that claptrap whole. I certainly did.

What I recall most vividly about Columbia, however, was the intellectual excitement I experienced there—not just the pleasure of acquiring knowledge, but the shared thrill of exploring & arguing the ideas our professors introduced us to, the excitement of disinterested intellectual pursuit. There was a respect & admiration for intellectual accomplishment that I've never known before or since. In a class in eighteenth-century English literature one day, a student made such an eloquent response to a difficult question that we all applauded him, including the professor. I loved that about Columbia. Thinking was viewed as one of life's most exciting & noble adventures, & as an aesthetic one at that, which is itself a beautiful idea. Our heros among our peers weren't jocks but junior Phi Beta Kappas & the students taking honors seminars with Lionel Trilling & Gilbert Highet. It was at Columbia that I first understood & was stirred by the phrase "the life of the mind," & where I first realized how profoundly the life of the mind impinges on the life of everything else. In its intellectual aspect, those four years were one of the great adventures of my life: some books & a sparsely furnished room, no distractions of getting & spending, the whole world focussed in the cone of light from a reading lamp as the words moved forward on the page, the fabric of knowledge rising in the expectant silence.

I experienced my second convalescence in life thanks to the appendectomy, & again it was unadulterated bliss. I had vast stretches of time for reading, the nurses pampered me, & I spent lazy hours sunning on a terrace until I had a respectable tan. Sam visited often (I begged him not to make me laugh, it hurt so much, but he kept me in additional stitches), & Larry Kert (then starring as Tony in *West Side Story*) sneaked in each night after the show with a bouquet of Sterling Silver roses, my favorites. Then a friend brought Ira Barmak, a student at Cornell Medical School who was peering out of the closet deeply worried that the gay world offered little in the way of sustained relationships. Ira had heard that my lover of the moment & I were an exemplary couple (a joke whose punch line was my affair with Larry) & had asked to meet me. We began a deep & abiding friendship, one of the few healthy relationships I was able to form during my golden boyman period. Ira was brilliant & spoke five languages, could recite Pushkin & Lermontov from memory, & he played the piano like a professional. He loved crossword puzzles, irony, lobster, etymologies, surprises, & midwestern blonds with substantial butts, & he could make us laugh until we cried. Born into a poor Russian Jewish family in Brooklyn, he was so charming that he'd scaled the heights of debutante New York in a single season (he was dating Wendy Vanderbilt when we met). But what most drew me to him was the sense that we were soulmates: we communicated in a kind of ESP, could flesh out each other's thoughts, sometimes spoke phrases & whole sentences in unison. Thank God for the friendship with Ira, for there were few spars in the storm-tossed seas I was embarking on.

Since Michael Kahn, a Columbia classmate & fledgling director, would be abroad for the summer, I sublet his apartment on Fifty-second between First Avenue & the East River, the Garbo block. (I saw her a few times—attempting anonymity in sunglasses & turbans, leaving passers-by dead in their tracks & staring after her as she strode up the street.) The apartment had a red living room with grand piano, a red dining room, a Moroccan bedroom with beaded curtains & tabourets, & a black cleaning woman who arrived one morning after I'd left for a booking to find a naked Yugoslavian sailor in the kitchen telling her in Serbo-Croatian to calm down. She never returned. "She was the *best* cleaning lady I've *ever* had," Michael said upon his return, repeatedly.

It was another summer of beach & gym & modelling & assiduous fucking. Though I loved a lot of the sex I had, I also felt an obligation to have sex. It came with the role of being a golden boyman. It was as if I'd auditioned for Hamlet and gotten the part, only to find that I had to fence. All the sex seemed a requisite for my reputation, yet I never had a libido large enough to have as much sex as I felt I should. Consecutive days were out of the question, so I reserved every other night & pretty much stuck to it. I realize that sounds mechanical & joyless, & some of it was, but there were memorable times too. When it was exceptional & the other guy was free (like the Yugoslavian sailor on shore leave), we'd hole up in Michael's apartment & go at it around the clock.

I'd heard intriguing stories about Cherry Grove on Fire Island, so on an impulse one Friday, I went out without a place to stay. (I'll say that much for the feeling of being desired—it gave me a courage I'd never had, knowing as I did that things would always work out fine.) Some people on the ferry invited me for dinner, after which I headed out for the Sea Shack, the woodframe bar on the beach where people gathered at night to drink & cruise. Suddenly the boardwalks were crowded—a little universe of gay men on the move.

The deck out back on the ocean side was lit with spotlights & jam-packed with folks beginning their weekend revels. As soon as I entered, I felt the familiar stir. Wherever I looked, people were staring, & here & there I heard my name. It was a hot, muggy night, so when some other

men took off their shirts, I did too. Again that sensation of observing myself from outside as people formed a circle around me, while those on the
fringes pressed closer for a better look. I soon had my invitation for the
weekend.

For years it was like that—people staring at me on the street, in super-
markets & museums, at the ballet & the laundromat. I got so that I
wouldn't even run out for a quart of milk without first checking in the
mirror to make sure I was fit for public consumption. And always, everywhere I went, I was treated. Though I loved it, I came to take it for
granted, more proof that I was unique & that life had finally devised a
way to compensate me for the past. Without ever phrasing it this way at
the time, I saw myself as exempt from the requirements & obligations of
ordinary mortals. I became, all in all, one of the most pampered & spoiled
young men going.

Yet the men in that world never called me on my arrogance & pre-
sumption. I sometimes accepted three & four invitations for the same
night, decided at the last minute where I wanted to go, & didn't bother to
cancel the other invitations. I stood people up left & right without giving
them a second thought. "I grew careless of the lives of others" is how
Wilde puts it in *De Profundis*. But the men I stood up usually called again
in a day or two with another invitation, so judging by the information I
got, my behavior was perfectly acceptable.

It was also full of a kind of cognitive dissonance that entered my life in
this period & would accompany me for the next two decades. Given that
my worst fear was of rejection & that being stood up was devastating for
me, you'd think the last thing I would have done would have been to
stand someone else up. Yet I never made that connection. Why not? Probably because people of low self-esteem have a hard time realizing that
they have any effect on others. In their worst fears, they count for so little
that they can't imagine they count for anything with anybody else. Since
I seemed so insignificant to myself, how could my not showing up matter
to anyone else? And yet my new role as a golden boyman involved me in
an exorbitant egotism whereby I conceived of myself as mattering enormously. Thus, as I went through that door into the gay world of the late
1950s, I reinforced the same contradictory attitudes that I'd developed in
childhood: I counted for a lot but I was worthless; I was in demand but
negligible; I mattered enormously but not at all.

That same summer of 1959, after having two teeth capped, I worked
with Richard Avedon for a week of all-day bookings doing face shots for

a toothpaste ad. "Gimme a big smile, Al . . . c'mon, a bigger smile . . . that's it, great, that's terrific!" Hour after hour, day after day of more smiles, bigger smiles, front face & three quarter smiles, sly & satisfied smiles, proud & delighted smiles until my face ached so much I thought I'd spasm. I asked Avedon how other models did it, & he said that most of the good models he worked with took acting classes. A week later I was enrolled in a beginners' class at the Herbert Berghof Acting Studio.

I was a conscientious acting student, doing my exercises & attending classes, quickly moving on to more advanced classes given by Uta Hagen, the original Stella in *A Streetcar Named Desire* & one of New York's best acting teachers. But from the beginning of my career as an actor, I had only one goal in mind: I didn't care about learning the craft of acting; I just wanted to be a star. Having had a taste of exciting desire in hundreds of gay men, I now wanted to excite desire in millions of American movie-goers. When Anne Baxter in *All About Eve* says she wants to feel those "waves of love" coming at her over the footlights, no one had to explain to me what she meant.

Around the same time I met a young photographer named Norman Kenneson who fell deeply & enduringly in love with me. Norman was a stocky, randy, good-time guy with a Roman boxer's nose & a meticulous Ahab beard long before the day of the butch clone. He took exceptionally good photographs of me—you never get better pictures than when the photographer is in love with you. Fortunately, Norman was willing to settle for friendship, & also to fetch & carry, bolster my ego, & help me cruise when we went out together. Since I never wore my glasses in public, much of life passed in a myopic blur. Norman kept clearing things up. I'd learned how to read a man's body through his clothes, & I could spot potential tricks by their shapes & how they moved, but except at close quarters, I was fuzzy on details.

"Norman, quick—that blond down at the water's edge."

"What blond? Where?"

"The one in the red trunks by the jettyhead."

"He's not blond, he's bald. That's the sunlight shining on his head."

Norman saved me from many a cruising disaster. He also helped me invent a new name for my modelling career. The agency was ready to launch me in a big way, but I couldn't be Al, they said, & Albert was out of the question. Norman & I spent a weekend inventing names in the style of the period: Cliff Granite, Rocky Studman, Brick Blast, Luke Montana. "I know," Norman said, "how about Rim Trap? If someone can be Rip Torn, why can't you be Rim Trap? Describes you to a T." We settled on "Alan"; the agency said fine & had a thousand head sheets printed for distribution to New York photographers & ad agencies. New nose, new teeth, new face, new body, new name, new career, new life.

That September Norman & I rented a huge apartment in a pre-war building on West Ninety-fourth Street between Broadway & West End Avenue. We moved in with a young Englishman, Michael Something-or-other, who worked as a hotel manager & devoted his spare time to exercise & sex. Norman was so perpetually horny he often had to see a dermatologist for the skin rashes he got from hours of cruising in the showers at the West Side Y. Between Norman, Michael, & me, the sexual traffic in our apartment was one continual rush hour.

We gave a New Year's Eve party that year, & our doorman kept calling on the house phone to report on the number of our guests. "Eighty people have arrived so far," "Latest count: A hundred & fifty," "You've got over three hundred guests! May I come too?" Half the *West Side Story* crowd was there & the whole *Five Finger Exercise* crowd, who brought along John Gielgud, who was instantly smitten & danced the night away with a young Gielgud look-alike. It was Ira's first huge gay bash & he was gaga at meeting so many dancers from *West Side Story*: "I now know that enduring gay love exists because I'm feeling it for half-a-dozen men at this party." What a bacchanal! It seemed that every time I opened a closet to hang up another coat, Norman was inside mounting another trick. Roddy MacDowell arrived minutes before midnight, peered in at the chaos careening toward its peak, said "I think not" & fled.

By six A.M., the place was a shambles & everyone had left except for my number of the night who was clearly disappointed by my bed. It was a perfectly normal double bed. "What's wrong with it?" "Nothing, I just heard you had a heart-shaped bed." Tricks told me they'd heard I had a heart-shaped bed or a circular bed, came five times a night, never came at all, brushed my teeth with vodka, slept on satin sheets or leather sheets or with a python, or in a room carpeted with mattresses, or on the floor, or only during the day, was a vegetarian &/or a Buddhist, made love only to Brahms. An opulently fictive Alan Helms was being composed of rumor & myth, & I thrilled each time a new fragment came my way.

Yet given my own libidinal preference, I would have looked entirely different—like one of those coal-eyed, raven-haired, big-nosed, thick-wristed, full-lipped, olive-skinned, slightly bow-legged Latins who turned my knees to milkshakes. I would have liked a thicker neck too, & larger calves, & an inch of bone inserted into each ankle. But no, I had to look like Norman Rockwell's all-American-boy-next-door. I wasn't at all my own type.

The greatly beautiful Bill Kramer certainly was though, & he was also the only serious competition I had for the title of gay New York's most desirable young man. "As many people want him as want you," said the voices. "Oooh, if only you could have him." Blond with dark eyebrows, he looked like a cowboy sired by a Russian prince, & his deep, smoky voice sounded like a panther purring in a cave. He moved like an animal too, & when he passed by, the air crackled with sexual electricity. He was an actor, & of all the male actors I've ever known, the one who, more than any other, should have become a really big star. But Bill, like me, was damaged goods.

He'd grown up in the Bronx where he'd been kicked out of the house at fourteen by a violent, alcoholic stepfather, and then spent a few years shunting back & forth between reformatories & the streets. He had the allure of a suave, gentle criminal. He was lurking in the garden at an East Side party the night we met, & everything about him said trouble, lots & lots of major trouble. I found him irresistible.

We left the party & went back to my place, where we made love & talked till dawn. Bill must have sensed an inner turmoil in me similar to his own. Whatever the case, we were clearly made for each other, so within twenty-four hours we were having an affair. I still recall the stir we caused whenever we appeared in public—the brunet & the blond, Diony-sus & Apollo, Narcissus & his bright reflection. "What do you live on?" someone once asked us. "Nectar & ambrosia," I replied.

That's certainly what it felt like. Wherever we went, people literally stopped & stared, for we really were a dazzling couple. We were also deeply wounded young men with tormented minds & hearts & souls, which was great for me since it let me think I could make the difference in Bill's life, save him & salve his hurt with my devoted love. That was a sce-nario I especially liked (like surrendering my place in the lifeboat to a stranger), but I no sooner began to enact it than Bill stopped returning my calls.

It turned out that his roommate, a Latin dancer/actor/singer/model/ waiter, was also his lover. "But we're breaking up," Bill assured me. Whew, for a minute there . . . Yet the breakup dragged on until it was clear Bill didn't want to end the relationship, especially when it became intoler-able. The worse things got between Bill & Latin Lover, the less I saw Bill; when things improved between them, Bill was back in my life. The guy worked Bill like an emotional yo-yo. If I'd had the sense to maltreat Bill he would have been mine, but I didn't see that at the time, & even if I had, emotional sadist wasn't one of my roles.

Being with Bill soon became fraught with the fear that at any moment he'd get up & walk out on me—a repeat of the Dick abandonment. It was the kind of guaranteed excitement & perpetual anxiety I hated but was ineluctably drawn to. When things were bad between Bill & me, I became catatonic, sitting for hours in my bedroom, not answering the phone, unable to leave the apartment except for the times I went down to the West Fifties & hid in a doorway to peer up at Bill's windows. To what end? I don't know; it was something I had to do, because the more unavailable Bill became, the more I had to have him.

After a couple months of transcendent sex & lots of public adulation alternating with abysmal loneliness & despair, I told Bill I was calling it quits. Suddenly, his interest was renewed. Then maybe we could work things out? Sure we could, except he didn't show for our next date. Okay, now it was completely over & that was that! But surely I understood I was the only person he wanted to be with, & would be with that very night? Surely I understood that? Well . . . I guessed I did, until around ten o'clock when it became clear he was standing me up again.

I called him at work one day to say *over, kaput, basta, don't ever call me again & this time I mean it*! He showed up minutes later hysterical & trembling, apologizing & pleading with me to reconsider. Okay then, *one last time,* but *absolutely the last*! We made a date for dinner that night. Need I tell you that he stood me up?

I couldn't see that Bill was typical of many gay men I knew in those days, myself foremost among them, in that the key to his affections lay in treating him with an indifference laced with rejection. Such behavior was irresistible to him, & to me too, since we both had a deep need to reenact a drama of rejection that confirmed our own poor estimates of ourselves— estimates formed by our troubled childhoods in cahoots with a social opprobrium that never slept. Actors both, each of us was starring in a drama of endless emotional turmoil. Anything settled & serene felt wholly alien to me, intolerable. I never understood why people looked forward to weekends in the country.

I've read, & believe, that Rembrandt used twenty-seven different blacks in his painting; I experienced as many dark moods in my life at that time. At one point I drew a razor blade across my wrists—an exploratory gesture more than a serious slashing, but enough to turn the bath water pink & leave scars that were visible for years. But at least I slept well. In the best of times I usually had insomnia & found myself at three & four & five in the morning rocking back & forth in a kneeling position with my head buried in the pillow, cursing & praying for sleep, at my wit's end waiting for release, feeling like I was losing my mind. Only depression guaranteed me a good night's sleep.

A letter arrived from the Draft Board in late 1959 announcing that I was being inducted, & I quailed at the thought of two lost years at the beginning of my gay celebrity & my careers as a model & actor. "Don't be silly," friends said. "Check the box." On the appointed day, I showed up at the induction center, stuck out my tongue, spread my cheeks, & checked the box that declared my "homosexual tendencies," certain I would be humiliated in front of hundreds of inductees. Fortunately I was sent to a waiting room where I was seen by a psychiatrist after he dealt with two guys who, taking no chances, had dressed themselves up as screaming drag queens. The doctor asked if it were true that I experienced erotic feelings for men. "Yes," I mumbled, feeling embarrassed & ashamed. The doctor said that in my case such feelings were probably temporary, & he would arrange for me to be called back in a year, by which time I would doubtless have outgrown such deviant desires. A year later, another summons came, but this time the doctor put me down as a hopeless case & exempt from the army. For years I explained the 4F status on my draft card as a result of the repeated lancings for abscessed ears I'd gone through in childhood.

I was therefore free when Michael Kahn called to offer me the part of Lysimachus in the *Pericles* he was directing that fall at Barnard. Barely fifty lines, but Lysimachus gets Marina in the end & I got to wear white tights with a powder blue doublet, a truly princely outfit. I also performed a few walk-ons, including a perilous minute during the shipwreck scene when I hung naked from the rigging, my back to the audience (more a hang-on than a walk-on really). I thus made my theatrical debut showing one of my finest features & made a tiny footnote in theatrical history by being one of the first people to appear nude on an American stage.

Since Michael's production was only the third *Pericles* ever presented in the United States, it was seen by a lot of theater buffs, including Stark Hesseltine, a theatrical agent at MCA. Stark asked me to audition for him; he also invited me out a few times before the audition, so I got to know him well enough to intimate the sturm und drang raging inside me because of the Bill Kramer affair. Stark urged me to see his therapist & I liked the idea, so twice a week I went to a Central Park West office where, with the help of a man I instantly disliked, I tried to plumb the depths of my misery. Within a couple of weeks, we settled into an invariable routine. Regardless of how the session began, I found my way to complaining about someone in my life, past or present, then ended by saying "But I don't like him."

"Why don't you like him, Mr. Helms?"

"Because I don't like myself."

The words came so automatically that it felt like they were wired in me somewhere, but they brought me up against an impenetrable wall. I knew they were supposed to unlock a door in the wall & let me through to the Eden on the other side, but they never did. They made my mind go blank instead, & then around the molding of the ceiling I imagined a neon sign blinking on & off, flashing the message "Bullshit . . . Bullshit . . . Bullshit . . ." Session after session, week after week, "Bullshit . . . Bullshit . . . Bullshit . . ."

During that first excursion into therapy, I met Tony Perkins at a party given by Michael Kahn. A reigning Hollywood star at the time, Tony had been nominated for an Academy Award for his performance in *Friendly Persuasion*, was starring in *On the Beach*, & within a few months would appear in *Psycho*. I was agog at meeting all six foot four of him in the living flesh—& what flesh it was, the smoothest skin I've ever touched. (He advised against soap: never on the body, & a special Spanish soap for the face, but only if you had to.) We were both reading *Justine* at the time, so there was that to talk about, & also my fledgling career & my upcoming audition with Stark, & of course my therapy (Tony was a devotee). He gave me his number & asked me to call two nights later at seven sharp.

When the fateful hour arrived, I delayed for precisely seven minutes to avoid appearing overly eager. God forbid that Tony Perkins should think I was keen on seeing him. He answered the phone by saying "Seven minutes, eh? I like that. Good move." As if we were playing chess. Off to an eerie start.

The whole affair was eerie. We usually met in Tony's "office": a studio apartment with a couple of chairs & a big bed, clearly a fuck pad. A block away on West Fifty-sixth Street, he lived with a German photographer named Helen Merrill in an apartment that Norman Bates might have fancied: a lugubrious floor-through with not a shred of chic, a homey place with grandmother furniture & lots of books. Tony & Helen were both great readers, & I seem to recall that Helen read Freud & Kant for fun. She certainly exercised a mysterious influence over Tony, but I never discovered its source. I was taken to meet her as a kind of test, more chess.

Tony had had some molars removed to accentuate his cheekbones (many people did that back then, to no discernable effect whatsoever), & he told me he'd seen a plastic surgeon about having his hips crushed & reset to make them narrower—surely one of the more bizarre desires in the history of human vanity. He also told me details of his long-lived affair with Tab Hunter (I swooned at the thought), a relationship apparently conducted with the same obsessive secrecy he brought to our affair. Gay stars in those days were so terrified of exposure that a "date" often meant a midnight rendezvous in an alley or an abandoned warehouse.

Tony was in fact so incredibly closeted (a few years later I saw him & his lover enter a party separately, then allow themselves to be introduced as if they were total strangers) & also so frightened of public recognition that I was amazed he tried to find me one night in a crowded cinema. We'd had a date that evening but he was called to a meeting, so I went to see him in *On the Beach* at the Times Square Loew's. (That was eerie too: seeing my lover's face projected on a screen fifty feet high.) When his meeting adjourned early, he came to look for me just as the movie ended & the lights went up. I heard a commotion in the balcony but thought little of it until he called later that night to say he'd been mobbed by adoring fans.

I told my therapist I was worried that maybe I liked Tony only because he was a movie star. The good doctor said, "I don't see why you're worried, Mr Helms. I'm treating three people who are frustrated because they can't even get to Tony Perkins." "Everybody wants him," the voices said, "and he wants you."

Word of our affair travelled quickly (a friend used to say that the three fastest forms of communication were telephone, telegram, & telefag), so I had the pleasure of running into Bill Kramer at the West Side Y & seeing his envy up close. "I hear you're seeing Tony Perkins. Wow! What's it like?"

Exciting, but now that I think of it, much like any experience of reflected glory. You have a friend or significant other who's special in some publicly acknowledged way, & you see the envy you inspire by being in that person's company. There was a lot of that in my affair with Tony, & to that extent being his lover let me think better of myself. I wasn't yet a star, but at least I was sleeping with one.

And it was also eerie, like I've said. No matter how I fiddled with Tony in my imagination, he stubbornly remained a movie star. It was hard getting through the distracting aureole of his fame. He seemed strange too— convoluted & pent & on the verge of flight, a young stag about to bolt. Even the apartment he shared with Helen was unsettling. You could enter his bedroom only by going through Helen's bedroom, as if she were the Cerberus of that dark portal. Once inside, a narrow iron bedstead like a penance filled the small room. On the wall above the bed hung a banquette of tiny lightbulbs spelling out Anthony Perkins. "I've always wanted to see my name up in lights," he said.

He got his wish a couple of months later when he opened in *Greenwillow* on Broadway. Not a failure because it was a Frank Loesser musical & Tony was a big draw, but not a hit, a two-month run. We'd broken up by then, but I sent Tony an opening night telegram telling him exactly how many adult lightbulbs it took to spell Anthony Perkins on the marquee.

In retrospect, I suppose I'd learned something from Tony about stars—that despite their celebrity & greater opportunities, they're much like you & me. In terms of the fundamentals—our need for love & dignity, hope & significant work—you can't tell the difference between a movie star & a monk. (I realize we're all supposed to know that, but we obviously don't.) Tony ended by being exceptional for me not because he was a star but because he was so bright, & that guaranteed a lot of good conversation.

I was learning a similar thing about famous people in the arts. At the time, I worshipped artists, & one of the best perks of my new life was that I got to meet most of the famous gay artists of the day. Nothing was more impressive to me than a successful, celebrated artist, for I'd always assumed great artists were morally superior to the rest of humankind. It made sense, right? Genius guaranteed nobility of soul. What a huge disappointment to discover that, their talent & genius notwithstanding, artists were as capable of being small-minded & mean-spirited as anybody else.

Once in a while, I found a nice exception. At a Christmas party given by Roddy McDowell, I was holding forth, arguing that of all the talents associated with *West Side Story,* the person who obviously deserved most credit for the show's success was Steve Sondheim. A man tapped me on the shoulder & said "You're wrong. The man who deserves most credit is Arthur Laurents."

"How would *you* know?"

"I'm Steve Sondheim."

When I told the therapist I was worried about how my audition had gone for Stark, he said, "You can relax, Mr. Helms. I know for a fact that it went quite well." This guy was indiscretion incarnate, besides which he used bad grammar & mispronounced a lot of words, & I was spending good money (Bernita's in fact: she'd have risen from the grave if she'd known) for the dim illumination that came from chanting my "Bullshit" mantra twice a week. I'm embarrassed I did anything as cornily obvious as wind up one day a few feet from his door with five minutes left of an appointment I'd completely "forgotten," but I did. And then thought "Bullshit" & switched to a Jungian therapist recommended by Ira.

She was an old woman who'd studied with Jung in Switzerland, then moved to Cannes where she'd treated the Begum Khan (an impeccable recommendation in my view); she was now living a semi-retired life in New York where she saw only a handful of patients. She was immeasurably kind & patient, & she told me I should be very careful not to overextend or tire myself. I don't know if she was cautioning me against the frenetic life I was living or she saw that the voices of my inner demons usurped a lot of my best energies, but her words made a deep & lasting impression on me. A proper Jungian, she had me record my dreams, & what Technicolor adventures they yielded. My favorite (you'll have to forgive me): I'm the captain of a ship in ancient Greece & we're sailing along when a temple suddenly rises out of the sea. I lead my men into the temple & down a flight of steps to the ocean's floor where a path winds through a coral forest. We follow the path until, turning a corner, there sits Poseidon enthroned in glory, surrounded by naiads & Tritons. (Everything's now looking very Rubenesque.) Poseidon gestures to a chest before me on the ground, & I understand that the contents are mine, a gift from the god. Inside are opals & emeralds, golden cups & coins & crowns, rings & necklaces of rubies, sapphires, enormous pearls—the abundant treasure I'd buried as a boy of twelve back in Indianapolis. A good thing I didn't know how long it would take to bring it back up into the light of day.

The audition for Stark had indeed gone well, so I became a client of MCA. Another of Stark's new clients was Elizabeth Ashley, & the two of us used to go for coffee & talk about how exciting life would be once we became stars. That Christmas, Stark gave a dinner for Liz & me & another new MCA client named Robert Redford. "*Very* good looking," I thought, & I'm sure I tried to charm him, but to no avail.

No matter, because by then I had a stable of fuckbuddies: a dozen sexy, well-built, well-hung guys I could call most any hour of the day or night & get to my apartment within half an hour, even when that meant they had to leave work in the middle of the day. It was a very efficient arrangement because you never had to spend any social time with a fuck-buddy. You met to fuck, then you parted until the next time. I liked them all, but only for sex. They were like a harem, except that instead of living in a wing of the palace, they were scattered all over Manhattan.

Then at one of the pimp parties Lester Persky gave for his celebrity friends, I met Henry Wilson, the most famous Hollywood agent of the day. Henry had discovered Lana Turner & Rock Hudson & Tab Hunter & that most beautiful of all male movie stars, Guy Madison. He also handled Robert Wagner & Rhonda Fleming & other movie stars known more for their looks than their talent. Henry was the living image of the Hollywood agent—a corpulent, cigar-smoking man in his fifties, vulgar but witty. He was a sleazy counterpart to Stark but much more powerful. A real starmaker, Henry could get anyone a screen test with a single phone call. Several people in a position to know had said I was destined to become a star, so when Henry invited me to dinner, I figured this was my chance to find out.

We met at the Pierre, where he was having a drink with Rock Hudson. I suspect Rock had been asked to look me over as potential star material—also as potential bedmate since Henry was solicitous of his actors, & none more than Hudson, the number one box office draw in America. But alas, Rock didn't fancy me, & no wonder. Anxious to make a good impression, I'd prepared for the evening by doing an especially arduous workout at the Y, after which I'd fallen asleep under a sun lamp. I was beet red, broiled to a turn. I'd also used hair spray, a common cosmetic blunder in those days (it made you look lacquered) & a surefire trap for someone as self-conscious as I was. Hudson opened the door on what must have looked like a young man disguised as a lobster.

Off we went, Henry & I, to a "progressive dinner," an immense inconvenience people pretended to like in those days: drinks in one place, appetizers in a second, entrees in a third, & so on. Sometime after midnight in a velvet booth of a plush night club, I was high enough to ask Henry point-blank: Did he think I could become a movie star? Henry zoomed in for a close-up & said yes, he was fairly certain of it. Enough of the sunlamp & the hair spray, & we'd have to get me in some Levi's & change my name. (Rock . . . Tab . . . Rim Trap?) "But yes, no doubt about it—if you're handled right, you could become a star." The thought of being "handled right" by Henry froze my blood, since he was notorious for nurturing new talent in bed. But never mind, the Hollywood oracle had spoken & I'd gotten what I wanted out of the evening.

Michael Kahn called to ask if I'd be interested in a very small part in a very small play by an unknown playwright. Was he *crazy?* But nothing else was brewing, so I read & got the part of the Angel of Death in *The Sandbox,* Edward Albee's early sketch of *The American Dream.* Small part, true, but what an exquisite little play it is, & since it took place at the beach, I got to wear a bathing suit.

Edward was always at rehearsals, pleasant but remote, lurking in dark corners in black turtlenecks. He'd had a success in Berlin with a play called *The Zoo Story,* & word was he was someone to keep an eye on. In the meantime, he kept an eye on us. We performed on weekends in an off-Broadway theater on West Fourth Street. The four one-act plays were called *Four in One,* & I seem to recall that *The Sandbox* was the lone success.

The next stage of my career took me to Fayetteville, Pennsylvania, for a season of summer stock at the Totem Pole Playhouse run by Bill Putch, husband of Jean Stapleton. It was there that my addiction to sweets shifted into full gear. It had begun during performances of *The Sandbox* when, after each matinee, I strolled up Second Avenue to an Italian bakery where I bought a dozen cannoli that I ate while strolling back to the theater. I hated myself for doing it, & vowed each time I made myself vomit that I'd never do it again. But after every matinee, I headed up Second Avenue like a catatonic for another dozen cannoli. It was one of the first signs I had that I was drifting into bulimia, but the subject wasn't talked about in 1960. I told my Jungian therapist about it & she said the Begum Khan had had a similar problem with candied pineapple. Begum Khan or no, I knew that what I did was odd & unhealthy, & I kept trying to stop but kept failing, then hating myself for failing, so vowing again to stop, then failing all over again, then putting it out of my mind because I couldn't think my way through it.

After Sunday matinees in Fayetteville, the company ate at a nearby restaurant where a prix fixe dinner allowed you unlimited helpings. I'd have four & five helpings of their apple pan dowdy, then make myself vomit before the evening's performance. The bulimia, however, was confined to Sundays for the most part, whereas I was now suffering almost nightly from insomnia. I tossed & turned from midnight till two & three in the morning, desperate for sleep, praying to God & Morpheus to *let me sleep,* until, exhausted at sunrise, I managed a couple of fitful hours of unconsciousness before it was time to get up & start a new day.

A perceptive man & a kind one, Bill Putch took me aside one afternoon & gave me a serious talking-to. He said I could definitely be a good actor if I worked at it, but he wondered if that was what I really wanted. Of course I wanted to become a good actor; it would help in becoming a star.

I was at least good enough by season's end to be chosen most popular male actor. (A group of Fayetteville girls had formed a fan club for me, & their acclamation placed me highest on the applausometer.) I got a wooden totem pole with an engraved plaque on it, along with the solid sense that things were going according to plan, that it was only a matter of time.

Back in New York, Cyril Landers, a Canadian producer, got me an apartment at 404 East Fifty-fifth Street, a block-long building with another entrance at 405 East Fifty-fourth. For people in the know, 405 was called "four out of five" because of the many gay tenants who lived there, but the building was better known as a place where celebrities lived: Lucille Ball, Van Johnson, Paulette Goddard & Erich Maria Remarque, Joan Fontaine, Hermione Gingold et luminous al. My next door neighbor was Lotte Lenya; Noel Coward lived on the floor below. Mine was a small studio apartment on the sixteenth floor that looked out to Queens & the Nabisco sign.

Cyril & I had met maybe a year before, & we had begun seeing a lot of each other once I moved into the building. Cyril was my greatest fan & convinced of my eventual stardom. "But of course, dear Alan, there's no question about it. You must simply press on & one day soon we'll see your name up in lights." He loaned me his Jaguar convertible whenever I asked, & invited me to plays & dinners & opening night parties, & fixed me up with visiting English actors & ballet dancers, & introduced me to my own crushes whenever possible (the young Alain Delon, mon Dieu!), & had me to his apartment for afternoon teas with cucumber sandwiches & pastries, & joked a lot about my odd eating habits, & every few weeks he begged to blow me. "It's such a *small* thing for you, & it means *so* much to me." I don't know how often I heard that hustle, yet it never occurred to me to say that, all things considered, dropping my pants for a blow job was in fact a small thing for them, while being pressed into the service of their fantasies was such a large, disorienting, wholly unpleasant thing for me. Though I wasn't easy to get, especially when I didn't desire the other man, anyone who persisted & wasn't downright rude could usually have his way with me if he bided his time, led me into a sense of obligation, persuaded me he cared about the "real whole me," plied me with liquor, then made his pitch. God forbid I should offend anyone, especially a "friend."

On the other hand, the heir to a pharmaceutical fortune whose family paid him to live outside the country had a more straightforward & effective approach. If on one of his rare, brief visits to the States I would come to his suite in the Plaza & have sex with one of the sailors or Marines he picked up in the bar on West Forty-fifth Street where servicemen hustlers hung out, he'd give me a hundred dollars. And he wouldn't touch, just wanted to watch. Those transactions helped with the rent, & it was always a thrill to have sex with a "straight" Marine or sailor, especially when one rolled over on his tight military stomach. If only that neat arrangement had lasted longer, but I arrived at the Plaza one night to find myself paired with Jim Stryker, the principal swoop of the physique magazines. I was so unnerved at confronting one of my major sexual fantasies that I couldn't perform. When I left the Plaza that night, I was toting a bottle of Seagram's in lieu of my usual fee.

One day in the elevator at 404, a neighbor introduced me to Noel Coward. "You must come for drinks this evening, dear boy," so I did, & Noel & I struck up a friendship that I still recall with immense pleasure. It was the kind of relationship I loved at the time: considerate attention from a bright, famous, older rich man who didn't paw me, the kind of friendship I had with Bill Inge. Noel invited me to lunches & dinners, sometimes just the two of us, & he invented the nickname "Alan Upstairs" as a sign of his affection. He also encouraged my acting ambitions, which was one reason he frequently called to invite me down for a drink. "Alan Upstairs? You must drop everything & come down im-*meed*-yutly. There's someone I want you to meet." The someones turned out to be Gielgud, the Lunts, Garland, Olivier, Dietrich—people known by a single name like Noel himself, the most celebrated denizens of the world I longed to inhabit. I served mostly as decoration & appreciative audience on those occasions, but I didn't care, for such times were always a guaranteed thrill. Noel was always on with his friends, delighting in their company & extremely amusing, for he was a great performer & the most effortlessly, brilliantly witty person I've ever known. When he was well-matched, as with Gielgud, the exchanges were vertiginously hilarious. I had a front row seat on the aisle for the best private theater in town. Seeing Noel on those occasions, I had no trouble crediting the story that he'd written *Private Lives* in four days propped up in a sickbed in Singapore, & "Someday I'll Find You" while stalled in a cab in midtown Manhattan.

Back upstairs to my apartment, for a fuzzy year taken up with auditions & modelling & weekends in the Hamptons, voice lessons with Katharine Hepburn's coach, dinners with Noel & Bill Inge & some of the *West Side*

Story crowd & the devoted Cyril, & lots of parties & plays & ballets & the gym & sex & more sex & still more sex until it was invading my dreams—all those coal black eyes & crystal blue eyes, hazel eyes glinting green in sunlight, curly hair & wavy hair, straight hair tousled & falling over the eyes, smooth white skin or black or dusty brown or olive skin, firm loins & muscled asses, firm chests with apricot nipples, bunches of pubic hair & the musky smells of crotch, the veins in calves & biceps & the tracery of veins on the inside of thighs & forearms, thick wrists circled with wispy hair, swollen lips & gleaming teeth parted in gasps & abandoned moans, flat saltlick stomachs & the curious dints running up & down the spine, the mysterious kneecaps & delicate hinges of arms & legs, the pliant ledges, sockets, mounds, clefts, & crevices of sex, & more sex, & still more sex.

Promiscuous? That's a hard word to define in a culture in which the average sexual experience now lasts all of two minutes (*The Harper's Index Book,* 1987, page 28). Besides, I was twenty-three or so & at the height of my sexual powers, such as they were. I didn't have a lover during most of this period, so there wasn't that to slow me down, & there was no AIDS to slow anybody down. And though I've said I didn't have a large libido, a lot of the sex I had came from lust manufactured in my head. That is, if you're weak in the self-acceptance department, then whatever your medium of exchange for acceptance, you can't get enough of it. Ask a diffident billionaire if he's got enough money.

It was tricky though, given my psychology. The guy had to turn me on enormously, convey that he wanted me a lot but not in a needy or cloying way, & then be able to lose himself in the sex. Then it was transcendent—like going through door after door into new worlds of sensual experience in which the boundaries of the self fell away, my mind was cleansed of the clutter of mentation, & I was open to the experience of melding with another, if not The Other. Then I could never get enough of it. My personal problems aside, the really good stuff we keep going back to for more, right? I've never known anybody to say "Beethoven's Ninth? Thanks but I've heard it."

Christmas, 1960. Cyril was in Toronto, Norman had gone home to his family, Ira had moved to California, & I don't know where Sam or anybody else was. Noel had loaned me his apartment, so I holed up there feeling lonesome & consoling myself with a sixteen-pound box of chocolates, a Christmas gift from an admirer. In early January, I went to the Bahamas on an assignment for *GQ* with two editors, the photographer &

his assistant, another male model (attractive but straight), & a petulant Miss Sweden who was sleeping with the photographer. Crazed with boredom by the end of the booking, I called a friend in Miami, who invited me to join him for a week. I decided not to let Stark know my whereabouts: something in New York might require my presence, & I wanted the pleasure the Bahamas hadn't provided. I got it: a week's romance with one of those Botticelli angels who normally appeared only in my dreams. Once back from Miami, I checked in with Stark. He was furious: Albee had wanted me for the lead in *The American Dream,* had even delayed rehearsals in hopes I would turn up but finally cast someone else. Too late, too bad, but so what? No role in any play, especially one by an unknown playwright, was commensurate with the pleasures of my week in Miami, & a gold Cartier ring showed up in the mail a few days later to prove it. Let Stark fume, & anyway, why such a fuss over Edward Albee?

I understood a couple of months later when I saw *The American Dream.* A perfect play in its savvy critique of American culture, it was also a perfect role for me—the beautiful young man unable to love or even feel who is universally desirable & who knows how to manipulate it. It was as if Edward had written the part expressly for me, or as if I had been born to play it. I took a dim satisfaction sitting in the audience that night thinking, "But *I'm* the American dream, not this substitute strutting about on stage. No one's seeing the real American dream."

By that point in my career as a Universal Type of Desire, I was so potentially dangerous I should have been put behind bars, in a jail or a zoo. At the very least, I should have had a printed warning to hand to people upon first meeting them: "I do not exist. I am merely an image, hence my ascendency over you. By fostering the illusion that I embody your desire, you grant me immense power; but because of who & what I am, I will abuse it. I don't want to cause you pain, but I will. It's not my fault; it's nobody's fault; it's the nature of things. Objects of desire always cause pain."

How so? In my case, by taking people for granted, standing them up & putting them down, leaving them hanging. By not listening or noticing or caring. By leading people on so the invitations & presents & compliments kept coming, & then dropping them for someone better. But all objects of desire cause pain because they exist only in the mind of the desirer. There's always a fatal gap between the real person who catalyzes the desire & the fictive person conceived by the desirer. (Buñuel makes the point in *That Obscure Object of Desire* by having his hero pursue a woman played by two actresses, the real woman & the hero's fantasy of her.) The desirer desires not the person but the image of the person. And any goal of happiness based on unreality is doomed to fail & thus cause pain.

Arthur Laurents cast me as the young woodsman in a production of *A Clearing in the Woods,* his own play starring Celeste Holm that he was directing for "Play of the Week," the most popular TV drama show of the time. Millions of Americans got to see me stripped to the waist, my torso covered with beads of glycerine simulating sweat. Then I took over a part in *La Ronde* on seven hours notice. I was a quick study so I had the part down in time for Noel to see me a couple nights later ("*Ab-so-lute-*ly *splen-*did, dahling boy!"). A friend brought Dorothy Kilgallen, doyenne of New York gossip columnists, who next day told her readers to watch for a rising new star on the theatrical horizon, or words to that effect. So despite having sabotaged myself out of *The American Dream,* my career was moving along quite nicely, which in a way makes it more surprising that now the bulimia & insomnia began raging in full force. Or maybe it makes it less surprising.

For three days at a stretch I lived on sweets: brownies & napoleons for breakfast, pecan pie à la mode for lunch, a couple of pounds of chocolates for dinner, self-induced vomiting after each meal. Then I'd become disgusted with myself, flush all the sweets down the toilet, & for the next three days live on lettuce & cottage cheese & go twice a day to the gym for two-hour workouts ending with half an hour in the steam room.

As for the insomnia, it's enough for now to point out that in all thirty-three rounds of Hell, Dante never allows his damned to sleep. His condemned souls share only two things: the eternity of their suffering & their sleeplessness.

Noel showed up in town to cast *Sail Away,* the musical comedy he'd written for Elaine Stritch that was about to go into production. He gave me the part of Glenn Crackerjack, son of Elmer & Mamie Crackerjack, a midwestern family on board the American cruise ship where the musical takes place. Four lines, five costume changes, one a bathing suit. (No, I didn't think I was becoming typecast.)

During rehearsals, I wandered into the world of José Quintero, then one of Broadway's best-known directors thanks to his excellent revivals of Eugene O'Neill. José was directing a Hugh Wheeler play, & I met & soon was seeing José's golden-haired boyman, a young Actor's Studio

Oklahoman Indian named Clint Kimbrough. Another lanky, tormented actor; another doomed gay love affair.

Things went badly from the start, & I confided in Elaine, who confided in Noel, who took me aside one day during rehearsals. "Dahling Alan, Elaine has told me *EV*rything. I'm *so* sorry. I *do* understand the troubles of the heart, so you *must* come see me if I can *evah* be of help."

A few nights later I met Clint for dinner at the home of one of his friends. Rehearsal had dragged on that day, so I arrived late to find Clint & host & somebody else deep in their cups. I drank fast to catch up, but it was one of those horrible evenings when I didn't get the allusions or the jokes & felt left out, & Clint seemed to be ignoring me, & then *boom* I was drunk & reeling. On an instant's impulse I excused myself to go to the john & walked out of the house & into a cab for home, determined to commit suicide.

Suicide seemed the best idea I'd had in a long time. I had the sleeping pills; all I had to do was write a few notes, tidy the apartment, clean up & put on something nice. I also needed to destroy my address book, which I could do by dropping it off the Fifty-ninth Street Bridge into the East River. And in fairness to whoever would have to clean up the life I was leaving behind, I should get rid of that pile of muscle magazines under the bed, & those abandoned journals in the closet, & pay a few bills, & what sweet vengeance to leave a message with Clint's answering service so he would discover he'd gotten it just as I was breathing my last. . . . Suddenly suicide seemed a complicated, arduous venture. Arriving back at 404, I went straight to Noel's & rang his bell. If that didn't help, *then* I would commit suicide.

I poured out my grief to Noel, who did the best a friend can do in such circumstances: he listened sympathetically & comforted me. He was under strict doctor's orders to maintain a health become precarious thanks to a lifetime of high-voltage living, so those hours taken from his sleep were precious ones for him. He had to be up at seven to be at the theater by 8:30 to begin rehearsals, but he was immensely kind & patient, & talking to him brought me great relief. At the end of my soliloquy, he applauded my decision to postpone suicide & assured me that everything would work out for the best. "*Yes*, dear Alan, *that's* the ticket. I know how *ghast*-ly it all must seem, but you'll see things differently in the morning, & *then* you must simply *press on & all will come right!*" I wouldn't want an Englishman for a therapist, but for that night no one could have helped me more than Noel did.

Might I spend the rest of the night sleeping on his couch? He preferred not, but come along, he would take me upstairs & tuck me into bed. He threw on a Balenciaga dressing gown & we climbed the service stairs to my apartment. When I let us in, I didn't register that the lights, turned off when I'd left that morning, were now on. Noel sat on the side of my bed arranging the folds of his dressing gown & patting the space beside him, saying "Come, dear Alan, into bed." "As soon as I go to the john," I said, but ooooh, was I ever nervous. If after a year of friendship & a night of commiseration, Noel was about to make a pass, I really *would* commit suicide.

Shutting myself in the bathroom, I found Clint standing behind the door making frightened "Shhhh!" signs. Rejoining Noel, I whispered the news that Clint was in the bathroom. Noel jumped up, strode to the door, opened it wide, & as he swept out he looked over his shoulder &, with a wink, said "I *raw*ther had a *hunch*!" Clunk went the door, period to a perfect exit.

The Clint affair petered out as *Sail Away* left to go on the road. We played two weeks in Boston & two in Philadelphia, during which I ate & vomited pastries by day & writhed in insomnia by night. We opened in New York on October 3, 1961, my first appearance on Broadway, if in fact such a minuscule part can be said to constitute an appearance. But it was enough to bring Mom & her oldest friend Mickey from Indianapolis.

Since Noel knew virtually everybody who was anybody, an exceptionally glamorous opening night party had been planned at Sardi's East, with Dietrich & Adlai Stevenson & Garland & Natalie Wood & Robert Wagner & the Lunts & Mary Martin & Myrna Loy & James Thurber & I don't know how many others of the great & famous. I didn't want to take Mom to the party because I would have been embarrassed by her; she didn't fit into the fictional life I'd invented for myself, a life that relied heavily on my aristocratic antecedents but omitted all reference to my working-class background & an overweight mother with bad taste in cheap clothes. But I didn't want to miss the opening night party either. Quite a dilemma, but my solution was simplicity itself: I simply stood Mom up, sneaked right past her out of the theater & into a cab for my apartment where I changed into a tux & went on to the party.

I've never done anything that makes me as ashamed as what I did to Mom that night. For someone as terrified of abandonment as I was to have been so unfeeling as to abandon my own mother, in the company of her best friend, after they'd driven eighteen hours from Indianapolis because she was proud of me & wanted to help me celebrate my first appearance on Broadway. I've often tried to imagine what it must have been like for her: her initial confusion, Mickey calming her & inventing excuses for my delay, then more confusion but now laced with fear as the certainty grew in her that I wasn't coming, & then the effort to imagine my reason, & then as they paced back & forth under the marquee glancing at their watches, the lights all turned out & the theater deserted, what a horrible, heartrending thing—the certain knowledge there was no other explanation for what was happening but the one now staring her in the face: her son was ashamed of her. She would have cried, & Mickey would have tried to console her, inventing lies to spare Mom from what Mickey too understood as the ugly fact of the matter. Over thirty years later, I still find it hard to forgive myself for what I did to Mom that night.

I don't remember the aftermath. There would have been an awkward telephone conversation next morning, & I obviously lied to gloss over my actions of the night before, then I think I took Mom & Mickey to lunch before they left on the long drive back to Indianapolis. What I do remember is that regardless of the cost, I had to have what I wanted, & I got it. I met still more famous people, & got a few promising phone numbers, & then as the party was breaking up, Noel invited me to join him & three friends back at his apartment: Stritch, Dietrich, Garland.

What did they say? All I remember is what they wore. Red, white, & blue: the colors of two empires. And two men in black tie, one of them a bona fide shit. But what an enviable experience it was, & all I'd had to do was betray my mother. Seemed like a pretty good deal to me at the time.

Sail Away got fair to middling reviews, Stritch got raves, & the show had a respectable run of five months. Early on, Elaine & I struck up a bizarre but wonderful friendship. We had intense crushes on each other, though where such benighted impulses were supposed to lead I have no idea. Elaine often remarked about how much I unsettled "the fags," & I know I thought of myself as in some sense her beau. Not her boyfriend, I was very clear about that in my own mind, but her beau. That sexual confusion aside, I've rarely laughed so hard or so much in my life. I remember having to grab ahold of parking meters & lampposts to keep from falling down in convulsions of laughter. True, our wit was oiled with an inordinate amount of booze. Elaine always kept a couple cases of champagne in her Beekman Place apartment, & the nights we went back to her place after the show, we often drank a bottle apiece. I usually left her at four or five in the morning & wove my way up First Avenue in the throes of my first hangover; after a few hours' fitful sleep, I'd awake to my second. Then time to get up & dress & go off to meet Elaine at Le Pavillon or another of those depressing beige-on-white restaurants where we began lunch with a few drinks & went on carousing until late in the afternoon, leaving ourselves little time to get ready for the evening's performance, after which we went back to Elaine's & began drinking all over again. Some nights we went out for supper with Noel or some of Elaine's friends, Arlene Francis & Martin Gabel or Kitty Carlisle & Moss Hart. In fact, that was the group one night at Joe Allen's when, in response to a waiter who asked which of the pastries I preferred from among the dozen or so on his tray, I said "I'll have them all." The others appeared amused as I ate the pastries one after another, then I picked up the bill for five people who each earned roughly a hundred times my salary per annum. Afterward I took Elaine home & joined her in a nightcap, then staggered back to my place at dawn to vomit & take a couple sleeping pills & crawl into bed.

Nights I didn't spend with Elaine or go out cruising, I went home to read Dickens. First, a sleeping pill (a double Tuinal), then into bed with a novel & a bottle of cheap red wine so bitter I had to sweeten it with saccharin & grape juice to make it potable. Half an hour of reading & drinking, then another double Tuinal. (Until Dorothy Kilgallen's death, we didn't know that barbiturates & booze can kill you.) Then more Dickens & drinking until I dozed off for three to four hours sleep. I read all of Dickens in that state, & in chronological order so I could follow the evolution of his style & themes. At the end, I remembered nothing. I saw the dawn five nights a week before I was able to fall asleep. Insomnia, bulimia, addictions to booze & pills & sex, but in my view things couldn't have been better.

One day in acting class after performing a scene in which I portrayed a young man angry with his girlfriend, Uta critiqued the actress, then turned to me & said "As for you, Alan, you have so much anger in you, you can't even focus it." Me, angry? What in the world was she talking about? What did I have to be angry about? Uta must have been crazy, but then I'd always heard she was better with women than men. I soon switched to Sandy Meisner, who appreciated me much more right from the start.

On another drunken evening with José on his terrace at 30 Fifth Ave, he was bemoaning his fate, asking "Why doesn't anybody like me just for

111

me?" I kept thinking "My sentiments exactly," & also how easy it would be, the act of an instant, to vault over the railing & out into thin air, then two seconds & twenty stories later (no time to think, I'd be numb with shock), an end to the torment of consciousness.

Then one day thanks to I don't know what, maybe the discontent festering in me like an open sore or the sheer accumulation of insanity in my life, my perspective shifted a few degrees & I suddenly saw that I hated my life. I'd known for a long time that I hated modelling; now I saw that I hated acting too. Until you get to the top, & often even then, you're always subservient, always at the mercy of so many things beyond your control: the director is bad, or you're bad, or the reviews are bad, or something's wrong with the lighting or the costumes or the other actors or . . . the possibilities are endless. I never had the satisfaction of doing or making something all my own, something I could point to with pride & say, "See that? I did that myself." I also saw that not only was I more unhappy than I'd realized, but everyone I knew was unhappy too. I was inhabiting a world of unhappy people. I suddenly saw Stark as pathetically lonely, Bill Inge as frightened & defeated, Noel as terrified of age & his declining success, Cyril as an importunate sycophant. Tony was forever anxious about the younger actor who would eventually replace him in the affections of the movie-going public, & Steve Sondheim took so little satisfaction in his accomplishments. Lenny Bernstein, who had written brilliant music & who with every year was more esteemed as a conductor, was an outrageous namedropper who tormented himself because he wasn't yet of the company of Bach & Brahms. Elaine was without question one of the great performers of the Broadway stage, but that hadn't kept her from becoming neurotic & alcoholic. Outside the world of entertainment, the people I knew seemed just as unhappy. I saw Sam Sloman as hysterical & self-loathing, Norman as sexually obsessed, Ira as selling his soul for a mess of Hollywood potage. And everybody was looking for some elusive secret of happiness in the next play or movie, trick or lover, deal or drink—as if all of living were perpetually postponed to some indefinite, elusive future. But more than anything else, it was the insomnia that finally did it. Night after night I writhed in bed unable to sleep, cursing sleep & praying for it, weeping as I rocked on knees & elbows with my head buried in the pillow, tormented from the sense that I was being tortured, crazed out of my mind. I had to escape that. At the time, the only thing that made sense was to leave New York.

I decided to clear out & as far away as I could get, perform a "geographic" as they say in AA. I'd always wanted to go to Europe, & Norman was game. We booked one-way passage on a Yugoslavian freighter bound for Tangier & sailed out of New York harbor on May Day, 1962, the day after my twenty-fifth birthday. Once out to sea, I slept soundly for the first time in years.

· 6 ·

If I'd had the disposition & wherewithal on that crossing to look carefully at my life, I might have asked what the previous three and a half years had amounted to & realized "Not a lot." True, there were all the social & sexual perks I've mentioned, & then the discovery that I didn't like modelling or acting & that I hated my life. And despite myself, I'd been led to a perception I couldn't credit & so couldn't make use of: the fact that I didn't like myself.

I'd also learned how to be gay. The genderfuck language & the secret lingo ("Is he a member of the fraternity? One of Bertha's boys?") had been easy; more important, I'd learned how to discern the secret signals coming at me from strangers in public, how to winnow through a crowd to find those discreet signs of shared identity I was seeking, & how to shift gears in an instant to hide my looking—which is to say I'd learned how to dissemble by living in a world of dissembling (an essential lesson for gay people but a deeply damaging one, for unless you learn how to unlearn the lesson, the deceit comes to figure in all relationships). What confusion—trying to be conspicuous in the gay world but invisible in the straight—& what quick-change routines it required: walking down a street in the middle of a straight June afternoon when *boom,* you catch the eye of a comely gay man, then back into the straight world for a few blocks & around a corner where *zap,* you exchange knowing glances with a gay couple, then on past them into the straight supermarket to buy some straight hamburger & orange juice & into the straight check-out line behind *bam,* a gay man with eager eyes & sexy body, now waiting in line while shunting in & out of an awareness of the straight world all around you with its watchful eyes & quick judgments of any sign of your desire for the man ahead of you who's looking back covertly, he too caught in the deadly awareness that if you're discovered in mutual desire right there in the straight supermarket you both run the risk of public humiliation & even violence. (Is it any wonder that for so long gay men have gathered in remote, dimly-lit places?)

Most important in terms of the life that was making me miserable, I'd learned how to be a Universal Type of Desire, or (to be on the safe side) an Almost Universal Type of Desire, or (to be as clear as possible) I'd learned how to cooperate in being considered an Almost Universal Type of Desire. That caused such confusion that even now it's hard for me to make sense of it. It meant that my looks & charms, such as they were, could be turned to so many advantages. In a culture where everything considered valuable is commodified, being desired can bring you so many benefits. If you're considered attractive in America, your attractiveness, like money, becomes fetishized, & if you're not a total fool, you become aware of the fact, which means you develop an acute & omnipresent self-consciousness about being desired.

At least I did, so much so that even when alone I used to check myself out in the mirror to make sure the gift of the look was still intact. I had learned well the lessons of my culture—to use my attractions as a means of exchange & to subvert the pleasures of sex through the mentality of profit & loss. But perhaps I'm not a good example of how beauty can be made to turn in on itself since I was such a self-conscious young man to begin with. Coming out into the gay world of New York in the late '50s & finding myself in demand simply exacerbated a psychological problem I'd developed in childhood. And yet, the beautiful Americans I've known have all spoken of the same self-consciousness, along with the fear that they're not really up to snuff, not as fully beautiful as they're made to feel. Get a beautiful American to relax enough to become confidential & you always discover a rift of diffidence—the eyes are too close or the calves too thin, the butt's too big or too small, the hair too curly or too straight or the wrong color, the lips too thin or too full.

"Better to be born a hunchback than to be born beautiful," says Voltaire, but Ira used to say "Let Voltaire try hunchback for a week & get back to us." *Pace* Ira, I suspect Voltaire understood the self-consciousness that comes with the gift of the look, & also the envy it inspires. That was perhaps the most unsettling part of being considered desirable, all the envy lurking in the admiration & the way it could turn to anger & rejection before my eyes. I saw it in so many men's faces—not just I want to be with you, get to know you, maybe even sleep with you, but I'd like to be you, or be like you, know what it feels like to be the living embodiment of others' desires. Then the rude about-face brought on by a fit of sour grapes. To meet an intelligent, successful man & realize that he would gladly have changed places with me, & then instead of turning into me might turn on me—that much self-repudiation, envy, & anger was unnerving.

So I felt charmed but I also felt cursed. Maybe cursed is too strong a word, yet I distinctly remember a recurrent fantasy of throwing acid in my face, thinking that such an action, drastic though it would be, might let me stop thinking about my looks & set my life on some saner course. I just never felt cursed enough to move beyond the fantasy, since I was addicted to being desired. Oh yes, I loved it—the flattery of so many people & the surefire knowledge that I could command a room merely by entering it. It thrilled me whenever I saw the heads turning as I entered a restaurant or strolled along a beach, & I loved the way, upon meeting me, so many people were startled, caught their breaths, forgot what they were saying. Doubtless many would have been susceptible to such attentions, but I'd become increasingly dependent on them for the sense that I mattered & my life had value. "Lucky *you*," the voices said, even when I thrashed in bed unable to sleep. "It must be wonderful," people said, "since all you have to do for sex is choose." It was wonderful, but that too confused me, for I often couldn't make up my mind until too late, by which time the contenders had gone home with someone else. I often failed to go after guys I desired (what if I chose wrong or someone better arrived later? & anyway, why put myself out when so many people offered themselves?), so I often went home alone.

Somewhere in all this mess & murk, I was dimly aware that I was becoming a vain, arrogant young man, despite my loathing of such things in others. Everything was somehow or other a reflection of me. W. H. Auden writes somewhere that "Narcissus does not fall in love with his reflection because it is beautiful but because it is *his*." Exactly—that was *my* reflection all around me: mine, mine, me, *me*, ME. I'd gotten to the point that I recalled little of the people I met, hardly heard what they were saying, usually forgot their names, often forgot to say thank you. I'd come to take so much for granted, & thus had become someone without humility or well-founded pride—precisely the sort of young gay man I go out of my way to avoid these days. I was a low-level monster of egotism & arrogance waiting to molt into . . . well, a David Cunningham, for example, a young man I'd met in Coconut Grove who was being kept by George Arendts, one of the richest men in America. I had dinner with them the night of their tenth anniversary, & I'll never forget how David complained about the Ferrari George had given him, saying that George knew perfectly well David was happiest in the back seat of a silver Rolls in the rain. David was impossibly arrogant & self-centered, though that wasn't why George finally kicked him out; George simply met a new & younger object of desire, whereupon David became disposable. David got forty-eight hours notice & twenty-five thousand dollars in cash. A few weeks later on an Easter Sunday in New York, he holed up in a West Forties flophouse & washed down a couple of dozen sleeping pills with a bottle of scotch—a common fate of the objects of desire I knew in those days.

In any case, as I set out for Tangier I didn't have the wherewithal or the self-acceptance necessary to make sense of my life. I'd taken this ship partly to escape such ponderings, & besides, all those turning heads kept turning my head. Somewhere in the future, maybe soon in Europe, I would find a way to be happy.

I was in fact incredibly happy on that trip, in witness whereof the bulimia stopped, never to return, & I slept halfway well for the first time in my life. I was so drawn to Europe that I devised ways to spend much of the next three years there, mostly in Italy. I was charmed by all the obvious things—the abundant art & history, the incomparable beauty of the cities, the quality of life with its unhurried ease—but I was attracted too by a different way of being gay, though I didn't know what to make of it at the time. The gay men I met in Europe seemed well-rounded people with a variety of interests; their conversation ranged more broadly than at home (they were readers to a man), & they seemed more substantial somehow, more mature, which is probably why I rarely got the sense of hidden sexual agendas. The beautiful ones among them were especially different from their American counterparts, for they seemed to have noted their attractions for others, filed the fact under "Nice but peripheral," & gone on with their lives. They weren't professional faggots of a kind I knew back in the States, men who devoted their lives to being desired & who therefore fetishized their sexuality as I myself did. When I was with European gay men, I sometimes found it possible to forget my own incomparable charms.

That first trip to Europe lasted six months. I returned to New York with fifty cents in my pocket & a French lover, an architect whom I'll call Paul since the mention of his real name would wreck his marriage & damage his career. He was proverbially tall, dark, & handsome, also rich & well connected. His address book was full of Orsinis & Rothschilds, & he knew improbable creatures like Chilean counts & pretenders to thrones.

He was also very bright & the most charming person I've ever known, but though I liked him enormously, I didn't love him, at least not after the first few months. By the time I realized my passion had waned, however, I was dining every night in New York's best restaurants in custom-tailored clothes with French dukes & Italian princes, & I was hooked—for this new, more glamorous life satisfied my two most important needs. It let me think that my life had value & it was proof positive of how far I'd travelled from 1214 Cruft Street.

It was a very posh life, with expense accounts at the best restaurants & a platoon of doormen & elevator men in our Park Avenue building (all of whom disapproved of my Levis), & a maid who woke us every morning with breakfast in bed (as deluxe a pleasure as good sex). The new doors that opened led me to the highest reaches of New York society—the dullest world I've ever known, full of people whose major subject of conversation was where they'd been & whom they'd seen, where they were going & who might show up. It was also a world with peculiar social standards, seeing that I was so obviously a kept boyman. I never thought of myself as being kept exactly. I'd met many kept young men & they'd always struck me as aimless & rather pathetic, so I rationalized that I was different. I never asked for money or presents, none of the Gucci loafers & Cartier watches that came with the role, & whenever I made money I put it in our common pot. That was enough to salve my conscience. But Paul paid for the rent, the food, the clothes, the travel, & the incidentals, which counts as being kept, wouldn't you agree? I soon had to drink a lot & take sleeping pills for the sex part; otherwise, time passed in a gilded haze. And every time I summoned enough sense of reality to consider pondering my situation, we were off on another trip, for Paul & I travelled constantly.

In the fall of '63, Paul decided he needed to see Frank Lloyd Wright's Imperial Hotel in Tokyo, & that soon turned into an excuse for a trip around the world, a terrific treat I'd never have managed save for the splendid, pointless life I was living. Istanbul, Bombay, Delhi, Agra, Benares, Bangkok, Angkor Wat, & then our first morning in Hong Kong we awoke to the news of John Kennedy's assassination. Since Paul was friendly with some of the Kennedys, he immediately returned to the States while I went on alone to Japan, then to Los Angeles to visit Ira, then made an obligatory stop in Indianapolis before returning to New York—which meant that though I thought I'd left that home far behind, there I was back in it again & more unhinged by it than ever.

The whole time I was there I was in shock from the look of the house.

Mom now had her own car, & her favorite pastime was driving for miles around to pick through people's trash. She'd become a bag lady on wheels. Everywhere you looked there were bags & boxes & piles of stuff: old magazines & newspapers, old clothes, broken blenders & TV sets & irons & sewing machines, broken toys & torn purses, lamps with torn shades & moldy shower curtains—you name it, there was a good chance she had it. Half the chairs were piled high with stuff, & the dining room had become a storage area for shopping bags full of old clothes. The stuff overflowed the front & back porches & spilled into the yard: card tables & ping-pong tables & ironing boards piled higgledy-piggledy against the back of the house, a few dozen old tires stacked along the driveway, mountains of old newspapers flanking the front door. The basement was full of more stuff, & the two-car garage had barely room for a single car. Stray cats wandered through the house like denizens of a ruined city.

I think all the stuff served Mom as a barricade between her & the world. She was so deeply frightened of abandonment & deprivation that she must have thought if she only had enough "stuff" she would somehow be safe. In any case, no one seemed to mind the mess; people joked about it or shrugged it off, & Mom kept saying "I'm gonna get on this house real soon," then got in her car & drove off to collect more trash.

Dad had been fired from the post office for getting drunk on the job a third time, so he was home a lot, which put a strain on everyone's nerves. Being fired gave him a brand new reason for feeling life was out to get him, so he was crabbier than ever, & drinking more too. The price of his folly was a reduced pension, but Bernita's money was easing that blow. Only five years old, Mom's inheritance was considerably diminished. She'd paid off the mortgage on the new house, repaid a large loan from Bead & Henry, given money to various members of the family, & made dubious loans to cousins who now weren't returning her calls. She'd also given Dad a cool ten thousand dollars, but it had been dissipated in big-spender inanities like sending roses to his favorite old-time movie stars with courtly notes praising their breasts. (I'd love to have seen Rita Hayworth's face as she read the note.) Ideally a source of security & satisfaction, Bernita's money had instead become the occasion for family quarrels. Everyone disapproved of how Mom was handling it & everyone knew a better way, especially those who had most benefitted from it. To hell with them all—the money was hers to do with as she saw fit, even if that meant it was fast disappearing. At least she was spreading some pleasure in the process, for Debbie, who loved horses, now had a pony, & Kent, who loved race cars, now had a race car.

Debbie, now ten, had just gone through a period of drawing graveyards with tombstones for everyone in our immediate family including
the dogs & cats & even the pony. The animals always survived longest,
but I was flattered that she laid me to rest last among the humans. Kent
was now so comatose when asleep that, in trying to wake him, Mom
poured water in his ears while setting off firecrackers under his bed. It
worked, but boy did he wake up in a foul mood. "Why don't you let him
be late a few mornings," I said. "Once his boss bawls him out, I'll bet he
starts waking up on time." "You're probably right," Mom said, but the
next morning: "Kent! Kent! Can you hear me? You're gonna be late for
work . . . Kent? . . ." Then a little agony waiting for the firecrackers to
explode.

My last evening home, they were all upstairs watching television & I
was rummaging in the basement in search of some high school yearbooks
when I came upon my old butterfly collection beneath a pile of moldy
clothes. Suddenly the memories flooded back—the happy summers I'd
spent wandering the alleys in quest of butterflies with my homemade net
& Susie by my side, the chase & the triumphant capture, then taking the
butterflies home to drown them in turpentine & dry them with their
wings spread just so before mounting them in the cardboard boxes I'd
made. The boxes were all crushed, their glass fronts broken, the butterflies in tatters. Bits of iridescent wings exhaled in tiny puffs as I picked up
each box in turn.

The tide of that old despair began rising in me, but I pushed it back
down. I gave the family the gifts I had bought for them on my trip &
boarded a plane for New York with a lighter bag & a heavier heart, convinced that despite its discontents, my present, curious life was far better
than what I was leaving behind.

I was back in New York in time for a New Year's Eve party with the
Duke & Duchess of Windsor, so let's say I've now hit my stride as a
Famous International Faggot. I'm living in custom-made suits, travelling
with a tuxedo, staying in the best hotels, sporting a boutonniere, & smoking Sobranies with a goddam gold-tipped cigarette holder. The Hoosier
has been bred out of me, & living with Paul has given me a social poise
I've never had before. I have all those charge accounts, & every few days
the phone rings with another German prince or Belgian banker inviting
me to the Schloss or the château. Lenny Bernstein has pronounced me
"sortable" (French for "take-outable"), meaning I can manage small talk
in three languages, catch most of the allusions, & won't confuse the
forks. You can take me anywhere, which is pretty much where I went. . . .

. . . In the palace of Avila, I've just complimented the Duchess on her paintings (Goyas & El Grecos mostly, some pocked with bullet holes from the Spanish Civil War) when she asks, "Would you like to see my favorite things?" "Very much," I say, because if this gal has Goyas with bullet holes, her prize possessions must be a knockout.

She takes me in a rickety lift down to the wine cellar where the walls of an entire room are lined with the framed ashtrays she's stolen from famous hotels around the world. On the one hand, I'm disappointed; on the other, the idea of a collection of stolen goods appeals to me, especially since the Duchess & I have stolen from some of the same hotels. . . .

. . . Though I know by now that the rich rarely remark on the food, I nevertheless compliment my host on his chef, for the tournedos are superb. That's when I feel a ferocious itch in one of my eyebrows. I scratch, dislodging a huge crab louse that falls kerplunk on its back in the middle of my plate (which once belonged to Catherine the Great, who would have sympathized). It's so big I can see its legs wiggling as I smother it in truffle sauce.

After dinner, in a living room as large as a mead hall with rugs that one normally sees only in museums, I play chess with my host on a sixteenth-century jade set given him by Chiang Kai-shek—for what reason I never discover or else can't remember since I keep drinking until the rest of the night fades into a blackout. . . .

. . . Dinner with Steve Sondheim again, & again his cleaning lady/cook has prepared our dinner in advance, so we open another bottle of Polish vodka & we're off. Steve has discovered my discontent with the life I'm living & likes that about me; I like it that he likes it & that he shares my views. I've always liked it that he's a night owl friend available for calls at three & four A.M.

He plays five new songs for me, then, diffident as ever, interrupts me in mid-praise to propose a new game based on recalling words associated with unrelated images on cards. With each new card, we have to recall all the words from the beginning. Incredibly, I win at forty-one (or was it thirty-one?). In the garden later, he shushes me so I can hear the voices of Katharine Hepburn & Spencer Tracy floating over the wall. I knew she lived next door but *wow!* Once again life turns into a movie.

As usual, we finish the vodka at dawn, so up the woozy avenue to home & bed, having had another delightful evening, though nothing more remains in ye olde memorie banke. . . .

. . . It's another party given by the chief of protocol at the United Nations. He's a Swedish count & I'm a great success but late for a humpy number. "Take the glass," he says as I start to chugalug, "& I'll call down & have my driver take you where you're going." Naturally I'm pleased, but this isn't special treatment; this is par for the course. . . .

Given such privileges & attentions, how could I not feel special? And given my deep self-doubt, how could I not cling to that feeling? And given the homophobia of my culture, how could I not prefer the safety of that safer world? And given no goal in life beyond treading more water as painlessly as possible, why not that life rather than another, for increasingly I was envied. I was confused about many things, but not about the fact that people envied me.

I passed the days in New York trying to write a novel that dwelt on the horrors of Mom's childhood, but writing was hard & lonely. I didn't like hard things & increasingly I didn't like being alone. Increasingly I drank more & took more sleeping pills to prepare myself for making love with Paul, for the romantic part of our relationship had begun to feel like a prison—which made me feel horrible, not for the prison part but because I felt so ungrateful & stupid. Paul was one of the most wonderful people I'd ever known: bright & curious about life, irresistably charming, even courageous. Someone once threatened to blackmail him for being gay, but he didn't panic or pay or leave town or commit suicide as others might have done; he called the FBI & arranged to meet the blackmailer in a restaurant. When the man repeated his threat, an agent stepped from behind a screen & arrested him. Paul was so devoted to me, so why couldn't I love him more, or better, or differently? Why did I do such stupid things, like the night after dinner with him & Bill Kramer when, again having had too much to drink, I jumped out of the cab at a red light, ran to the intersection, dropped my pants & mooned them both, then took off down a street with a DO NOT ENTER sign.

The rest of that night was a blackout. There were lots of blackouts in those years & a lot of things happening in waves of darkness & nausea. There were times when I suddenly came to, feeling like a visitor in my life, wondering who those people were & why they were looking at me like that (had I just said something shocking or rude?). Sometimes friends had to tell me what I'd done or said, which always felt like getting news of a stranger. Sometimes I'd meet a man & think, "I *know* I know him," then a day or a week later I'd recall that we'd had sex, sometimes even a little affair. The hours & days of vanished time began to worry me, & the worship was becoming wearisome.

Ira often said that I seemed to be living a joyless life. He was right, but what was the source of my discontent? I had no financial cares, I was socially more in demand than ever, & my sexual activity was at an all-time high. I had everything I wanted, & over & over again the voices reminded me of what an enviable life I was living. "Lucky you," they said, "everybody wants to be you!" So why such a recurrent sense of discontent & sadness & even despair? If only I could figure out a way to be happy . . . if only I could stop smoking . . . if only my life had focus & direction . . . if only I had some sort of career . . . or that book from Scribner's, the facsimile edition of the *Farnese Book of Hours* in the leather slipcase, so off for some more shoplifting & then to the gym & back to the apartment for another date with another trick, another party or opening night, another affair, another anything I could come up with to ignore the dark tides gathering beneath the surface of my life.

Looking back, I don't know whether to laugh or cry, or maybe just cheer that this is now so far behind me. What I couldn't see at the time was that my self-absorption doomed me to unhappiness. But my childhood had made me desperately needy for acceptance, I now found it wherever I turned, & the voices kept reinforcing the delusion that the life I was living certified me as someone who mattered. According to them, other golden boymen were frittering their twenties away to little purpose, but I was in a different league. My friendships with Noel & Lenny were of a different order; the tricks I pursued were superior to others' tricks; the treats of my special life marked me as someone wholly apart. Other boymen were wasting their lives; I was living in an empyrean of glamor.

Yet even in my ignorance & at my unhappiest, something kept me stumbling forward toward something better. I couldn't identify the impulse or articulate the "something better," but I somehow managed to keep alive not just the thought, "I want to be happy," but also, "Somehow or other I can become happy." Despite myself, the struggle stayed alive in me. It also led me to people who helped me, people like Ira, & Paul in his way, & a man I want to tell you about because of the difference he made for the better.

In May, 1963, Paul & I were travelling in Egypt, & everywhere we went we kept running into the same group of twenty or thirty Italians. At Giza, Memphis, the Temple of Karnak: twenty to thirty Italians led by a regal man in his fifties to whom the others paid conspicuous deference. On to Aswan & Abu Simbel—sunset in a felucca in the middle of the Nile, an orange sky streaked with purple clouds, herons flying low overhead—the Italians in tow.

We returned to Cairo with the Italians on a flight that was delayed six hours & nearly crashed in a sand storm. Arriving at around four in the morning, we found that the only taxis at the airport were reserved for the Italians, but their leader offered to drop us at our hotel. Once under way, he gestured to his companion & in halting English said, "May I present Dino de Laurentiis. I am Luchino Visconti." I recognized de Laurentiis' name because of the many Italian movies he'd produced, but Visconti's meant little to me. By ride's end, however, Luchino & I had discovered that a month hence, after Paul had returned to the States, we would both be in Spoleto for the Festival of Two Worlds. That coincidence, plus our having travelled in tandem throughout Egypt & nearly been killed in each other's company, created a bond. As if already friends, we parted with pleasure at the prospect of an imminent reunion.

I'd seen from the first how charming Luchino was, but only in Spoleto did I learn that he was admired throughout Europe as the founder of Italian neorealism & a director of the first rank in film, theater, & opera. My new friend, I discovered, was one of the most famous directors in the world, & was from a family that had ruled Milan in the Middle Ages & that appears in *The Canterbury Tales* & *The Divine Comedy*. He seemed to know everyone—all the Italian glitterati of stage & screen & opera plus an endless crowd of famous foreigners. We lunched with Jeanne Moreau & Louis Malle, dined with Anna Magnani & Marcello Mastroianni, & day after day I found myself with people I'd admired from afar for years. It was a much more interesting world than its American counterpart, more intelligent & tasteful & full of people who talked philosophy & history & art & politics. It was fun too, for Luchino was playful & courtly & a great host, a real padrone. I was dazzled & delighted.

Toward the end of the festival, Luchino asked my plans, which were to spend a few weeks in Rome before returning to the States. In that case I would be his guest, & for as long as I pleased. The matter was decided, not that I ever demurred.

Once I took up residence in Luchino's villa in Rome, I found myself living the most luxurious life I've ever known. Each morning, Ignazio, the majordomo, woke me with breakfast in bed, then vanished to supervise the running of the house with the help of five other domestics, a gardener, a night watchman, & a chef of fabled skill who prepared dinner for twelve even on nights when Luchino & I dined alone. With its paintings & tapestries, its Renaissance bronzes, its blackamoor floorlamps & Russian icons, the villa looked & felt to me like a friendly palace. Save for Luchino's quarters & the servants' wing, I was given the run of the place, also the use of the five cars in the garage. Whenever I missed a meal or became hungry at odd hours, I called the kitchen, whereupon Ignazio appeared in his handsome livery bearing a silver tray.

I'd known rich people before, but no one who lived like a king. Better, actually, for Luchino not only had the means but also a freedom of movement in public that kings don't enjoy. Those in the know recognized him but kept a respectful distance, while to others he was merely an imposing stranger. He was immensely rich, or at least he lived like he was, for I never knew him to count the cost of anything. He had six homes when we first met, others before & after, & he spent lavishly rehabing & furnishing them. He sometimes rented a couple of railway cars & took a dozen friends to Paris for the weekend. Hotels, restaurants, theater & opera—everything was his treat, for he was always the host, the grand seigneur. People called him "the Emperor of Rome."

For a man whose mother cut coupons out of the newspaper to save a nickle on a box of Tide, the wealth & glamor of Luchino's life were of course impressive, but it was our friendship that soon mattered much more to me. I became one of the beautiful young men who were with Luchino wherever he went, a group that at different times included Franco Zeffirelli, Alain Delon, Helmut Burger, & lo & behold, Massimo Girotti, the scantily clad Roman slave who'd catalyzed my adolescent libido in the Garfield Park Cinema years before. Unlike the others, however, I didn't have designs on Luchino—didn't want him to be my patron or lover or give me gifts or star me in a movie or hire me as an assistant or a set or costume designer or any of the other innumerable possiblities brewing in the minds of the other young men. Luchino knew that my affection wasn't contaminated by desire for material or professional gain, & besides, he never expressed desire for me, thank God. No doubt I wasn't difficult enough, wasn't essentially straight like Delon & Girotti, or contentious like Zeffirelli, or intractable like Burger. Luchino's affection for me was genuine too, untrammeled by lust & motivated by something kindly & paternal. For the next thirteen years (which is to say, until he died), we had a mostly honest, trusting, loyal friendship, bolstered by our understanding that since we weren't romantically involved, we would never disappoint each other the way our lovers had done.

What was he like? So huge a presence that he gave new meaning to the phrase "larger than life." In his fifties, he was more imposing than merely handsome, but he nevertheless still showed vestiges of the extraordinary good looks that had enthralled Chanel & Cocteau when he lived in Paris in his late twenties. Age & a life lived at a pitch of white heat had turned his looks into something pared, intense, austerely regal. The passions were so concentrated in him that his love was more deep & enduring than any I've ever known, his anger more fierce & unyielding. He was extremely bright & knowledgeable (he read four & five books a week), extremely cultivated, immensely gracious & irresistibly charming when he put his mind to it. That was the angel half of Luchino.

The devil half? Imperious pride combined with a streak of cruelty that sometimes led him to humiliate others. During those first weeks in the villa, I often saw him humiliate his lover of the moment, Fred Williams, a German Alain Delon who appears as the handsome Hindu in Fellini's *Juliet of the Spirits*. It's true that Fred was vain & ignorant & given to remarks like "Hitler wasn't all bad." At times like that, I too wanted to tear out first my hair & then Fred's, but I couldn't bear seeing what Luchino did—taunt Fred for his stupidity & ignorance & his lack of talent, real failings that Fred himself was embarrassed by. I felt pain for Fred, but also for Luchino, for at those times his behavior bespoke some deep, unhealed wound from the past. (Luchino was mean to me only once, & awful as it was—he berated me in front of thirty people because I'd allowed Tab Hunter to pick up the check for a dinner in London—it passed quickly.)

I loved Luchino very much, & I loved all our times together—the nights we sat in the drawing room after dinner reading or listening to music, & the nights a dozen people came to dinner & more dropped in afterward for impromptu parties with charades & those vicious truth-telling games so many Italians enjoy, & the nights we went out to dinner with a crowd of people, & the afternoons we drove in the countryside around Rome to visit special places he wanted me to see. Setting out from Rome one morning on a drive that would take us to Volterra where he was beginning a new film, he asked "Have you ever seen the cathedral in Orvieto?" No, I hadn't. "You must," he said, & took an hour's detour so that I could.

I especially loved the ordinary times when we passed the morning in his study or in a shady corner of the garden talking of this & that over another cup of coffee. I loved it that our language together was Italian, & that he helped me with my vocabulary & grammar, & that he taught me the shockingly vulgar idioms I produced at mealtimes to the discomfort of his guests & his own feigned alarm. He took time to explain his politics to me (he was a Communist & though in poor health at the time, stood as an honor guard at the bier of Togliatti, the leader of the Italian Communist Party who died during my first stay at the villa). He quizzed me about my museum goings, & encouraged me to find my way (I would be a writer, that was it), & trusted me by authorizing me to deal with his affairs in the United States. He took me with him into the world of his blood family, the ducal brothers & countess sisters & princeling nephews who constituted a world apart from the more public world of his career & his elective family. He joked with me & teased me & told me intimate details of his personal life & loved me like the son he never had, while I loved him like the father I was always seeking. Luchino changed my life for the better, for his love let me glimpse an Alan I could begin to respect & take pride in.

Luchino's love wasn't enough, however, to keep me from drifting—no one's love would have been. I was hooked on my aimless, mesmerizing life, for so many adventures kept coming my way: lunch with Ezra Pound in Spoleto & with Fellini in Rome (he gave me a small part in 8½), a drunken evening in Philadelphia with Ava Gardner & Nat King Cole, a splendid affair in London with another American movie star who to my dazzled eyes was the most beautiful man on earth, encounters with European royalty, a Papal Mass in the Palace of the Popes in Avignon, late nights with Rudy Nureyev roaming the by-ways of Venice in a gondola, & the afternoon in a French train from Cannes to Paris when a man entered my compartment looking like the archtypal English schoolteacher, all tweeds & spectacles and with a frazzled, absentminded air. Every twenty minutes or so, in what was clearly a foreigner's French, he asked to borrow a pen. I handed it over, he wrote something down, he handed it back with "*Merci beaucoup.*" Outside Paris, I took out a *Time* magazine.

"You speak English?" he asked in an Oxbridge accent. We began talking, & I soon asked the inevitable American question: "What do you do?"

"I teach at Cambridge."

"Aha. And what do you teach?"

"Well, I don't teach actually. I suppose you could say I counsel & advise."

"What do you counsel & advise?"

"Well, I don't counsel really. Actually, I'm a writer."

"Really? And have you written anything I might have read?"

Leaning toward me now & beaming like a delighted child, he said confidentially: "Actually, I've written one book that's really quite, quite famous."

"Really? What's it called?"

"*A Passage to India.*"

The man I admired most in the world was leaning toward me with excitement & pride, & I was speechless, flabbergasted, astounded—there should be a new word for the way I felt. The year before, I'd read everything he'd written, & ever since I'd known that if God had said, "You can meet any one person alive on earth," I would have chosen E. M. Forster. Miraculously, there he was, my hero, sitting across from me in a French train inviting me to tea in Cambridge.

It's exciting to meet your hero, but events like that don't contribute toward shaping a meaningful life. As best I knew at the time, the only way to create meaning in my life besides keeping in the swim of my gay celebrity was to embark on another love affair, for I bought wholly into the nutty American notion that I was less than half whole unless I was part of a couple, no matter the couple. So after a couple of years with Paul, I walked out on him for a gorgeous Neapolitan-Sicilian who guaranteed me so much emotional turmoil that I once found myself in the emergency ward at Bellevue having my stomach pumped because of a rigged suicide attempt designed to keep him from rearranging my face with a claw hammer. (Lethally jealous, he had discovered one of my many infidelities & gone berserk, breaking everything in the apartment that he knew I loved, & then coming at me with the hammer. The only way I knew to stop him was to lock myself in the bathroom & take twenty double sleeping pills. It worked.) I was so miserable during the three years of that affair that the friends I confided in often said, "You must want to be unhappy," but I knew how wrong that formulation was the first time I heard it. Barring the occasional masochist, no one ever wants to be unhappy; some people just need to be unhappy to act out a narrative devised by the dark voices in their minds, a narrative that confirms their own poor estimate of themselves & their sense that they don't deserve better. But didn't I deserve better? What was it in me that needed such turmoil & misery?

That love affair gave way to another, & then to another, & then it's easy to lose track since I pursued lovers the way some people go about shopping, in which the point isn't to find something & have done with it but to keep on shopping. So my hectic quests for the next lover occupied most of my time while I worked at part-time jobs & indulged the fiction that I was writing fiction. In the fall of '66 after the failure of yet another affair, I met Frank Scavullo & voilà—my modelling career was off & running again when I met Brian Thompson, a California surfer Adonis who was taking a Ph.D. in history at Princeton.

Around the time I met Brian, I'd begun to realize that my career as a golden boyman couldn't last forever. I was on the verge of my thirtieth birthday, & though I looked younger, I knew I couldn't count on being a cynosure for many more years. I began thinking of possible careers, something that would pay the bills but that I would enjoy as well, something absorbing enough to engage me for a lifetime. Partly because I'd met Brian, teaching appeared as the obvious choice, for I'd always loved school & admired my teachers & thought a professor's life altogether desirable. Literature had always been a source of great pleasure for me, & the fact that you could make a living teaching Shakespeare & Whitman seemed too good to be true. In a sense, it was. Though I knew some professors at Columbia & NYU, I knew nothing about the practical realities of academe. When I imagined a future as a professor, I saw myself discussing great books with eager undergraduates, teaching a maximum of three courses a year like my Columbia professors had done, lunching with fascinating, humane colleagues, spending winter vacations in the Caribbean & summers in Europe. As for the money part, that never crossed my mind, & a good thing too.

I applied to Columbia, Princeton, & Yale, since everything had to be the best & I would rather have failed spectacularly than come in second at anything. Then I met a professor from Rutgers, & after persistent recruiting on his part, I applied to Rutgers as well.

I took the day-long GREs & afterward went to dinner with Brian, who suddenly expressed reservations at our becoming lovers. But there was nothing to worry about, I explained. We would have a legendary love affair that would make us the envy of gay New York. We would never be jealous. We would be free & easy & honest, thereby growing into the rich, full people we'd always longed to be. We would be good friends as well as turned-on bedmates. And for me, this would be the good love affair at long last. All the previous affairs had taught me everything I needed to know; they had failed that this new relationship might succeed. Nothing could be simpler or more desirable than that Brian & I become lovers.

Brian soon saw things my way, so he moved in & we became an official couple. And if I do say so myself, we really *were* special—a dazzling duo ripe for the most avid public consumption of gay New York. Some of my friends found Brian a tight-assed WASP, a charge I found hard to credit since I myself was a tight-assed WASP. "That Nazi dyke" is how another golden boyman described me at the time. Albert Earl, Hanya, Al & Alanino (Luchino's nickname), Celeste, that Nazi dyke, a Universal Type (Almost) of Desire, a Famous International Faggot, a model & a graduate student, and then around this time "the marquesa" & "Matilda Mild Reprimand"—where was I in that melange of names & identities? Never mind—I was Brian's lover, that's who I was, & that's all that mattered.

I chose Rutgers for graduate school since they came through with a government fellowship for three years with more money to follow in case I dawdled. (Remember when Sputnik alarmed our masters so much that they invested in education for a change?) Yet again, another door opened into another new world. Once classes began, however, I found myself reenacting the same scenario of fear & trembling I'd gone through as a freshman at Columbia. Everything was over my head, I felt stupid & therefore ugly & pointless, & when Brian went home to California for a visit, my sense of intellectual deficiency grew worse. I couldn't scan Pope or grasp *Ulysses* or remember the tenets of Neoplatonism. I was so miserable I was crying myself to sleep at night in my rented room in New Brunswick, & sleeping no more than three or four hours at a clip, & staring at myself in the mirror thinking that life wasn't worth living. But a month later I was into the swing of graduate school & loving it. Students who'd arrived directly from college were blasé about reading *King Lear* for the third time in as many years, but I thought, "Boyohboy, Lear again after all these years!"

At Christmas, Brian went to LA for two weeks while I wrote term papers & took exams. I had so much work that I asked my doctor for something to see me through, & he gave me a prescription (a hundred pills, renewable five times) for Escatrol—a speed time capsule pretty as a pointillist rainbow. I loved my Escatrol, for it increased my energy & focussed my attention & kept me at my work around the clock. In eight days I slept four nights for maybe four hours a night.

After handing in my last paper, I stopped the pills & plunged into a depression so profound that I thought I was losing my mind. Afraid to leave the apartment because of free-floating paranoia, I sat on the couch & cried. Each time Brian called from LA, I pretended to be fine; as soon as he hung up, I relapsed into weeping. Christmas Eve on a dash to the corner for cigarettes, I ran into Joel Schumacher, who took one look & said, "*Boy*, are YOU ever *crash*ing!" What, pray tell, was "crashing"? Joel's explanation helped me weather a couple of more days until the withdrawal was over, leaving me enough time before Brian's return for some horny infidelities & *The Way of All Flesh*. But despite the horror of my first withdrawal from speed, I still loved my Escatrol, & I had no inkling I was beginning a new addiction. At that point in my life, the addictions consisted of cigarettes, booze, the gym, sex, adulation, the envy of others, & the voices inside my head. Then along came the drugs.

Next, marijuana. I didn't feel anything the first time, but Brian clearly loved it. I felt something the second time though, & more the third, & by the fourth or fifth time we were smoking out of our own stock. We bought by the pound—eighty to one hundred dollars for superb grass with odd names & accompanying myths: "Ice Pack" was grown on top of a sacred mountain in Mexico that was under ice half the year, blah, blah, blah. Hash followed soon after, then seco synatan (a "set-up," part upper & part downer, speed without the jagged edges) which we called the "love pill" since it allowed us to have marathon sex. Then acid & mescaline, & cocaine occurred somewhere in there, along with kef & occasionally opium, & always Tuinals & Valiums & Percocets & Placidils (all sleeping pills or pain killers), & once we encountered it MDA whenever we could get it. And of course Methedrine, the Dom Perignon of speed. The poppers had been there from the beginning; then Ben, my barber, began shooting me up.

Within a few months after we began living together, Brian was tending a cash box whose compartments were kept full of the aforementioned drugs, plus the necessary paraphernalia for consuming them. We took drugs most nights we were together, most weekend days too, & I had my own cache at Rutgers. I loved smoking a joint late at night & reading poetry since the grass distended time & the words grew large until they filled my room & I lived in the world of the poem to the exclusion of everything else. Always easily distracted, it was a blessing to be able to focus with single-minded clarity on anything, & bliss when the anything was poetry. On weekend evenings in New York, friends stopped by to smoke some of Brian's anal-retentive joints produced on his little rolling machine. Then out for a night of dancing, for it was the dawn of the gay disco—the Sewer, the Sanctuary, the Stonewall—where the songs were all about love & sex & the dancers were all on drugs.

Was there anyone in the late '60s who didn't take drugs except Nixon & Kissinger? The lure of drugs was powerful for Brian, who said they helped him relax & be more spontaneous & expressive. They had me hooked because they obliterated my discontents & created extraordinary sensuous experiences. In those days, I knew of few highs higher than taking speed & getting stoned in Fire Island Pines, paddling a raft out into the ocean, maneuvering myself into a cresting wave, & snorting poppers split seconds before the wave broke & tumbled me in the surf. And of course the drugs gave an extraordinary intensity to sex, taking me further outside myself than anything I'd ever known.

Over the next ten years, I never had sex without grass & poppers, & often used other drugs as well. I studied & attended class & wrote papers & much of my dissertation & even taught on grass & speed. During the entire relationship with Brian, whenever someone asked if I'd seen a movie, I was never sure since we always went to the movies stoned & thus everything I saw melded together—except for *2001*, which we must have seen a dozen times, stoned & tripping while lying on the floor in front of the first row seats, exclaiming over & over again, "Wow, oh man, wow! I don't be-*lieve* it! *Innnn*-credible!" The drugs must have made us stupidly tolerant, for I don't recall getting bored with such inane talk, & we endured years of it.

Besides the drugs, what remains in bold relief from those three and a half years of the longest & last love affair of my life? There was the gorgeous couple part, being a "UC," a Universal Couple. Now people said they swooned when *we* walked by on the beach, & they heard that *we* slept in a heart-shaped bed, & they wished that *we* would make a pornographic movie. I revelled in how much we were envied.

There was also Brian's body (it spoke of swimming & gymnastics & the favor of the gods), & some good conversation, & some fun (a discovery for sobersided me, who'd long thought that if it weren't serious, it couldn't matter), & then the fact that Brian was preparing for an academic career supported my own efforts in that direction.

There were also the summers we spent at Fire Island Pines, three words of lament for Paradise Lost. What it is these days I don't know; what it was then beggars description. Each time the ferry left Long Island & headed for that enchanted sliver of scrub pine & windswept dunes, it felt like leaving the moorings of all the mores & social taboos I'd ever known. Once on the island, it was like living inside the most romantic of Technicolor movies: no cars, no traffic but tanned bodies in bathing suits no matter where, on the beach or in the stores or strolling the boardwalks on the way to another lunch or brunch or tea dance or trick or dinner or party. Every weekend, a dozen parties. Was it the Black & White party, or the Red, White, & Blue party, or the Black & Blue party where the deck gave way under the weight of a hundred gyrating pumped & polished bodies & then after a moment's shocked pause everyone resumed dancing, but now on a tilt? Was it the South Seas party or the Aztec party or the Cleopatra party where Sam Sloman as Mae West made his entrance from the bay borne in a litter by half-a-dozen bodybuilders?

Sam was often there, washing down uppers & downers with margaritas & Black Russians; & Halston, wafting about in a caftan sniffing the rose in the Roman vial he wore on a gold chain around his neck, & Joel Schumacher, popping pills while biding time between careers as the Revlon designer & the Hollywood director.

Brian & I shared a house with Joel one season, & Joel used to greet me on Friday evenings with a Methedrine cocktail that kept me going the whole weekend. One Saturday night Joel gave a party; Brian & I spent the night out, & when we returned next morning, half of everything was broken & the walls were covered with splattered popcorn outlined in raspberry Day-Glow paint. Even the pines flanking the front walk had been sprayed, & the front walk too of course. That was also the summer some friends rented a house with a slat-board floor in the living room, & on Labor Day weekend they tore up the floor to get at the blackbirds & yellowbirds & all the other pills that had fallen between the slats over the course of the summer.

A few years before when Paul & I had gone to the Pines, the parties had been elaborate, with queens spending weeks of time & salary on their costumes. I recall a Roman orgy party Paul & I attended with a couple of friends, me dressed as Tutankhamen attended by three Egyptian gods. Our pleated linen skirts were made at Hattie Carnegie's, our gold lamé crowns at Lily Daché's. By the time I knew Brian, however, the parties had become much more simple & relaxed. Someone was giving a poolside party with a Tahitian theme? You threw on a bathing suit, stuck a flower behind your ear & a joint in your basket, downed a tab of mescaline, & you were out the door. Ahhhh, all those brilliant colors in the sparkling sunlight, all those glistening bodies on parade, all those pink & turquoise drinks, all those pills & tabs & joints.

I was high one afternoon lying on the beach (Brian was in LA) when out of the water came Cal Culver, soon to become America's first gay porn star as Casey Donovan in *Boys in the Sand*. It happened exactly like it does at the beginning of that movie: he walked up to me, I got up, & without saying a word we walked into the woods. I was still high later that day when I said my name to the clerk in the grocery store so I could charge the food. That's when the guy behind me said, "Did you ever write a poem called 'Vermeer'?" I had, & he'd read it in the Berkeley literary magazine; in fact, it was one of his favorite poems. What a nice feeling that was—but so unusual, for I'd grown unaccustomed to relating to people on any basis other than my looks.

We talked outside the store & agreed to meet next morning for breakfast to continue our conversation. Then I met a terrific kid on my way back to the house, & that made me late for drinks, after which I stopped by another trick's place to say we'd better move things back an hour, but one thing led to another until I was two hours late for dinner, which meant I lingered over coffee to compensate, & then some people insisted I stop by for another joint on my way back to the second trick's place before going to the Boatel, & that must have been where I passed out. I awoke the next day around noon, having forgotten my breakfast date with the guy who'd liked my poems, having forgotten I'd ever published poems or done much of anything I could take pride in besides being constantly desired & envied.

That was one of the two summers a friend rented a room in his house to Brian & me for a hundred dollars. The friend knew dozens of beautiful young boymen, which meant that every weekend the house was glutted with beauties, so there were interminable waits for the bathroom & quarrels over who usurped it most. I was actually fairly fast: a shave & a shower & a final primp, then the injection in the right cheek of my ass with one of the syringes Ben had prepared for me back in the city. Then off into a night of dancing at the Boatel on another of the highest highs I've ever known.

Ben, my barber, was a friend of Dr. Max Jacobson, aka "Dr. Feelgood" & "Miracle Max." Max used to shoot up Jack & Jackie Kennedy (quite legally) along with an equally glamorous bunch of exhausted or depressed or otherwise ailing movie stars & models & politicians & socialites. I saw Max in his office once for a ten o'clock appointment, & he gave me a shot that produced the clearest, coolest, most focussed head I've ever known, along with a solid forty-eight hours of smooth, inexhaustible energy & the confidence that I could swim the Atlantic with one hand tied behind my back, both ways. Truman Capote described the effect of a Max treatment as "instant euphoria." That & then some.

Miracle Max with his little black bag of amphetamines & vitamins & steroids, & the calcium for the warm flush accompanying takeoff, had passed on his secret recipes to Ben. Ben fortunately lusted for me ("With a joint & a popper, I can have you in imagination"), so he gave me injections along with my haircuts. I loved seeing my veins dilate when he tied the tourniquet & swabbed the spot he'd chosen, & I felt an intensity I'd never known when the needle entered my arm & the clear liquid disappeared into my bloodstream. On Ben's instructions I stood, breathed deeply, & the bliss was upon me. Then, "So long, Ben" & out the door for a day of errands & bookings & go-sees & the gym & cleaning the apartment before drinks & dinner & sex of a superlative order, & then a second day of the same all over again, for I was on cloud ninety-nine—wholly charged, carefree, invincible. Each time Ben shot me up, I felt physically the way for years I'd felt socially—like a prince or a star or a godling.

Since I couldn't give myself an intravenous injection on my own, Ben taught me how to administer an intramuscular shot (same effect without the rush), warning me that a single inch the wrong way & I would be paralyzed for life. He prepared syringes for my weekends in the Pines, & fortunately I always aimed right. Joints, acid & mescaline, speed & Ben's shots—the drugs were an inevitable accompaniment to life in the Pines, along with a lot of booze of course. We spent entirely stoned weekends there, & lots of guys fell off the boardwalk into the poison ivy each night from being stoned or high on drugs or booze or both. Ronnie, Brian's best friend, used to shoot up two & three tabs of acid at a time before joining us for an afternoon on the beach or around the pool, & I'm sure we all smoked grass & took hallucinogens the night we gathered on the beach to scatter Ronnie's ashes in the waves.

Poor, sweet, bright, funny, damaged Ronnie, always ricocheting between frenetic acid highs & a private despair so steered by the demons inside his head that he finally took an overdose of sleeping pills one night while listening to his favorite music. And how odd that in setting out to describe the pleasures of those sun-filled days, I end up with this waste of a life. I begin writing about what I recall as a good thing, & it turns into a bad thing, or a sad thing, a thing that mars the past, another lame lament of memory.

The same thing happens when I think about the love affair with Brian, for although there were pleasures & good times, what stays with me is that our sex got better & better because essentially we remained strangers since we were almost constantly stoned. Strangers? It was only when we were breaking up that I learned of Brian's penchant for prepubescent boys, & he never knew a quarter of my infidelities. But that's only part of it. We learned all the obvious things about each other, histories & tastes & beliefs & so on, but our souls remained closed books. Some trips to the Caribbean, lots of drugged sex, a few happy days on sunny beaches—that's mostly what remains.

I'd arranged to take my Ph.D. orals on April 30, 1970, for the satisfaction of achieving that goal on my birthday. I couldn't sleep the night before—all I knew of English & American literature kept rewinding inside my head—so I was dim at the beginning of the ordeal, but I perked up & passed.

Then the bus into New York for my thirty-third birthday party, thinking "How odd, becoming thirty-three. What does thirty-three mean?" In modelling I'd been told to lie about my age so often that I myself became confused sometimes. "How old are you?" tricks would ask (the question is an inevitable component of American gay male sex), & I'd say "Twenty-six, I mean twenty-five. No, wait a minute, I'm twenty-seven. Yeah, that's right, twenty-seven." Then at twenty-seven or so, age had begun to confuse me since I couldn't figure out what significance my age was supposed to have, so I'd put it out of my mind until the bus ride from Rutgers into Manhattan the afternoon of my birthday. It was my own version of the tired joke about the man who moves to LA, falls asleep beside the pool, & wakes to find he's eighty years old. As far as my own awareness of my age was concerned, I'd fallen asleep at twenty-seven & awakened to find myself thirty-three. All I could think of was that by that age, Keats, Shelley, & Schubert were dead, leaving behind works that assured their immortality. What could I count to my credit at that advanced age? A lot of sex with humpy guys on two continents & being admired & lots of travel & the memories of some interesting people; a couple of solid friendships; some good, hard work at my education; an exorbitant number of hours at the gym; the fastidious cultivation of the gift of the look; a few lovers I rarely saw any more; a closetful of addictions old & new. It didn't amount to much, I thought, looking out at the oil refineries of northern New Jersey. Then I thought of the last line of Rilke's "On An Archaic Torso of Apollo": "You must change your life." Yes, yes, but *how*? Where could I go to learn how to change my life?

I hadn't wanted the guests at my birthday party to feel obliged to buy me presents, so I'd asked Brian not to tell them it was my birthday. Damned if he hadn't complied. In lieu of presents, however, I got some phone numbers on the sly. One from that tall stud sweetheart as near to perfection as anyone gets, but alas, he would be dead before I could call, the only death by vanity I've ever known. He wanted a cleft in his magnificent chin, so he made a date with the plastic surgeon who's appeared in these pages &, once under the anaesthesia, his heart stopped. I also got a model's number that night, another worthless piece of paper since he soon committed suicide over a failed affair with another model. There was a soulfully handsome Columbia student at the party, a shy, tormented philosophy major who also killed himself a few months later, & I recall that some of the guests remarked on Ronnie's absence. That may also have been the night we got word of a friend who'd taken home an S&M trick from Central Park who tied him up & put him through several versions of hell with a razor blade before cutting his dick off & stuffing it in his mouth, then slitting his throat. "You have to be really sick to do such a thing," people said. About our friend, that is. "Howzabout-anotherjoint?"

The following weekend, Brian & his friend Tony & I took mescaline & went to a Jefferson Airplane concert at the Fillmore East. It was a wonderful concert till toward the end when I began hallucinating: everyone in the audience turned into fourteen & fifteen year olds but I was old, the only old person in the audience. I felt a lacerating shame at being so old, & when it came time to leave, I was convinced all the exits led to cattle chutes with Nazis waiting outside to club us & slit our throats. On the cab ride home, Manhattan looked like an abandoned concentration camp, all concrete & chainlink fences & litter.

Back in the apartment, Brian & Tony grilled me about why I was having such a bad trip. They were having a great time, so I should relax & enjoy myself. What was the *matter* with me? This was fun! Why couldn't I relax and have fun?!

Off they went for more nighttime revels; I stayed behind, terrified & ashamed. I was still up when Brian came in at dawn, having had a wonderful time & clearly disappointed in me. A week or so later, Brian announced that he wanted to move out in the hope we might thereby rediscover what had brought us together in the first place. In the meantime, he would spend the summer in Princeton working on his dissertation.

Now, Ira swore that months before, I'd told him I was deeply unhappy with the relationship & wanted out. He said I told him that my life with Brian had become sterile & unrewarding, & he claimed I told him that repeatedly. All I know is that during & after the breakup, my experience was one of being abandoned. I'd never known such obsessive, crippling despair. And to think that if Ira was right (& he swore he was right), I created it all myself, & out of a relationship that mattered so little.

Tormenting gossip began drifting in at second- & thirdhand: Brian was spending time at Tony's in the Pines; Brian had moved into Tony's house; Brian & Tony were having an affair. I went out to the Pines one afternoon to talk with Brian, but there were so many golden boymen in the house (all much younger than I was, with more luxuriant hair & smoother skin) that it was hard getting him aside for a conversation; by the time I managed, he was tripping. "Sure I'm in love with Tony. I'm in love with everybody, aren't you? I don't know anything about the future, Alan; all I know about is this afternoon. You should try some of this mesc, it's outta sight. Why don't you just relax & take it easy? Go with the flow & live in the moment, it's the only reality we have. Wanna joint?"

Week by tortured week, I began falling apart. Everything seemed such an immense effort that there were times when I didn't bother to shower or shop for food or eat. I passed days at my summer job (selling plants at Bendel's) & paranoid nights alone in the apartment. I became so incapacitated that I decided to see a therapist, the first in over ten years, but it was a wasted hour since only in the final minutes was I able to focus enough to articulate my pain & confusion. What troubled me most was that three and a half years with Brian were turning out to mean nothing, another huge waste in a life that looked more & more like a wasteland of lost time.

The voices took possession of me: "You're being abandoned again because you're unworthy of love, Brian's or anyone else's, & you've wasted all that time & now you're a worthless, older, almost middle-aged man. Your time's running out, & everything you've ever done has been botched, stupid, wrong." I stayed home as much as possible, terrified of meeting someone who would give me news of Brian, though all I wanted was news of Brian. I began to hate New York because it meant the certainty of running into Brian, or worse yet, Brian & Tony together. Morning noon & night, week after week, my mind was a chaos & my heart a misery. The only thing that solaced me was The Beatles' "Let It Be," which I played over & over & over again. Otherwise, life was a continuous anxiety attack—except, that is, for the times I spent in the baths.

Seymour got me going: he enjoyed them so much he went for entire weekends armed with a cache of drugs & a hair dryer. Seymour was my best friend & most faithful companion during the Brian period. Short & Semitic & sexy, brilliant & rich & spoiled, a genius of visual design, Seymour was the trick du jour in Cherry Grove the summer he was seventeen. Already his designs were decorating the land in the form of wallpapers & fabrics, & he was the on-again, off-again lover of Angelo D'Onghia, a dean of American design. If Matisse & Vuillard had had a baby, it would have grown up to be Seymour. His apartment in Angelo's townhouse was filled with a gorgeous cacophony of fabrics & upholsteries & rugs, & he'd laid the floor throughout with a geometric pattern of tiles in chocolate brown, butter yellow, sky blue, & salmon. I'd never seen a floor decorated before, & a happy plaid at that. Seymour painted

Regency tables Chinese red, & painted a rainbow-colored picket fence on the walls of his bedroom, & wore eyeglass frames of ruby red & emerald green, & bought Eskimo masks & Gallé vases & seashell picture frames long before people collected such things. When later he moved to a loft in Chelsea, he ordered boxes of floor tiles in eight colors, dumped them on the floor, & had the workman lay them in the order in which they came to hand—thereby creating a dazzling Dada-Constructivist design. An ardent proponent of the freest personal expression & the Brian breakup, he was also a loyal & hilariously funny friend, & he helped me through that horrible time.

"Forget that desiccated WASP, darling, & come with me to the baths. They're fabulous, you'll love them. What are you waiting for? Get off your high horse for a change & down on your knees." I'd always thought there was something desperate & sleazy about the baths, & in any case I'd always been able to get most of the men I wanted so I hadn't needed them.

But Seymour was right. Once I got off my high horse &, er, in the right frame of mind, I loved the baths—all those shadowy shapes moving along dimly-lit corridors, the naked quarry spotted in the showers, the sudden encounters with Mr. Right for the Night, then the tentative groping & quick seclusion behind the locked doors of a room whose claustrophobic dimensions focussed the lust while the sounds of sex erupted into the halls, men making love in the sauna & the steam room & the orgy room, the living pornography of it all, the anonymity that gave greater intensity to the coupling, that sense of crossing a boundary into a world where knowledge of the other consists entirely of the body, seeing & touching the body, nothing but the single, well-hung, proportioned, beautiful body, all communication concentrated into physical response & the transported moans of excitement, surrender, gratification. Dispensing with as much of the cultural & psychological baggage as is possible for people of our time & place, the men in the baths embraced the purely physical & erotic, & oh yes, Seymour was right—I *loved* it, all those naked, responsive, beautiful bodies. And none of the dreary ditz, thank God, of conventional cruising, no "You've gotta be kidding—my *cousin* went to Columbia!"

I also loved the baths for the strange democracy that reigned there, or rather the inverted oligarchy in which stock boy & student took precedence over lawyer & banker. Like any post–hunter & gatherer world, the baths had their own hierarchy of exclusionary values that created haves & have nots, but youth & face & body & sexual equipment were the determining factors, & thus that sense of exhilaration that comes from entering a topsy-turvy world where customary values are inverted—Fire Island Pines, Mykonos, Alice's Wonderland, the Lenten carnival where jesters rule & outlaws set norms. You might think it was easy for me to enjoy such a world since I could compete with success, but men far less desired than I was got their chance with a humpy guy so horny he couldn't see beyond the need of his tumescent dick, or so into the bacchanalian spirit of it all that one mouth or ass served as well as another.

My first time, Seymour took me to the Continental Baths on West Seventy-fifth Street, where in the swimming pool I met up with a barely legal, pearly skinned cowpoke from Montana. A couple of delectable hours later (he came three times, so yes, thank God, he'd *really* wanted me, so I could relax for a while), I emerged into the dance-floor area & saw a crowd of well-dressed men & women seated in rows of folding chairs in front of a makeshift stage. Here & there, I recognized a familiar face from the worlds of art & theater. What in the world . . . ? Then a raucous young woman fueled by some intergalactic energy began to entertain, a singer by the name of Bette Midler. I wouldn't be surprised, I opined to my towel-clad neighbors, if that woman went somewhere, though with a face like that you could never tell.

After Midler's performance, most of the audience departed save for a few attractive young men who sent their dates home & remained behind to dance, first without their jackets, then their shirts, until, splendid torsos now glistening with sweat, they took a room & a shower & settled in to explore the rest of the night.

Strolling home at dawn, the sky like a Tiepolo above the Plaza, sensually slaked, happy with having been so repeatedly, fully, satisfyingly desired, my pockets full of telephone numbers for future encounters . . . at those times I felt contented. If only heaven were a Turkish bath for gay men where you were wildly wanted & where Italian angels served pasta three times a day. But earth itself didn't fall short of my desires on those satisfied Sunday mornings.

Then I was back in my apartment & into the despair of breaking up with Brian all over again. The pain was always fresh, & it always took me to a deeper & sadder place than any I'd ever known. Yet how could anything with so little meaning matter so much? That was part of the pain, the realization that there had been so little real love & intimacy between Brian & me. Another part was the dawning awareness that I had lost my glamorous life. Together, Brian & I had represented something others had envied; alone, I was little more than a lonely man approaching middle age.

At summer's end I went with a friend to Vermont for a week. While there I went down one Saturday to Concord, Massachusetts, to see a therapist by the name of Robert Coles. It was a good thing I didn't know Bob was a well-known therapist & writer (his picture would appear on the cover of *Time* magazine a year later). There was no one to impress, just a bright, amiable, attentive man to talk with. Though I'd been told we would meet for an hour, we talked for well over two. In ending the session, Bob said he thought that, yes, I could definitely benefit from therapy, & further that it was a shame I didn't live nearby since if I did, he would treat me free. Hmmmm . . . Might I think that over & get back to him?

On Labor Day weekend, Seymour & I drove into Provincetown in early evening in a borrowed convertible, the top down & the wind in our hair, the sky laced with pink clouds, the dunes immaculate & the light pristine, & both of us filled with mounting exhilaration. "Darling, this is going to be *fabulous!*" It *was* fabulous: the main street crowded with holiday merrymakers, little shops & restaurants with their doors invitingly open, quiet side streets of snug cottages behind picket fences where it looked like you'd wandered through a time warp into a Van Gogh painting, & everywhere a riot of flowers nodding in the breeze off the bay. We soon met two art majors from Bard College, so after dinner, much beast with two backs in a tawdry motel on the outskirts of town. Next day on the beach at Truro, in the midst of a sparkling afternoon out of the Golden Age & without an inkling why, I was in such torment that I imagined my head as a glass globe full of writhing snakes, each one with news from hell. I wanted to take a hammer to my head, or just to make sure, a gun. (That must be why people who shoot themselves go for the head: to silence the voices.)

Seymour was so smitten with Provincetown that before the weekend was over he'd rented a house for a year. For the next few weeks, I drove from New York to Coles' place in Concord where we talked for two or three hours, then out to Seymour's for a couple days, then back to Coles for another session, then on to New York where a couple days later I'd set out again. Seymour was soon the center of a motley crew of P'town hippies who dropped acid at the slightest pretext—they were down, they were up, they were in love or out, they couldn't think of a name for their baby (Reardon? . . . Ashanti? . . . *Sky!*). Glenn Milstead, later known as Divine, entertained us on drugged weekends in a house with a swing hung from a rafter in the living room. Glenn dressed up in southern belle drag with big picture hats & sang drawly songs while swooshing back & forth in the swing, which miraculously didn't break.

There were artists & dropouts & carpenters & cooks & waiters & bartenders & a sprinkling of townies, & everyone drafting a letter of application for Janov's Primal Scream Therapy Workshop. Like me, everyone I met in Provincetown was suffering from some wound or other & was hot on the trail of the latest get-well therapy: transcendental meditation or macrobiotic food or H. D. Laing's latest book or the primal scream or hatha yoga or EST or self-actualization or the latest California touchy-feely stuff. We were all convinced that somewhere, somehow, there was a solution to our pain & to the pervasive sense of not fitting well into our skins. So we talked of the news from the get-well front, & compared our wounds, & drafted our letters to Janov, & prepared our wild rice & bancha tea, & every night we dropped acid or mescaline & went to Piggy's where we danced our brains out—by far the most successful therapy most of us ever managed.

Soon I was spending all my time on the road, or in Coles's study in Concord sifting through the debris of the past, or in Provincetown & New York biding time before the next session with Coles. After a month, the therapy had come to matter so much I was willing to do anything to help it out, so I rented a room in Boston's South End & closed up shop in New York.

It was October of 1970 & I was thirty-three—the worst case of arrested development since Marie Antoinette. I packed the borrowed convertible with some clothes & the books for my dissertation & took a farewell drive around Manhattan. A couple of hours later as I was crossing from Connecticut into Massachusetts, James Taylor came over the radio singing about "the turnpike from Stockbridge to Boston / With ten miles behind & ten thousand more to go." Sounded just right, so maybe there was a God after all. At the very least, there was Robert Coles.

Part Three

· 7 ·

I settled into my room in a house owned by two unremittingly butch, quarrelsome lovers, & into a schedule of seeing Coles three or four times a week for two to three hour sessions & working on my dissertation in the time between. At night I frequented gay bars where I glowered in dark corners daring people to speak to me, furious that they didn't. Being so thoroughly therapized, plunging into a dissertation I didn't want or know how to write, making sullen, hobbled attempts to create a new social life for myself—the combination didn't improve my disposition.

I probably wasn't a charming patient for Bob either, though he said I was a hopeful one since I was so eager for help. We met in his office at Harvard or his study in Concord, & I can still see his tired face as he sat across from me in crewneck sweaters with holes in the elbows, nodding encouragement while tracking me through the maze of my misery. He even participated in our sessions, praise the Lord—none of that lonely Freudian monologue I'd hated so much with my first therapist ten years before. When Bob revealed himself as a man struggling with his own doubts & dilemmas, it became possible to open my heart & show him what was inside.

Inside was a world of unarticulated misery & disgust with myself for the life I'd been leading, but I was so confused I couldn't think about it clearly. Suddenly I was being helped to some clarity by a man I admired immensely, probably too much for my own good. I saw how hard Bob worked to help others, & his love of literature & his ascetic bent struck responsive chords in me. The people he associated with had a new kind of glamor for me—the Kennedys, the Berrigan brothers, Anna Freud, William Carlos Williams—& when I learned that he himself was famous, I seemed to acquire value by association (that old failing again). His treating me free also made me feel special, even though he treated his few other patients free as well. Then it turned out he not only liked me, but, to my amazement, expressed admiration for the part of me that wanted to be a better, more decent man. If Bob Coles could admire me, maybe I could too.

He certainly worked hard in the beginning to gain my trust—getting me a guest pass to the Harvard gyms, loaning me his library card, allowing me the off-hours use of his office for my work. When I was arrested for speeding near Bard College & thrown in the Poughkeepsie jail for possession of enough marijuana to qualify for a felony, it was Bob who got a local attorney to bail me out of a holding cell where a seedy kid terrified me with tales of the times he'd been raped in prison. When it looked like I'd be spending my first Boston Thanksgiving alone, Bob invited me to join him & his family for dinner.

Why such special treatment? Bob must have seen that my trust in people had been severely damaged, & he was willing to take extraordinary measures to restore it for our work together. He was wholly undoctrinaire & willing to experiment with unconventional methods that his more staid, theory-bound colleagues would doubtless have disapproved of. A teacher himself, he also must have seen that in my present condition I was capable of wreaking havoc in the lives of my students unless someone intervened before I began my career. As for so many hours of so many sessions each week, he must have taken one look & decided I needed radical treatment.

I was desperate for a quick solution, a name or a label for my plight that would let me speedily dispel it, but Bob hated the quick fixes of psychiatric cliché. One of his strengths came from his ability to see his patients not as types but as individuals with their own reservoirs of truth & resilience. He kept countering my desire for a fast, clean transformation with his sense of the irony & complexity of life. Didn't I find any redeeming features of my recent past? If I were so deeply unhappy at being gay & really believed that gay life was an emotional dead end, there was an article I might want to read about changing one's sexuality (having to do, as best I could tell, with superhuman will & a long dearth of pleasure), but in the meantime, what about the contented male couples who lived quiet lives & who probably didn't frequent the bars & discos & parties that comprised such a large part of my own social world? Yes, happiness was no doubt a good & desirable thing, although perhaps less exciting than many supposed, sometimes much less exciting. Granted that my childhood had been traumatic, was it only that & nothing more? Hadn't I learned any sustaining values as a child along with the terrors of violence & abandonment?

Bob got me to slow down & think about my life in a far more rigorous, honest way than I'd ever managed before. And even when our sessions were painful, I usually loved them, for I almost always left Bob feeling fortified & encouraged, lighter somehow, as if I'd put down a burden of the past or made a new connection or cleared a space by way of preparing for a new life. Ten years before, a therapist had led me to the perception that I didn't like myself & immediately an impenetrable wall had gone up; now Bob helped me explore the wall. It was hard work, but I learned that even the most painful truths, once expressed, are liberating. "The truth shall make you free," St. John tells us, & that was certainly my experience in the mind- & soul- & heart-work Bob & I did together.

When Bob talked, he often brought me news of another world. "All pain is honorable," he once said, "if it's genuine & honest & soul-searching." (Then maybe my past wasn't a total waste.) Simple words I'd once known revived in his conversation & took on powerful meaning—words like honesty, soul, humility, dignity, conscience, joy.

"What *is* joy?" I once asked.

"I don't know. Freud said joy is love and work."

"Love makes sense, but work?"

"Don't you find joy in your work?"

What an alien thought that was at first, like many others Bob sent my way. One day I was berating myself for not wanting to sleep with someone who had been kind & generous to me.

"Are you physically attracted to him?"

"Not at all."

"Well then?"

Could it be that simple?

In his quizzical way, he sometimes expressed an astonishment at my notions & ways that gave me a new perspective on them, but most of that perspective came from the activity of talking about my life with an earnest, modest, caring man whom I came to love. In that talking—a story-telling really, the construction of a new narrative of my life—it was amazing how saying something to Bob made it real in a new way. I'd long known it was unconscionable to stand people up, but the day I told Bob of my habit was the day I suddenly & vividly saw how odious it was. I never stood anyone up again. "It takes two to make a truth," Bob quoted one day from Nietzsche (meaning that nothing is fully real or significant until it's been shared), & doors sprang open throughout my mind revealing the secret of the healing powers of friendship, love, teaching, prayer, this therapy itself.

Around Christmas we assessed our progress to decide whether or not to continue. Oh yes, I wanted desperately to continue because at long last I had real hope in my life. Often during that period I thought of William Carlos Williams's remark that he could divide his life into *Before Pound* and *After Pound,* for I began dividing mine into *Before Coles* and *After Coles.* When Bob's biography of Erik Erikson came out, he gave me a copy with an inscription that included a poem by Emily Dickinson:

> A Death blow is a Life blow to Some
> Who till they died, did not alive become—
> Who had they lived, had died but when
> They died, Vitality begun.

Oh dear God, let it be—that I was dying to an old life & being born to a new one. The poem felt right, I felt more right than ever, & Bob's prognosis was good.

Yet the contrast between my life & Bob's was daunting: he was selfless, I was selfish; he was established in his career, I was beginning mine; he'd published hundreds of books & essays & reviews, I'd published a few flawed poems; he devoted his time to his work & his family while I divided mine between my new career & my old reputation, which meant continued devotion to the gym & the lotions & the midnight researches into the image in the mirror. So while gaining a glimpse of a different & better me than I'd ever known, I continued to think of myself as unworthy, a D student in the school of life. I sometimes found myself acting in ways that, I later saw, were designed to gain Bob's approval.

Driving home after a session one winter night, I had stopped for a red light when I spied a young man on crutches peering into a bar. He turned to leave, looked back into the bar, then hobbled down the street. I made the light &, pulling ahead, jumped out of the car & approached him holding out a five-dollar bill. He halted & shook his head, "No...no..." "It's all right, don't be afraid. Someone's helping me & it makes me want to help someone else, that's all." Calmer now, he took the money & shyly asked if we could talk. Inside the car, he told me he'd been wounded in Vietnam & was disabled, & that his family & friends wanted nothing to do with him. His girlfriend had abandoned him too, & he felt himself drifting into an addiction to alcohol that he was trying but failing to conquer. He wasn't angry, just deeply sad & confused. And extremely beautiful, which was the main reason I'd stopped to help him. Was there somewhere we could go to talk some more, maybe spend the night together?

No, for I couldn't bear the thought of subjecting him to the scrutiny of my predatory landlords. He hobbled off into the night & I drove home. But I had given him some money & listened to the story of his pain.

Another night I was at a party talking with a handsome Harvard undergraduate who rowed crew & a young painter whose face was hideously scarred. As we talked, the Harvard boy turned into a two-dimensional cartoon while the artist became so beautiful he began to glow. I invited the artist home where we made love & talked throughout the night. He told me that during his childhood he'd been used as a prime example of his disease (fulminating acne) — trotted out before platoons of interns, examined by specialists, photographed for medical textbooks. When we woke next morning, the spell was broken: I saw again how disfigured he was, also how disappointed when I ignored his suggestions for another meeting. No way, not in the clear light of a new day, but at least I could tell Bob that I'd made love with someone not because of his looks but because I had found something beautiful in his soul, if only for a single night.

I wanted so much for Bob to be proud of me, for in predictable fashion I had turned him into my father & best friend, my confessor & teacher, my moral guide & model. If only I could be like Bob. . . . I even wondered in dreams why he didn't abandon his family & career to go off & live with me in a cabin in the woods somewhere. You can imagine my dismay when he became furious with me one time (I'd let myself be taken for two hundred dollars in a rigged dope deal), & another time when he said that for him, the happiest day of our association would be the day I walked out of his office for the last time.

I did walk out finally, with Theodore Roethke's help. I was reading Roethke one night when two lines suddenly leapt from the page:

> I take this cadence from a man named Yeats,
> I take it, and I give it back again . . .

Could taking, worked right, mean giving too? Could I give back the love others had given me? Conceiving of myself as not just a selfish taker but a passer-on & partaker in the wealthy procession of love suddenly made the world seem right, & gave me hope of feeling right in the world. Then Blake stepped in with a proverb: "Everything possible to be imagined is an image of truth." If I could imagine Roethke's lines as I had, surely I could change & become a better man, a man I could learn to live with & even take pride in.

The night I told Bob about my reading of Roethke, we reached out &

took each other's hand, & it was only then that I realized his hand was deformed. "Now you see," he said, referring not just to his hand but to what I'd understood—that I could learn to love. Bob was flawed but he was all right; I was flawed but I could become all right. At long last, I saw the door in the wall. I hadn't gone through it, but at least I saw it. The wall was no longer an insurmountable barrier between me & a decent life.

Given our goal to help me find value and meaning in my life, the therapy had succeeded & it was time to part. I now see, however, that I retained most of my conflicted feelings about my past. Bob himself was never judgmental about my life as a golden boyman, but I began to judge myself by unconsciously adopting some of his attitudes about the sham attractions of celebrity, glamor, fame, the New York I'd recently left. There was a lot more healing left to do, but with Bob's help I had clarified some of the past & talked the conception of a better life into being. It was little more than the sketch of a new life laid over the old, but it would have to do until I was able to design something more permanent.

By the summer of '71, I'd taken a job as an assistant professor at the University of Massachusetts in Boston, finished my dissertation (on Austen's *Persuasion*, Marvell's Mower poems, & punctuation as prosody from Shakespeare to Frost), & moved into a large floor-through apartment on Beacon Street (fireplaces, built-in bookcases, walk-in closets, very deluxe) with an interior decorator-weightlifter-socialite roommate. With time freed up from ending therapy & finishing the dissertation, I set about making a Boston life for myself.

Leaving New York had been much harder than I'd expected, for during the fifteen years I'd lived there, the city itself had become one of my principal addictions. A typical week of my life in New York had included a conversation with Katharine Hepburn in Scribner's on Fifth Avenue (about Elizabethan biography; she knew lots), an evening at the Blue Angel to hear a new young singer named Barbra Streisand, & a small party for King Hussein of Jordan. New York had been full of such choice excitements for me. The constant stimulation of the city, its busy cultural life & engaged people, its abundant sexual opportunities, its ability to entertain the eye on a twenty-four-hour basis, the ease with which it harbored social marginals like me—I'd become hooked without realizing it.

But my last summer there I'd lived in dread of running into Brian, & I'd also seen the city decline in ways that suggested worse to come. The subways were falling apart, Central Park had become dirty & dangerous, & the habitual rudeness of the natives was acquiring a harder edge that was wearying to deal with. Crime was on the rise—my apartment was robbed twice the same week the *New York Times* published an article claiming that if you lived in New York for the next twenty years, chances were one in five you would witness a murder or be murdered yourself. The city was becoming marred with graffiti & littered with trash, while new buildings of unparalleled banality were causing the sky over Manhattan to disappear, the canyon streets to be plunged into gloom.

In Boston I could see the sky; in the Public Garden, I rediscovered the miracle of trees for the first time since childhood. The city was beautiful by American standards, also much cleaner than New York & the pace much slower. Like Paris, Boston went to sleep at night, which was some help in my doing the same.

Yet Boston didn't feel right in the beginning. People were cool & distant & their lives seemed colorless compared to those I'd known in New York. No kings or movie stars or *GQ* cover men, not even much in the way of civility. Books were still banned in Boston & sharp lines drawn between races & ethnic groups & even professions. In New York, a party meant a potpourri of people from different backgrounds & careers— artists & doctors & hookers & writers & lawyers & models, the whole shebang; in Boston, bankers gave parties for bankers, academics for academics, & the banks & universities didn't mix. My clothes felt wrong in Boston, & maybe they were, for why else did people stare at me with such unfriendly curiosity? As if all this weren't bad enough, I began to realize that in leaving New York I'd left behind my reputation as a Famous International Faggot. I could still operate on the gay meat market with success, but now when I entered a gay bar there was no flurry of excitement at the arrival of a celebrity.

My reputation still held in New York, though, so down I went that first summer to the Pines where I had a splendid affair with huge, sexy, Jesus Christ–look-alike Howard Collins. The gift of the look also worked wondrously well in San Francisco for two weeks at the end of the summer. So great, no problem, & fuck Boston.

Time to take the shaky new self Bob had helped me cobble together & begin my career as a professor. Finally, I had the first serious, full-time job of my life: at thirty-four, I would now teach. But what in the world, I found myself wondering the night before my first classes, was "teaching"? We'd never discussed it in graduate school, & it was only on the verge of doing it that I realized I didn't have a clue how to go about "teaching."

My first day of classes terrified me. Seated in front of forty students in a class on "Poetry Since 1750," all I knew to calm myself was to talk non-stop (the novice professor's Solution To Absolutely Everything) & to place my hands beneath the desk as if to lift it off the ground—an old orator's trick for calming the nerves back in the days when we still had orators. But in "Poetry Since 1750" there was at least a clearly defined subject spread over thirteen weeks in clear, chronological order, so I could follow my own outline & that should somehow add up to "teaching." What, however, was I supposed to do in "Freshman Composition"? Teach them to write well, yes, but what did that mean, & how was I supposed to do it? And how could I spark interest in those students: a dour middle-aged nun, a squirmy boy, & twenty girls fresh out of high school whose faces betrayed not the slightest impression of thought. Have them read Whitman, that was how—all of "Song of Myself," every glorious word, for since I loved it so much, they would too. And have them read other things I loved: Freud's *Civilization and Its Discontents* and Rilke's *Letters to a Young Poet*, & maybe Dickinson, & why not *Walden* & Faulkner & Flannery O'Connor, & we would analyze our reading & they would all write better. Once they saw how great writers did it, they would do it too, right? Flat dead-ass wrong & a disaster from start to finish. They didn't understand Whitman & Freud, found Thoreau "boring," resented Rilke for saying that young people don't know how to love. They hated everything—except the nun & the squirmy boy, who parroted my enthusiasms until I wanted to strangle them & flunk their dead bodies.

Teaching was much less exciting than I'd expected. It was far more interesting hearing Luchino describe his problems with a production at La Scala than hearing a freshman decipher an incoherent essay. No glamor, just an interminable amount of mostly god-awful student writing, & committee meetings of such excruciating boredom that I writhed & fled.

Suddenly, a slew of new anxieties. What if I never got the hang of "teaching"? What if students didn't like my classes, or worse, didn't like me? Even if I learned how to teach my students to read & write better, how could I teach them to change their lives, which was what most of them needed most of all? What if I never learned to talk the way they did in committee meetings? ". . . & therefore I wonder whether or not we might not consider the possibility of allocating funds for a perhaps not altogether different purpose in view of whatever it is that we do or don't finally decide to do." As for my critical writing, would it be good enough to get published? No matter what—annual review, reappointment, promotion, publication—the odds were against me. But my darkest fear was that I wasn't bright enough, & one day soon someone would discover I was faking it, pretending to be intelligent when I was just superficially smart.

Through all my fears wormed a growing disappointment at discovering that many of my colleagues weren't the ethically & morally superior people I'd assumed they would be—just smug intellectuals adept at masking their biases with a veneer of logic replete with five reasons for everything. What a sad & painful disillusionment that was, just like the discovery I made about all those famous gay artists when I first came out. And how it made my skin crawl to witness the kid-gloved viciousness of the bright & vengeful.

"What are you going to do?" Luchino asked me in the winter of '72, standing in his underwear in a suite in the Pierre Hotel in New York. "What am I to do?" I was moved that he would show himself to me almost naked, & moved too that his body looked so old.

Luchino was speaking English, & although his English was better than I'd ever known it, he spoke in a perpetual present, transposing all tenses to the now of his narration. What was I supposed to do, he was asking, "when I find he is so . . . so . . . incredible selfish? A monster of selfish." His voice was calm & controlled as he described the failure of his seven-year relationship with Helmut Berger. "So I send him to live in his own house & now I live alone."

But they were travelling together that winter, for Helmut stopped in to say goodnight before going off to dinner with Raquel Welch. A Hollywood producer couple arrived to take Luchino to dinner. They were loud & dressed in obnoxiously expensive clothes, & I couldn't conceive of Luchino in their company. I'd last seen him a couple years before at a party Frank Scavullo had given for him, where we'd sat talking politics with Simone Signoret & Yves Montand—old friends who understood & respected Luchino & moved in his world. That was his element, not these vulgar Hollywood types.

As we parted (it was to be the last time we ever saw each other) he seemed almost defeated somehow. Certainly chastened & sad. Something was terribly wrong.

Something was wrong back in Boston too because the therapy with Coles wasn't turning out the way I'd expected. True, I lived my life differently now—avoiding egregious lies, showing up when I said I would, being conscientious about my work, honoring my promises even when they inconvenienced me—but there was something joyless & doggedly dutiful about my new life. I'd learned how to "function" but not how to live well.

I embarked on a series of what I now see were penances designed to make amends for the old life I'd come to repudiate without giving it up. Since I'd often charmed people in the past, I became blunt & sometimes rude. Since I'd used my looks & my body as lures, I now wore baggy clothes & went unshaven. Since my custom-made wardrobe had been a sign of my privileged past (& since my students were mostly working-class folks who had a hard time making ends meet), I packed two suitcases full of tailored suits & monogrammed shirts & jackets with hand-carved buttons & dropped them off at the Salvation Army, not knowing at the time what homophobes those glum bell ringers are.

Then I had an affair with a sweet blond hippy from Ogunquit, Maine, that was its own kind of penance, since Rob was a raving alcoholic & drug addict. Winter weekends I went up to visit him & his eclectic friends—Indians & heiresses & rich young queens, a grandfather poet & his orphaned grandchildren, married hippies who made their living from making driftwood mobiles & selling drugs. We passed the time like others housebound in Maine during long, severe winters—we smoked acres of dope & drank till we passed out.

The following summer I rented a room from Rob for June. I would stop smoking & winnow through years of correspondence & diaries & journals—two easy tasks that would leave me lots of time for the beach. But it rained for twenty-nine of the thirty days; my resolve to stop smoking failed daily; & at June's end on the one clear day, I gathered all the letters & journals & diaries into a pile in the backyard & burned them, thinking (I think) that doing so would help sever me from a past I despised. Up in flames went the epistolary remains of half a dozen love affairs, the record of my friendships with Noel & Luchino, hundreds of Christmas & birthday cards, years of letters from Mom & Dad who were both entertaining correspondents, & all the journals & diaries that would have made writing the middle part of this book a breeze. In five minutes, I reduced the written evidence of years of love & affection to ashes—another penance that didn't make any difference. It did however serve to inspire one of the few enduring regrets of my life, but how could I have known then that I would ever value my life enough to treasure its written record?

It may have rained all June in Ogunquit, but when Walter Giegold lay down beside me on the beach at the Pines in July, I'd never known the sun to shine so brightly. Walter was a twenty-two-year-old German golden boyman who'd been kept by Arendt Krupp, final scion of the family that brought us World War II, & even considering that Arendt could choose from the cream of international rent boys, he'd chosen well. Tall & lean with full lips & green eyes, Walter had a feral look, moved like a panther, was a total knockout—right up my alley. There we were sunning side by side, & there I was smackdab back in the old life & loving it.

Where would I be Labor Day weekend? In Provincetown? Walter would come too, he'd find me. He did, to my amazement. Fantastic—Walter could have anybody & he wanted me!

After our weekend we made a date & parted, then people began calling from New York to ask about Walter's whereabouts, for he'd disappeared & I was one of the last to see him. I didn't know where he was, hardly anybody knew until three months later when they matched the dental records from Munich with the teeth of the corpse they dredged from the East River.

Something was definitely wrong but I couldn't figure out what it was. Why was I eating during the night & sometimes thinking someone was in the apartment when I was alone & feeling so lonely so much of the time? And why couldn't I figure it out & fix it? Maybe if I went shopping, bought something, cleaned the apartment or watched TV or ate some ice cream or cruised & came home with a guy so far below my glory day expectations that I didn't want to think about it. Maybe if I smoked a joint & took the phone off the hook.

Maybe if I became a hippie . . . Oh, if *only* I were a hippie, like beautiful, brilliant Deborah who was a student at Hampshire College, & brilliant, sensitive David who wrote poetry he didn't publish because that was a countercultural thing to do. Even Seymour had become a hippie, which in his case meant that he'd grown his hair long & expanded his sexual horizons by sleeping with women. Hippies understood American society much better than I did, & they actually did something to bring about a better world in which people were no longer oppressed & it was all right to be gay. Their actions were based on love & sympathy, & they seemed happy & carefree & tuned into some secret of good living that continued to elude me.

> Come on people now
> Smile on each other
> Everybody get together
> Try to love one another right now.

If only I could love people—everybody no matter who, like Christ had done & hippies did—but the voices were relentless in pointing out others' flaws. Hippies were tolerant & accepting but I was critical & judgmental. Hippies were sexually adventurous but I was sexually picky. Hippies lived lyrical lives & rolled with the punches, but my life was one of routine in which I was unhinged by the unexpected. Maybe if I became a hippie, *that* would make things right.

I bought some flowered shirts & had an admirer embroider my jeans with roses & dated my letters "on a high" & "amid the flowers." I smoked dope to watch the sun set & inflated my grades & gave my phone number to students the way my hippie colleagues did. But the students called at midnight & rang my doorbell at two & three A.M. with tales of abusive boyfriends & rapes & nervous breakdowns & drug busts. I bought some popular records but I couldn't understand the words, I never got the hang of the frisbee, it was agony sitting crosslegged on the floor, & it turned out that hippies were cavalier about appointments & sometimes stood me up (*me,* who had abandoned that odious habit forever). When I started dealing drugs & a little coke on the side (to eke out my modest salary & because it was a hippie thing to do), I marked up my goods as modestly as possible since hippies didn't make money off their friends; but my customers were amused when I charged $22.85 or $23.15 for an ounce of grass, & they seemed to think I was absurd. I felt a sham, & a bit too old for the part.

Maybe if I grew my hair long I would at least *look* like a hippie. I looked as young as many of them, younger even than the fathers in their mid-twenties toting babies in knapsacks (how that sight pierced my heart). I let my hair grow & grew a beard, just a short one, & then a longer one, then shaved it off & tried a moustache, then a moustache & beard together but closely trimmed. Then I shaved off the moustache à la Ahab, then cut my hair short à la Fort Bragg. I studied myself in the mirror day long & night late, certain there must be a way to look that would let me feel . . . different & . . . better, somehow. But each time I searched, the man staring back (nearing middle age now but not showing it, thank God) looked all wrong, especially given that unfamiliar trace of fear in his eyes.

When my roommate moved out, I rented his bedroom to a black Harvard undergraduate who passed for white & lived a hippie sort of life. He talked endlessly of how much he loved people, especially the interminable parade of tricks he marched in & out of the apartment. He cruised so much that one morning I met one of his tricks on my way into the shower & another on leaving it. He'd accompanied trick #1 downstairs to say goodbye, spied trick #2 passing in the street, & invited him up for coffee & sex. I couldn't keep the names straight, they changed so fast. I told him it was like seeing a B movie of my own life, knowing it would hurt him, but I didn't care. His promiscuity made me so tense with envy and disgust that I felt like I had a demon on my back, an incubus digging its claws into my flesh, & nothing I could do would get it off—not yoga or heat or massage or drugs or sex or booze—until my roommate moved out & took the incubus with him.

Howard Collins was a hippie, which in his case meant a luxuriant mane of hair & lots of drugs & an ability to roll with the punches so accomplished that he'd long forgiven me for the unceremonious way I'd rejected him at the end of our affair, the previous summer of '71. This summer, my second in Boston, Howard had taken a house in the Pines, so down I went for a week, timing my arrival for a Sunday afternoon to miss the weekend's sexual feeding frenzy. I suspected I might not be as desired as in the past, & I certainly didn't want any old-timers comparing Boston Alan with New York Alan.

The Pines, the Pines, those beautiful Pines—scene of so many social & sexual triumphs over the years where I'd always been one of the most desired of all the beautiful young men. What a feeling of power that had been, & how much it had confused me. But this time I would focus on the immaculate beaches, the scrub pine woods dotted with wildflowers, the seashore dawns & bayside sunsets. This time, I would be adult & sane, even in Fire Island Pines.

Howard met me at the ferry & we walked back to his house smoking a joint. We had a drink while I unpacked, then another joint & some hash before strolling to the bay to watch the sunset. Back to the house for more talk & more hash before time to clean up, drop mescaline, & head out for the Boatel. We danced & drank while Howard introduced me all around, filling me in on vital statistics: "Nine & a half inches, thick but crooked. That one? Best ass in the Pines. That's a glass fist on the chain around his neck." After the Boatel, we were invited to an impromptu party (someone had bought some uncut coke) where the cream of the beauty crowd had gathered, which should have made it easy choosing a bedmate for the night. Compliant as always, however, & relieved to avoid the risk of rejection, I let myself be chosen. Back at Howard's, more grass & cocaine & then, at the guy's insistence, I fistfucked him, my first experience of that delicate operation. I was accomplished at a kind of sex in which the partner resolves into a zoom-lens, sharp-focus part of his body—a dick with adjoining loins or an ass for the most part—but I'd never known sex in which I felt so uninvolved.

Next day I awoke to an empty bed in an empty house. I wandered onto the beach & into an equatorially hot morning in which a viscous haze hung over a sullen sea. Then in a flash it came clear: in less than twenty-four hours I'd smoked a dozen joints & lots of hash, drunk almost a fifth of scotch, dropped mescaline, snorted enough coke to render half of Hollywood comatose, & fistfucked a sexy, eager, anonymous ass without experiencing a shred of pleasure. The air was so heavy it was hard to breathe, & then I ran into an old acquaintance who invited me back to his place for coffee & acid. An hour later I was on the ferry heading back to Boston.

The entire decade of the '70s was like that—I'd become aware of a feeling or mood only in retrospect, my awareness lagging behind my living, as if I were existing in different time zones or pulled by contending gravities. That dissociation was in part an inheritance of my childhood; in part, it came from the effort to balance or combine three entirely different lives: the new life of teaching & scholarship, the old life of gay celebrity, & an ideal, almost saintly life I'd conceived on Cruft Street & revived in therapy with Bob Coles. New York Alan (getting older but still looking great) found class preparation & student papers boring; Boston Alan (now enjoying teaching but still worried he wasn't bright enough) was dismayed at all the time New York Alan frittered away in the bars & baths; Saint Alan wanted nothing to do with the other two guys & constantly urged me to give up all worldly concerns & retire into a monastery for the good of my soul. The "me" being urged was a fourth Alan living yet another life that wound around & through the others. It was such a confusion trying to hold the disparate selves together, especially since at the time my favorite guides to life were Blake's "The road of excess leads to the palace of wisdom" & Aristotle's "Nothing in excess."

In the discombobulated meantime, Boston still didn't feel right. It was staid & stuffy & Irish Catholic, which meant it was anti-gay & anti-sex & anti-body, which meant I saw guys in the U Mass gym showering in their underwear & pulling their pants on over wet shorts, even in the winter, which was invariably, unspeakably cold. I learned with grim satisfaction that long after discovering the South Pole, Admiral Byrd had been asked where on earth he'd been coldest. "In Boston in February," he said. The wind came at you like freshly-honed scimitars, so fierce you sometimes saw old people grabbing parking meters to keep from being dragged down the street.

I was getting a cold reception in the bars too, which was surely why I started namedropping—figuring that if people understood who & what I was, they'd warm up a bit. I heard myself doing it, hated myself for it, but couldn't stop, even though it never worked since people were unimpressed or intimidated or annoyed by it. And increasingly I had to explain the names: the younger guys didn't know who Noel was & even the bright ones hadn't heard of Luchino, though they nodded in doubtful recollection when I mentioned *Death in Venice* & *The Damned*. If only I were back in New York where people knew I knew famous people & I myself was celebrated. If only I didn't have to work this new crowd with its oddly different ethos. If only I had a lover, then I would be happy, but the world outside the walls of my apartment seemed increasingly intractable.

In the old days, people stared after me in the street, & gushy guys told me they jerked off to my picture in ads. No such welcome in tight-assed, Puritanical Boston. There I was, hardly thirty-five, only thirty-six, barely thirty-seven, but for some of the guys in the bars, I was no longer "hot." The young ones especially looked through me, & I began to experience the eerie sensation of being invisible in the world of the hungry cruise. Is that what I'd done? Looked through people I wasn't attracted to as if they weren't there? That's exactly what I'd done. I was now being treated the way for years I'd treated others—which in a way didn't matter since now whenever I saw an attractive young man, even one who expressed interest in me, I found it almost impossible to act. As I entered middle age, I imagined the younger guys I desired as versions of myself when young—pestered by importunate, older men, pawed & fawned on & revolted by it all. I began to see myself as one of the importunate, older men. An astute guy in a bar one night put my hand around his waist, saying "It's okay, I want you to touch me." Without such unequivocal signs, I was usually unable to act on my desires. When I did, or when someone maneuvered me into bed, I rarely enjoyed the sex any more—which in a way didn't matter since more & more often now I was impotent.

I was sitting at a sidewalk cafe one afternoon when along came George, Glenn/Divine's partner back in the days of their art deco shop in Provincetown. "Darling, it's been forever. How in the world are you?" We chatted awhile, then George said, "Isn't it horrible about Seymour! You mean you haven't heard? Dead as a doornail! A fire in the apartment, asphyxiated, he must have been on drugs because the dog died too. Ghastly, a real tragedy, here today & gone tomorrow, but what can I say? Listen, hon, I gotta run, but it's been fabulous & you're looking terrific. Catcha later."

Seymour dead? My brilliant, loving, funny friend was dead? The person I'd cruised & drugged & laughed with so much over the years, who had helped me through the Brian breakup . . . dead? & at thirty-one? Could a life be so stupidly, pointlessly wasted? And turned into the small change of gossip on a summer afternoon? How could anyone's life end up meaning so little?

I was now thirty-eight & beginning to lose my hair. Male pattern balding had been with me since my early twenties, but because of some genetic grace period or the dermatologists I'd seen over the years, it hadn't made much headway. Now my midnight examinations in the mirror showed it was on the march. The tiny wrinkles beginning to show under my eyes were hardly detectable, but my hair, my glorious hair was falling out. "Not enough to notice," my barber said, but he was being nice, & anyway he wasn't going down on teenagers in broad daylight. I began seeing a Park Avenue dermatologist who injected my scalp with estrogen (would that make me nelly?) & gave me a sticky application for bedtime use, then forty transplants & another forty a couple years after that. Those appointments drew me back to New York, & a few old friends, & the exhibitions & the baths & the occasional romance—like the one with the Italian who worked in a Fifty-seventh Street art gallery & picked me up one late afternoon on his way back from a coffee break to close the gallery, where we started off on a desk flanked by a couple of Cy Twombly paintings before moving into the main room and onto the floor surrounded by Warhol & Rauschenberg & Kelly & Johns, all of whom would surely have enjoyed being pressed into witness. Sex in front of an Ellsworth Kelly—now that was elegant! That was a happy dose of the good old days.

So were the visits to Paul's estate in the Caribbean. Yet even there, attended by servants as I lounged in a hammock on the edge of a cliff, wild orchids blooming overhead & green waves crashing below, I seethed with discontent.

"You look terrific," the old-timers said, the way New Yorkers do even when you're in the throes of terminal typhoid. "You look fabulous. How's life in Boston?"

It was always a hard question. In one sense, my Boston life was going well. I loved teaching by now, was reviewing poetry for *Partisan Review,* knew some interesting people, & was enjoying the charms of the city. Increasingly I missed New York less. I gave great parties (I prided myself on being able to collect a lot of interesting & attractive people), one for Alan Ginsberg (five times he disappeared into the john with different young men), & Tab Hunter came to another party (I loaned him my current trick for the night). There was even a new & different glamor in my life — a growing friendship with Denise Levertov, evenings with Frank Bidart, & through them I met people like Alice Walker & Robert Lowell. Yet in another sense, things were increasingly shaky. I was experiencing the initial stages of alcoholism along with a growing eating disorder (snacks at three & four in the morning but no vomiting, no more bulimia, thank God), & had settled into a habit of smoking at least two joints after dinner each night. My romances were all short-lived, & no matter who I had dinner with, I was fretful if there was no possibility of concluding the night with a sexual adventure.

The sexual adventures were harder to come by, however, & the whole gay world had become confusing & even daunting for me. It bewildered me that I got such different responses in the bars — most guys passed me by but some knockouts lingered & stared. Was I all washed up or still hot stuff? Another confusion: gay men now wore handkerchiefs in their hip pockets to signify their sexual tastes, but I could never remember what the colors meant — except for light blue which was cocksucking, yellow which was water sports, & brown which was . . . was the word "scat"? Where the handkerchief appeared also signified — left pocket meant one thing & right another — passive & active, I knew that, but I couldn't keep them straight, especially when I learned that different sides meant different things on different coasts. As for the daunting part, gay life now seemed rude & mean & hard-edged. Guys who wanted me didn't smile; they glowered & sneered, though people said that was a sure sign they wanted me. The ones who didn't want me cut me dead — especially the men who now wore black leather & swastikas, as if Hitler were merely a footnote in the history of fashion. So many gay men had turned into grotesque mirror images of the worst in American straight men: the insensitivity & intolerance, the swaggering macho bullshit, the failure of imagination, the immense self-absorption. Bars & discos were now full of mirrors, & men danced with their reflections as if cruising themselves. Gay life had become something narrow & brutal & depressing, & I felt shame & sorrow for gay men, & thus more shame & sorrow for myself.

And growing hatred for a culture that despised people for their sexual difference while blinding them to their oppression by shaming & judging them, then blurring their minds with the frenzy of late twentieth-century consumer capitalism. Aside from a few close gay male friends, my favorite companions became lesbians & straight women. At least the coming out I had to go through every time I met someone new was endurable with women.

"Well, it's been great," the old-timers said, going off with their young lovers as I went home alone.

If only I had a lover. I'd never gone more than a few months between lovers, but in Boston there was such a long wait before the next lover.

"Bisexual law student, 22, model, very handsome & well-built, 5'11", 160 lbs, br/br, seeks similar for sexual adventure. Photo a must." I was now thirty-nine so not exactly "similar," but I passed for ten years younger, & around the time I came upon the ad I'd been carded in a bar—a Maine bar, truth to tell, but nevertheless. I sent a Scavullo bathing suit shot & it did the trick. When Dan came by he said he'd received responses from eighty-two people & was seeing only two of them. Hurrah, *winning again!* We had a one month affair & that was that.

Dan was the only guy I met through the ads who represented himself honestly. "Football player's build" meant a prominent gut; "sensitive" meant bad skin or a receding chin; "thinning hair" turned up bald as a billiard; "unconventional" was a guarantee of kinky sex. Nevertheless, I kept combing the ads & sending off photos & notes in which I lied about my age, figuring what the hell, the guys in the ads lied too.

The baths proved much more reliable, & what great times I had in the Boston baths through the 1970s & early '80s. Even Cal Culver praised the Boston baths when he came for a visit, & Cal pretty much had his pick since by then he was America's reigning gay male porn star. How odd & dismaying to find myself existing in Cal's reflected glory that weekend as I took him on a tour of the Boston bars. It had always been the other way around.

People up from New York called to ask if we could meet for a drink. We met, but I soon realized that all they wanted was to check me out. While we sat making small talk, they scrutinized me from head to toe to see how the fabled Alan Helms was holding up, the fucking necrophiliacs.

I was in fact holding up quite well. It's hard not to hold up well when you're as devoted to the gym & the creams & lotions & your overall appearance as I was. And despite a growing diffidence about my physical charms, I still occasionally scored well. There was glorious Tim Clarke (hit & run: 1978) with peerless Praxitelean body & head wreathed in golden light, & seventeen-year-old Billy Porter (AIDS: 1989) who picked me up in a Cambridge bookstore, & Luke DiAngelo (AIDS: 1990) who was that year's Mr. Teenage Georgia, & languid, feral Paul Ruiz (AIDS: 1986) who looked like a Cuban Paul Newman, & endlessly sexy Bruce Leo (suicide: 1978), a lean Marine I met in a john at Harvard, & dozens more of really memorable numbers. But I lived as if each encounter would probably be the last, as if any morning I would wake up looking my age, as if any moment my history of sexual success would become a thing of the past, another thing to mourn.

So many things to mourn—my glamorous past, my sexual success, my reputation as a golden boyman with the gift of the look, the look itself now fading, everything fading & lost, life nothing but a mourning, a penance, a holding action, a shame, & that growing fear in the eyes of the man in the mirror.

Actually though, things weren't all that bad, all things considered, granting that there were a lot of things to consider. But later. For tonight I would relax & "become the music while the music lasts," as T. S. Eliot puts it. There in Boston Symphony Hall during those quiet couple of hours, I would do absolutely nothing but surrender myself to the music of Chopin, a nocturne drenched in a lush poignancy in which the bass tremolo makes everything turn ominous as suddenly I'm walking down an alley where I see a woman's legs jutting out from behind a trash can, one shoe off, the foot splayed at an angle that says dead, murdered, then panic as I turn to flee just as he claps an iron hand over my mouth & presses a knife into my side, forcing me toward a basement door. I'm frozen with terror but maybe I can break away, bolt & scream for help, but he's inhumanly strong like something insane, & now we're through the door & into the dark interior reeking of urine & despair where he plunges the knife into my stomach, twists it, & is gone. So it all comes down to this: I'm dying in agony in a piss-drenched darkness, abandoned & alone, murdered by a faceless stranger. Then a burst of applause jolts me back into the present, the concert over, the pianist taking his measured bows.

Times like that made me furious. The voices had now taken over such vast tracts of my mind that I was hopeless for concerts & readings & movies & ballets & even evenings with friends—as if my attention had been trained by cruising in gay bars. When would it be over, I wondered—the concert, the movie, the dinner, the evening, the weekend, the

ALAN HELMS

years with their eternity of waiting . . . for what? What in God's name was I waiting for? *"Pay attention,"* I screamed at myself, furious at all the wasted time, all the lost living.

Increasingly it seemed that whatever of importance I planned or hoped for met with disappointment, so I developed an unconscious strategy for postponing important things. It was a strategy of first things last, except I wasn't in on the secret. I would get up in the morning & go through a mental rigamarole that went something like this: "My writing is very important, so I'll get to it immediately, right after tidying the apartment & watering the plants & answering those letters, & then I'll be free & . . . okay, okay, I'll answer just this one call since I'm not yet under way. . . .

"Imagine calling your professor at home to ask what went on during the classes you missed! If we'd done that at Columbia, they'd have had our heads on a platter, & quite right too. Never mind, back to work as soon as I glance at the mail since I'm now interrupted & . . . damned if the bank hasn't screwed up again! Better call right away & it'll be off my mind, & I should call Charlie while I'm at it to see if we're still on for Friday. Busy, busy, so a few minutes with *Time* magazine & I'll try again, & if it's still busy, right down to work. Only 9:45, the morning's still young.

"So, my God, is Brooke Shields! Why does America go crazy over a teenager with a face blank as a pie plate? What an infantile, ageist culture. Why couldn't I have been born in Italy where everything is gorgeous & they have the civility to keep their homophobia to themselves. Three months in Europe & I never once saw any homophobia except that night on the Kurfurstendam when those guys screamed '*Ya fuckin' faggot!*' Wouldn't you know it would be Americans. If only I had a secret weapon so I could zap the shit out of guys like that, swaggering assholes with beer for brains, like those guys who piled out of that car that night & came at Tim & me, & me with my arm bandaged from wrist to elbow. 'Quick, Alan, run,' Tim yelled & got away, but I was mesmerized by the guy in front. I'd never seen such a crazed expression, such a blood lust for violence, & that's all he needed. Then the fight at the intersection, Tim running back to pull me free, the cars lined up waiting for the light & everyone seeing but no one helping or honking, & the one who chased me inside my building where I made it to the landing & turned to kick him down the stairs in case he followed since I couldn't use my arm, the bandages torn off now & him at the bottom screaming '*Why don't ya fight, ya chicken faggot*' even though he could see I was bleeding. If I'd had a gun I would've shot him, not to kill but to scare the shit out of him, first the foot, then the ankle, then the knee (he'll limp for the rest of his life), & now he's begging me to stop so I pause to give him hope before I shoot again—in the thigh, the hand, the forearm, & he's lying in a pool of blood now begging for his life as I take longer between each shot to make him hope again.

"I hate straight men, or American straight men at least. We should have testosterone deposit centers where they could go once a week to be drained. Is that why most of my former lovers are married, to avoid the threat & make life easier? I wonder what it's like to be married, or to be a husband, or a wife, or a dyke, or a black dyke, or a Jewish black dyke, or a Jewish black dyke comedian since under those circumstances life would surely appear as a joke. How many black men have I made love with? I should have kept a list, & photographs . . . if only I had photographs, what a book *that* would make. I wonder whatever happened to Richmond Carver, & Horace René, & that sailor in the Mine Shaft. If I were black & poor I'd have machine-gunned half the neighborhood by now, starting with those three-piece guys with briefcases marching home after work. A winter night, people dining at the Ritz, the room aglitter with crystal & silver & rich folks' talk, & with unerring aim I lob a bomb through the window . . . POW KaBOOM! No more Lodges & Cabots. Or banks, why don't people blow up banks instead of each other? Aha—a piece by John Ciardi that might come in handy for the poetry class. Better clip it now so I don't forget. And so . . . 10:20? I'd better get this show on the road.

"Where was I? 'During the past twenty years or so, American poetry has shown signs of . . .' 'Or so' sounds diffident. 'During the past twenty years, American poetry has shown . . .' Now I sound smug. 'During the past generation,' I forgot to take my vitamins. Too long after breakfast? Why doesn't someone tell us if it's okay to take vitamins on an empty stomach? Amazing the things we don't know about health. If I could revise the college curriculum, I'd definitely stick in a course on health & the body & CPR, all those people dying in subways & walking along the street—plop, dead—because no one knows how to resuscitate them. And you'll spend a year outside the country, kids, & learn the language & have a job & live with a family & pay foreign taxes & *then* maybe we'd have a generation of Americans who could see their culture with objectivity, see how fucked up it's becoming, how violent & unjust. And politicians should have to take public transportation & send their kids to public schools & get their health care in clinics, but they're not listening or giving a damn beyond protecting their own selfish asses before the next election. Disgusting, all the hypocrisy & waste. . . . 'It gives me great pleasure to introduce our new Secretary of College Curricula & Aesthetics' (applause, applause), & I'd have an expense account & a sexy Italian driver & ride around saying 'Remove that billboard, plant trees on that street, & don't you ever again, madam, appear in public in those haircurlers & that lime-green pants suit!' I'd also decree that they'd learn to floss, all those rotten teeth because millions don't bother to floss. Oops—forgot myself, so better do it now, with flossing sooner's better, though I can't imagine flossing after every meal, & certainly not after sex, whatever sex is any more. If you have lots of sex, you could end up with rotten teeth like that leper who accosted me in Angkor Wat, though his teeth weren't the most striking feature of his physiognomy. What if I became a leper? Or woke up one morning blind? Or was buried alive in an earthquake until I starved to death but remained conscious the whole time? What if returning home alone one night from a bar, I entered my bedroom to find a psychopath waiting to tie me up & gag me & then carve me up with a razor blade before cutting off my dick & stuffing it in my mouth & slitting my throat? Imagine the gleam of hell in his eyes, the terror in mine.

"*Damn* Johnson & Johnson & their economy size cheap floss so you end up going back to the smaller, more expensive size, & the stores not stocking the economy size anyway, & rearranging the stock so it takes forever to find what you want since the goddam marketing researchers have discovered that people buy more when they see new things, regardless of the things. Everything's greed, greed, greed in this society, morning noon & night. What a disgusting society we've become, producing products that don't work & food that doesn't taste & flowers that don't smell & people who don't think or vote or love each other. . . .

"But I *really* have got to get to work!

"'During the past generation, American poetry has become . . .' C'mon brain, do your stuff. 'Has become' . . . tired? How could I be tired? The morning's still young, unlike guess who? Oh, to hell with it—I'll take a nap, then to the bank after lunch when there's not much of a line, & on to the supermarket which, if I go to the gym, shoots the afternoon. But I'll be free after dinner, & then I'll spend a few uninterrupted hours on the essay. I will, I really *will*!"

Years of that, day in & day out, & years of rage at the wasted time. Such a long string of daily deflections & defeats that gradually I developed a compensatory attitude that said why bother with anything? If so little came of my efforts to attend to first things first, why bother, why not after frittering away the entire day smoke a couple of joints after dinner & pull out the porn & poppers & manufacture another prolonged session of horniness culminating in an orgasm so unsatisfying that after an hour of roaming the apartment I found myself again thinking of masturbating until I recalled that I'd already done that, for that night anyway. Always reasons why if first things first didn't work, I could do first things last & last things first. So the first things rarely got done, but I was fastidious about the last things.

Waking at two or three or four in the morning, I would get up & smoke a joint or two & rearrange the apartment. It's hard to convey the lunatic satisfaction I got from fiddling with the apartment—finding precisely the right place for the Dogon mask, or discovering that hanging the Matisse next to the Hockney created an interesting historical continuity while providing a foil for the Gallé vase. A pint of ice cream & back to bed with a real sense of accomplishment for a change. Getting up around noon, I spent another hour or so restoring everything to its original place, sometimes on the verge of tears.

Some nights I lay in bed reviewing the list of all the things I could have had but didn't get: that icon in London, Ahmed in Cairo, that lacquer box in Tokyo, the blond on the Esplanade. . . . Other nights I awoke to a disabling sense of the enormity of all the things I'd once known but forgotten. It seemed my life was moving backwards from knowledge to ignorance, & I thought that if I could retrieve my lost knowledge, perhaps that would let me feel better, hold things together, provide me with the key to a happier life. Then freight trains of questions trundled through my brain for hours: Who was Prester John again? It's Egyptians, Babylonians, Persians, then Greeks. But who were the Hittites? And do the Phoenicians have a period or were they just all over the place a lot of the time? Vale, dale, swale . . . tor, tarn? Heian, then Kamakura, then what? An elf has pointed ears, but a gnome? And are gnomes bad? Once & for all, what's Occam's razor & *why* won't it stick in my head? Do mosquitos need blood to survive or do they just like it? TNT stands for . . . ? Was it Kierkegaard or Schopenhauer who said that if you could imagine all the suffering in the world, your next logical act would be suicide?

Other nights, other questions: How could I be a kind & thoughtful man yet still look out for myself? When did looking out for yourself spill over into selfishness? How could I derive pleasure from the past but fully inhabit the present? How could the present have meaning without laying plans for the future to allay the anxiety I increasingly felt at growing older? Which part of my discontent came from my psychic disposition, which part from losing my glamorous past, which part from growing older, & which part from society? Would I ever break out of the fear-inducing prison house of American culture so I could finally be free to live my own life (whatever that was), not one dictated by the mind-managers of Hollywood & Madison Avenue & the media? And when those kids swerved to scare me, hanging out the window yelling "*Ya fuckin' faggot,*" what did it mean? When I first came out, "nigger" was the word men used to demean other men, but now their insult of choice was "faggot." Was "faggot" merely a part of those kids' scare game or had they seen something in me that I sometimes saw in other gay men—a lack of freedom in the body, something tight about the mouth, a self-conscious, defensive mien, that trace of fear in the eyes? Did I look like that or were they just guessing, or were they not even thinking? Which was it? I asked the man in the mirror, but he wasn't talking.

Increasingly I was less present for the living of my life, which is probably why I was arrested in the drugstore that time for stealing those vitamins. When they took me in the back room, I remembered that I'd half noticed the plainclothesman tagging along from aisle to aisle, yet I *had* to have those vitamins, *had* to get something free, some compensation for the insufficiency of my life.

Increasingly it seemed I never had enough of anything—vitamins, energy, attention, time, money, love—so I came to portion those things out in small doses, afraid I might run out if I weren't careful. I was becoming a stingy man, a miser of love & friendship, & I knew it & hated myself for it.

But if I had a lover, surely everything would be all right. I went through my address book & made a list of a dozen people I could ask to introduce me to a likely lover. "What do you have in mind?" "Well, my ideal would be a guy in his early thirties who looks ten years younger, with a superb body, sharp as a whip & hung like a firehose, a Latin with lupine eyes & slightly bowed legs, & a love of the aesthetic with a meditative cast of mind & a circle of friends that includes a periodontist & a plumber. I don't care what he does as long as it's something in the arts or the helping professions, & it would be great if he were a swimmer & spoke some French or Italian. But I don't want to be picky. Let's just say someone who's bright & presentable, not seriously fucked up, & likes older men. There's got to be at least one guy like that in all of metropolitan Boston, no?"

Apparently not. At least no one ever called back.

Fuck 'em, fuck everybody. I could manage nicely on my own, thank you. I was still invited around & I went around a lot. But increasingly it seemed an effort to dress & go out. That sweater didn't fit right, & those pants didn't show my ass to advantage, & the pants that did didn't go with the sweater, which would probably be too warm anyway, though it might bring a healthy flush to my face which tonight was looking tired & faintly . . . old? But I wasn't old. Thirty-nine & forty & forty-one surely wasn't old. Then how would you describe that face in the mirror with the fear in its eyes? Just older than I'd ever been, with wrinkles under the eyes & a few etched on the forehead now. I didn't have any clothes to hide those wrinkles or that fear, & even if I went out I'd probably come home alone. I hung up the clothes, took a valium, & went to bed, knowing that the depression I felt was my guarantee of a good night's sleep.

Forty-two obviously wasn't that old either, for otherwise when Deborah & I ran into Lenny Bernstein in that club in SoHo, Lenny wouldn't have exclaimed, "Alan Helms, *still* the most attractive man in New York!" Then when he grabbed me in a bearhug & whispered, "Almost," how I loved it, for in refusing to flatter me completely, Lenny made it clear that I was still worth flattering.

He invited Deborah & me to join him, & the tug on my jacket meant that Deborah wanted me to accept—so into a limo & off to a party, then another party, & then there was or wasn't another party, but I do recall that around four in the morning we ended up back where I was staying. Deborah, by now smitten with Lenny (he could do that to people in a night), went to bed; Lenny, by now smitten with me (hadn't we travelled this same dead-end route twenty years before?), was indulging himself in boozy sentimentalities. "Sit still, don't move—I just want to look at you. It's been such a long time, Alan. Too long." Maybe not long enough, I thought, but I managed to ease him out by dawn.

He called next day to invite me to dinner that night—just the two of us, "to renew old acquaintance." Lenny was such a raving egomaniac, & his diffidence was worse than ever judging by the namedropping of the night before. Besides, I couldn't bear being mooned over through another night. And yet he was one of the most scintillating people alive, at least sometimes, & also loveable in a maddeningly on-again, off-again way. Poignant really, all that accomplishment & fame riddled with so much doubt. If only he weren't so addicted to the adulation. I'd once seen him put the White House on hold because forty Hare Krishnas had gathered in his foyer to chant a hymn of praise in his honor, but later that night he turned the phone off so we wouldn't be disturbed while he played the piano. There were so many Lennys it seemed he'd decided to run a gamut of selves from the sublime to the ridiculous, plumbing each for all it was worth—or wasn't worth. Yet how wonderful to feel the flush of that familiar attention & be back in that dazzling world I knew so well from the old days. To be flattered & entertained by one of the most brilliant & famous people on earth—it was well-nigh irresistible. I'd be a fool to resist, right?

"I'd love to, Lenny, but please, *please* can we go somewhere where they won't make a huge fuss over you?"

"I know just the place."

The place turned out to be an Italian restaurant on West Fifty-fourth Street where, the moment we entered, the maître d' looked up from a far corner & bellowed "*Maestro!*" whereupon everyone in the room burst into applause. Never mind, Lenny was in great form that night & the way I liked him best—not mercurial & maudlin, but calm, thoughtful, fully present. In that mood, no one was more captivating than Lenny. Then he was like a prodigy kid off on a spree, all the brilliance & knowledge employed not to impress but out of a sense of fun & intellectual adventure. Then the gossip was amusing or made a point, & the soulful moments were honest & deeply felt. During dessert, he quoted a long passage from Eliot's *Four Quartets* without a mistake—a feat that astonished & moved me. Oh, how wonderful, being ushered through a time warp back into the choicest excitements of the past. As I glanced around the room, I saw that once again I was a cynosure. "You're actually more attractive than ever," Lenny said. "More mature, a grown man now."

Did I want to go to a party given by his business manager, just a few people, a quiet affair? Absolutely, for this was turning out to be one of the best nights of my life. So into a cab ("How stupid of us, Alan, that we never had an affair; we would have been wonderful lovers"), to what was indeed a quiet affair—just Lenny's manager & a dozen golden boymen, half of them hustlers rolling joints & cutting coke in a bedroom, the other half musicians intent on worshipping Lenny. Why was it always that way with Lenny—first *Four Quartets* & then tricks smoking dope, the soul always accompanied by sleaze? And why were the boymen so slavishly adoring?

When Lenny asked me to dance, the young men all sat down to watch. That was bad enough, but when he broke away &, still holding my hand, asked the onlookers, "Would you believe this man is *forty-two years old*?!"—I wanted to cut his tongue out. I stormed out, he pursued me into a cab, I insisted we part, he protested, I dropped him at the Dakota, he called later that night. "What did I DO?" Oh, just twist the time warp so that I was suddenly confronted with the down side of the good old days, that's all. Just send me reeling back to a time when the only value I'd ever had was based on my looks in that expense of spirit that had passed for my life. But though Lenny's behavior was cheap & degrading, my reaction wasn't his fault. How could he have known how confused I still was about my past, how torn between adoring & despising it?

He apologized, we made up, I went to dinner at his place, & when it came time for the dreaded, inevitable pass, I fled his apartment & ran down Central Park West like a thing pursued through another dark night of the soul.

Never mind, it didn't matter, nothing much mattered anymore, & if it did I could blot it out with pornography. Nothing focussed my attention like porn, at least until I became disgusted with it or myself or the world & tossed it all out. Then after feeling virtuous for a few weeks, I ambled down to the Combat Zone (Boston's red-light district) & bought another magazine & began to accumulate another cache, until I became disgusted with it or myself or the world & tossed it all out, over & over again, because hopelessness repeats itself.

When I looked at the porn, I took the pictures not as images of lust scripted & produced for public consumption, but as images of mutual acceptance. It was the same mistake I'd made twenty years before, when I'd believed that all those men who wanted me liked me. I thought those guys in the pictures liked each other, & that their tumescence was the sign of a full acceptance, & that if I could concentrate hard enough I could participate vicariously in their relationship, such as I imagined it. I bought into the fictions, never thinking that after each shooting the actors parted & went their separate ways. Porn lured me too because I'd always yearned for a world in which it was safe to be gay, & the only places I knew where that was possible were gay bars & parties & the baths & my fantasies. No one ever screamed "Ya fuckin' faggot" in my fantasies. But beyond that, porn was irresistible to me because it took me back to the time when I'd had guys that good & better. Some of the pictures I pored over were of guys I'd known who had wanted me in the past. Oh, all those beautiful bodies I'd made love to without thinking about it since I'd assumed there would always be many more. What an abundant sexual luxury that had been, & now the only way I could reproduce it was through the porn.

But as time passed I had to work harder to make the porn work. It was only good when the actors became so lost in lust they forgot the camera, & that rarely happened. More & more I had to manufacture the lust, work harder at getting myself in the mood, smoke more dope & peruse more pictures & work harder at coming. There were nights when I spent upwards of three hours masturbating, repeatedly failing at orgasm & so smoking another joint & trying a different arrangement of the pictures on my bed & snorting more poppers. By then my body was aching, my heart pounding, my brain shooting with pain so intense that I reeled when I stood & had to grab ahold of something to keep from falling. But still I kept at it, for if I'd gotten some new porn & it was good & my libido had stored up enough stuff & I could get my imagination in the right groove & working off the pictures in a way that conjured the past, I could relive what it had been like when I could have anyone I wanted.

Some of those nights turned into blackouts, but I'd had blackouts for years. In going through my desk I sometimes came upon poems I had no recollection of having written—poems composed in some netherworld lost to memory.

> Mind carries me back,
> Time carries me forward.
> Torn two ways,
> I drift as if drowning.

> A handful of pins,
> The right curse,
> The face in the mirror.

I thought about writing a book about my life, but it would have to begin in Indianapolis, & every time I thought of Indianapolis I was filled with rage & sorrow. I went back as seldom as possible, once every two or three years at most. It took a week to brace myself for the trip, a week of drugs to endure it, & a week to recover. All my recollections of those trips are fuzzy because of the drugs, but I do recall a dinner at Bead & Henry's when everyone was remarking on Henry's senility. He'd retired long ago & now had Alzheimer's interspersed with moments of acute clarity that were wasted on the others, who kept saying "Poor Henry, failing before our very eyes." They said it that evening talking across him at the table, yet for years, whenever I called at Thanksgiving or Christmas, while they nattered on about their blood sugar counts & bank accounts & medications & tests, it was Henry who asked "How's your teaching going? Are you enjoying your classes? And your life in Boston?"

After dinner, I sat with him in the back yard & I asked, "How are you,

Grandpa?" He said "Oh, just tired, Albert Earl. Tired of hearing them talk about me. I just want to die."

He did die a short time later, two days after they committed him to a rest home where he was tied down in bed & made to lie in his feces. "If only we'd known he was so close to death," they said—oblivious to the fact that he knew what they'd done &, in despair at being abandoned, had died of a broken heart.

When Bead died (we'd become close again & she'd told me she was ready to die: "I can't get warm anymore, I'm cold in August"), Mom called with the news. "Are you coming for the funeral?" "Of course." "Well, you can't stay here," she said, which meant the house was worse than ever. "Where will I stay?" "I'll call Mary Agnes & we'll figure something out." She called back to say they'd solved the problem: I could sleep in Bead's bed. I arrived at noon for the funeral & returned to Boston the same evening.

For the most part, the hopelessness I felt wasn't dramatic, just a gray pall over everything, a listlessness, life drained of affect or color or dimension—what in the Middle Ages people called accidie or acedia, meaning spiritual exhaustion. It wasn't that any one day of my life was intolerable so much as the accumulation of such days over years, the repetition of hopelessness in blackouts, booze & drug bouts, marathons with porn, 4:00 A.M. pigouts, & a little lifetime spent redecorating the apartment. Into that relentless round of obsession, the most ordinary events now intruded like cataclysms in the lives of the unwary.

One night under the desk lamp, I saw a reticulation of faint wrinkles spreading over the back of my hand. It seemed to be happening as I watched. My beautiful body was aging before my eyes. I was filled with revulsion.

"How old are you?" the young men asked before, during, or after sex. Always that same question, even from hustlers who should have known better, but it was a point of honor with me to tell the truth. "You're as old as my father," they said, & "You're older than my father!"

I began looking for men in their mid-thirties, but they were looking for men in their early twenties. I began looking for men who were damaged or marred or scarred, men in slings or on crutches or with wine-stain birthmarks, men who were as wounded or marred on the outside as I felt on the inside. I thought they'd be easy to get & even grateful, but they weren't.

Leaving the subway one night, I saw a man walking toward me &

thought, "Not bad but not good. A far cry from the *GQ* guys who used to be my daily fare. No one I'd give a second glance." I then realized I was looking at my own reflection in a plate glass window.

Nights when I was hoping for a call from someone special, I became so deranged with wondering & waiting that I took the phone off the hook, took a valium, & went to bed. It usually turned out he'd called, "but your line was constantly busy." The news never assuaged me; it filled me with rage. "You coward, you cripple, you *pathetic failure!*"

My face began to twitch, a cheek or an eyelid, always in company. I left the room so no one would see. Whenever I heard the phrase "roll with the punches," I wanted to scream.

"You're so nervous, Alan. You should try to relax, maybe take a walk." But where did you go when you took a walk if you weren't heading anywhere in particular? How did you know when you got there? How could you tell how long it would take? What if you ran out of money? I'd never heard a dumber idea in my life.

In 1975 I was asked to serve on a Ph.D. examination committee at Boston University. The candidate was doing a doctorate in nineteenth-century American literature & religion; my job was to examine him on the literature part. Amazed at how uninformed he was, I voted "No" & left the B.U. professors to their embarrassed deliberations, then walked home along the Charles River through a dazzlingly beautiful early June afternoon. An hour later, behind the locked door of my bedroom with the shades drawn, stoned on two joints with poppers at the ready, kneeling on the floor in front of the porn spread over my bed & arranged with meticulous care, I perused the pictures as I inhaled some popper to make them come alive—praying to pornography, the god of my sexuality, to *make life do what I wanted*. Later, wandering through the apartment in a paranoia so severe I was afraid to answer the phone, I rearranged the furniture for a couple of hours, for if only I could find the right place for things, maybe then I would feel . . . better, somehow. If only I could create a world where I was surrounded by beauty, & where everything had its appointed place, & where everything was immutable.

Then the familiar sense of a growing despair. Never mind, it didn't matter, & if it did it would pass, it always had. In the meantime I could smoke a couple of joints & masturbate, there was always that. Then the sinking sensation when I recalled I'd just done that, & then the sense of peering into an abyss as everything swirled into a dark emptiness, the black hole at the center of my life.

Through it all, I socialized & went to concerts & had people in to dinner; I published essays & gave papers at conferences; I got tenure & bought an eighteenth-century Japanese painting to celebrate: a monkey perched on a clump of rocks reaching for the reflection of a full moon in a swirling stream—a creature entranced by illusion, a metaphor for my life. I kept redecorating the apartment & travelled & even became mortgaged, thus doing my bit for consumer capitalism. I had friends, though I grant you they don't appear much in these pages; I felt I couldn't ask them to listen to my unhappiness. It seemed hopeless or impossible to explain. But my life kept moving along, & I even had good times now & then: a museum with David, an exciting class, a visit from Ira, a dinner with Deborah. It's just that on balance I was losing, becoming more isolated, more controlled by the voices saying that everything was insufficient, wrong, spoiled, lost, doomed. I began thinking that maybe my unhappiness was a schooling in the rigors of age, & that I was thus getting a headstart on my friends: when the going got tough for them, I would be used to it. But where was the compensating serenity of age?—for increasingly the voices wouldn't leave me alone, & sometimes for days & even weeks at a time an incubus was on my back, digging deep into my flesh until I wanted to scream from the torment. Nevertheless, I still had good times.

Ira & I had a great time in Amsterdam over the Christmas holidays in 1976. Ira was now my oldest friend & one of the few people who could pull me back from the edge, adjust my vision, show me reasons why I should be, if not happy, at least less miserable. Our friendship was one of the few things I took pride in—twenty years of mutual love & support—despite the fact that Ira's success sometimes rankled with me. In his medical school days he often ate Jell-O for dinner, but now he was a millionaire several times over. He'd also acquired a certain celebrity in the entertainment industry for inventing "The Dating Game" (a fact he preferred to keep secret) & winning an Emmy for writing & producing a CBS Special. When I thought of his homes on both coasts & his beautiful lovers & famous friends & expensive cars & frequent travels, I was often filled with envy. But we'd had our own memorable trips over the years, & Amsterdam that Christmas was one of the best—Vermeer & Rembrandt, herring & beer, the hearty Dutch in a holiday mood, some great international tricks, hours of transport in the Rijksmuseum thanks to Van Ruisdael. Then one night in a bar I noticed a booth of young men talking about me, saying scabrous, humiliating things. But was that so? Often now I produced a distorted version of reality that had nothing to do with what was really going on, so this one time at least, safe on foreign soil, I had to test my perception. Summoning my courage, I walked over & asked for a cigarette. Of course, have two or three, join them for a drink, be their guest; they wouldn't take no for an answer.

Years of reading the signals wrong, turning them on their heads to create a twisted version of reality in which I was unwanted, scorned, unloved, mocked & humiliated. Years of not being able to trust my perceptions, as if I myself were the distortion that intervened between me & a reality so different from what I perceived.

Years of thinking, "That boy, the one in the Gay Pride March in the khaki shorts with those muscular legs & flawless skin & that thick tousle of hair & the fresh expression in his eyes, if only I could have that boy. But I can't, he wouldn't want me, my days with those boys are over." And that same night in bed with that very boy, it never made any difference, never called into question my own reading of my life, never halted the onward march of doubt & diffidence.

And time was marching on, moving faster & faster. If I weren't careful I'd run out of time, along with all the money & love & energy & attention & hair & sexual attractions I never had enough of anymore. More & more of less & less of everything, including time, so I'd better move faster myself, & be more careful, & hold on tight, & *relax* for a change. . . .

"Ah, tranquillity," I thought as I settled in for a cozy evening at home with a good book, surely one of life's greatest pleasures. But hardly had I begun to read when I heard them outside—all the people galloping forward in the daily sweepstakes of life & me at home taken unawares, the race already under way, the competition already lost as the hole at the center of my life gaped & devoured my peace of mind, clippety-clop, clippety-clop, losing again, everything lost.

All those things going on outside—those dinners & dances & parties & movies & concerts & people meeting each other & cruising & tricking & falling in love—& I wasn't there. If only I could be in two places at the same time, or better yet three, so I did what I could to contrive such a reality, inhabiting it psychologically by being with David thinking of Bruce who was with Jack waiting for me at Styx before going on to Paradise where we would meet Fred who might or might not (probably not) turn out to be trick number 2000 more or less, though who was counting?

I was, counting & judging & weighing & measuring & totting up the eternal balance sheet of my life in which I kept coming out a loser—so more, dear God, give me more, that's all I want. Better yet: give me three wishes & I'll never ask for anything again. Let me be desired, let me have my pick, give me three more wishes. Make me brighter, & my writing brilliant, & give me three more wishes. Bring in the invitations, also the lovers, give me three more wishes. Let me win, let others lose, give me three more wishes. Let me be there yesterday, make the waiting stop, give me three more wishes. If only, if only, if only . . . for years & years & years.

Then one night there was a man standing on the fire escape outside my bedroom window. A creature more than a man really, a thing immensely powerful & determined to do me harm, patiently watching & waiting his chance. Every couple of weeks I dreamed that same dream—that I had awakened, & then the shock as the terror descended, for he was there again, standing in shadow just beyond the window where I couldn't see him, biding his time until I fell asleep again when he would have his way with me. I knew that he wanted my life & that if I made the slightest mistake he would have it. Always the sense that if only I could raise myself & look at whatever it was, actually confront it, I could save myself; & always the terror that froze me, lying in bed in the middle of the night.

The trembling fits began around the same time. I was always alone & studying at my desk when they happened. The first one frightened me so much I tried to call the police, thinking that perhaps I was having a stroke, but I was shaking so badly I couldn't dial the phone. I crawled to my bed where I lay for an hour or so, shaking from head to foot, then it subsided. They went on like that for a few years, interspersed with the nightmares, always leaving me spent & frightened. I never told anyone, I was so ashamed.

Something was clearly, seriously wrong, and clearly it wasn't my fault. It wasn't my fault that so many of my students were unprepared for college work, or that I didn't have a lover, or that my friends were flawed, or that my telephone rang so seldom, or that I spent holidays in bed on valium, or that my cruising was increasingly unsuccessful. Or that after years of struggling to find my way to a better life, I still felt thwarted. Or that all in all I was miserable, hated myself & my life more than ever, & was obsessed by the increasingly insistent voices in my head reciting an interminable series of "If only's": If only Ira carried through on his promises, our friendship would be stronger; if only my students were brighter & better educated, I could enjoy teaching more; if only I made more money, I could feel more secure; if only my hair would stop falling out, I could become competitive in the gay world again; if only my parents would die, I could be released from the obligation of those agonizing trips to Indianapolis.

"If only," I was complaining to Deborah one evening at dinner before leaving for a month in Europe; then suddenly, since it usually does take two to make a truth, I heard myself repeating the same tedious litany of familiar woes. Deborah had heard my grievances dozens of times by now. Sympathetically, sadly, she nodded, & it was her expression that brought me to my senses.

"I'm sorry, Deborah. I'm very sorry."

"You needn't apologize, Alan. You know I love you, & if you need to do this I'll listen. It's just that whole years of a life can pass this way. While you're talking about these things, your life is still going on. We don't get time out for this sort of thing. Nothing goes on hold while we're unhappy."

What a horrifying shock—the notion that my life was passing while I was caught up in an orgy of resentment at a world that had other things to do besides attend to my grievances. Suddenly I saw myself with a new clarity.

But I could think about that later, or better yet, I could use this new perception as a new torment, thinking that if only I could stop complaining, if only there weren't so many reasons to complain, if only my lot in life were better, if only this & only that, years of it, & of the trembling fits, & the thing on the fire escape wanting my life.

Always now the sense that I needed to do something drastic, & always the sense that it was too late. Besides, what else could I do? I'd tried everything I knew—more therapy & a mid-life crisis group, transcendental meditation, yoga & reading the great thinkers, the advice & help of friends, prayer & drugs & every self-help book I could lay my hands on—& though everything had helped, nothing had made the final difference. I kept feeling closer to some essential discovery that would let me become a happy man, but always the sense that I was moving forward at a snail's pace, a blind man groping in the dark, a mountain climber inching upward on his knees. And now whenever I felt within striking distance of a new clarity, of seeing myself & my life clearly enough to move beyond my misery, I would free-fall into an anxiety attack so horrible that I knew if it lasted longer than a week I would kill myself.

I was so rendingly, agonizingly confused. I wasn't a cruel or stupid man, I kept my promises, I worked hard at my job. I still had a lively curiosity about the world. I was a decent man, & I even experienced pleasure now & then. Yet I hated myself for what I'd become: a man consumed with envy of others' good fortune. At least "envy" was the euphemism I used to mask the worse truth—that I hated it when others were happy, for if others were winning I had to be losing. Because I no longer took pleasure in my friends' success, I feared that I had lost the capacity to love. If that were so, the future stretched before me into a long, unpeopled vista where I would wander alone until death. And if that were my fate, why go living? The thought of suicide became a solace to me, a pressure cooker valve that relieved my anxiety whenever I felt trapped by life.

The sight of lovers—gay or straight, young or old—filled me with envy & sadness. In the old days I'd never gone more than a couple of months without a lover, but now it had been three & four years, then six & seven, then nine & ten & eleven until, crawling into bed alone on cold winter nights, I thought that if I had to do that much longer I would rather die. If that was what my life came down to—a loveless, lonely future of nights in an empty bed hating others' joy—I'd rather be dead.

The voices became cacophonous. I began to drink & drug more, to pore over the porn more, to eat more three & four & five A.M. meals, to have more nightmares & trembling fits, & to stockpile sleeping pills. The man in the mirror said nothing. He'd become a stranger except for that fear in his rheumy eyes. Sometimes now his eyes didn't focus. It was the look of someone who's had a stroke & suffered nerve damage. What did that look come from—self-abuse? self-hatred? both in equal measures? I hated his face so much that sometimes I couldn't bear looking at him.

Toward the end of a spring vacation shortly before my forty-fifth birthday, I ran into a gay guy who lived across the street, a model who travelled with a high-powered Boston beauty crowd. Not pretty, he was handsome; not a boyman, he was a manly twenty-five or so, big & broadshouldered with a hearty, open smile. Now & then he'd flashed that smile my way but I'd avoided him, for he was a former me, & I well knew what trouble that could mean. This day, however, receiving his big, warm smile from across the street, I thought "Why not?" I crossed over & introduced myself.

Amazingly, he was bright & a good conversationalist. In that case, would he like to come for coffee? Yes, he would—in, say, about an hour?

I ran like a crazed thing to finish my errands, but I made it home just before he rang the bell. We talked & smoked a couple of joints & sketched our lives for each other. He was unhappy with his lover, didn't like modelling, hadn't spoken to his father in five years, had been on the swimming team in high school, thought he might like to go to college, smoked a dozen joints a day. We stood as if on signal & came together in a long hug, & he said "I've hoped for this for a long time. I can't believe it's happening." I couldn't either, & the more it happened, the more I couldn't.

Afterward, we were lying in bed talking when his eyes suddenly transfixed me, they were so connected not to what we were saying but to some essential me I had forgotten or never known. We fell silent & then I saw him as if for the first time. He was kneeling on the bed in front of the window, silhouetted against the rainy afternoon outside, & inside I thought "This is incredible & he knows it too." Then the phone rang & rang & rang & stopped & he smiled, we smiled together, for it hadn't broken our communion, had in fact sealed it—two men looking into each other more & more deeply, entering every nook & cranny of their beings, mingling their souls until I was flooded with bliss. Never in my life had I looked at another person that long without feeling a fret or shame that broke the hold. We kept smiling together; then when it reached its fullest, it held & kept on going. I'd never known such harmony, peace, call it what you will, such transcendence.

When it came time to speak, I said "I feel like I'm in heaven, or the Caribbean. Heaven's in the Caribbean, right?" He laughed & I poked the sheet up with my knees; it billowed as he fell into my arms again.

He called a week later. "Did that really happen or did I dream it?" My sentiments exactly. He came by ten minutes later & it was the same way again, an experience that I'd never known, that I could describe to myself only with the word "bliss." Afterward, he told me that he sometimes sat in his living room window hoping I would pass by, he so liked the way I walked, the way I moved.

I was very clever: I never asked for his phone or proposed another meeting or did anything to make him feel constrained. And it was working: he was returning of his own desire, just like in the old days. He came for dinner a week later (he was leaving his lover, hurrah!) & next day we went swimming at the university. He had superb form & a powerful stroke, & he was magnificent in a pair of racing trunks, & it was so erotic being with him in the showers. In my office afterward, locking the door, he asked "Have you ever made love here?"

It was working out according to plan. I couldn't believe it: life was *finally doing what I wanted it to*!

Then suddenly I was on a roller coaster careening out of control. I couldn't think of anything but Tom—his smiling face, his man's voice that in excitement cracked with the inflections of youth, his muscular legs & broad shoulders & the veins in his forearms & on the inside of his thighs, his big, strong body as he swam laps in the pool, his playful ways & the bliss—yes, that's the word—that I knew each time we made love. It was like being pulled into a cyclone that tore me apart & hurled the pieces back to earth.

I was going crazy; I had to *do* something. So a few nights later, scheming how to keep this passionate romance going while retaining some semblance of sanity, I decided to go to the baths. The baths would take my mind off Tom & I might meet another attractive guy; with someone else on the hook, I could relax with Tom. In any case, at the baths I wouldn't think about Tom. How clever I was, even in the midst of such anxiety, how full of foresight. This time I wouldn't fuck up. I would become more relaxed & easygoing, & soon Tom would move in with me & put his life in order, get a steady job, smoke less dope & maybe learn some Italian so we could go to Europe, maybe that same summer, & he would understand that I didn't have a strong sex drive so we would make love only every other night, making up in intensity what we lacked in frequency, & he would begin to read substantial things, Dickens at first & then James & Joyce, & gradually he would come to prefer quiet nights at home with me & a good book to partying & drugs & discos, & no one would believe my luck in landing such a bright, handsome, sexy, affectionate young man. Good as my glamor days had been, they couldn't compare with *this* affair. Everything had been worth it—my painful childhood, Dick's abandonment, the years of confusion & pain in New York, the growing despair of my life in Boston. It was all going to finally work out *exactly right*!

Turning a corner in the baths, I bumped into Tom. I could hardly answer his cheerful hello except to mumble that I was leaving. But back at my locker, a saner voice said "You'll ruin everything if you leave. He'll feel freighted with so much responsibility for your happiness that he won't want to see you anymore. You've made this mistake many times before, don't do it again." Arming myself with a joint, I made my way back to Tom, who was now chatting with a spectacular guy, a Latin version of himself. I feigned insouciance, we smoked the joint, they headed off for a private room.

We'd planned to meet the next day but Tom didn't show. I left a message & camped out by the phone but he didn't call. Next day, another message & another silence, & the same thing the next day, & then to ward off the tide of grief & sorrow rising inside me, I smoked a joint & began some yoga when suddenly I began to cry, the first time in more than ten years, huge heaving sobs that wracked me, coming in waves that mounted higher until I thought I would drown in despair. Everything I wanted in life existed in Tom's big smile, but he was abandoning me &

the feeling went deep into the fault line of my psyche, opening me to all the living misery of the past. I crawled to the full-length mirror on my bedroom wall & looked up at the man in the mirror. "What in God's name is the *matter* with you? What is so *wrong,* & why can't you figure it out? *Why are you constantly so unhappy???*"

For what seemed like the millionth time, I had worked my way to the threshold of an ineffable joy only to be thwarted; & for the millionth time, the fault was mine. I had behaved blindly, stupidly, whatever, & for the millionth time I was the thing that had gotten between me & my happiness. For the millionth time, but never with such force, I wanted to die.

Days passed in which I wandered around in a limbo on the verge of suicide, disabled by a lethargy so profound I couldn't even read to escape myself. I could pass a tolerable hour by lying in bed as still as possible & emptying my mind until I achieved a state bordering on coma, but then the voices started up again & my mind became a firestorm of recrimination. "You've done it again, fucked up royally, brandished your bottomless well of need & so of course he abandoned you. It's all your fault! And it was your last chance. Now nothing will ever change, except that you'll become older & more alone, crawling into that cold, empty bed until you're a miserable, pathetic, lonely old man. But you have the pills, there's always that. . . ."

Then one night another trembling fit began, & again I was barely able to make it into bed. Lying there racked with spasms, I thought, "All right, whatever you are, you can have your way with me. I'm too tired to fight you anymore. Even if you're death, you can take me." Instantly the trembling stopped, & in my mind's eye I saw a flashing sign moving across the ceiling. In white lower-case letters on a black background, it said "accept . . . accept . . . accept. . . ." All right, all right, but accept *WHAT???*

That Saturday, I ran into a neighbor on his way to an Alanon meeting. Alanon? He said it was a program for people whose lives had been affected by alcoholism, adding that there was a beginner's meeting next afternoon in a nearby church.

The next day, Dad called drunk. He'd done that for years, & each time it happened it unhinged me for days. It trapped me in a dilemma: if I complained, he remembered & resented my complaint; if I didn't complain, he forgot he'd called & called again. This time it seemed better not to complain, so I listened while he rambled on about how misguided Kent & Debbie were, & Mom too (sloppy & foolish with money, though the best woman in the world), & so on in that vein. I hung up feeling the old tide of sadness & anger pulling me out into the black sea of despair, & then I recalled the Alanon meeting that would begin in half an hour. I went but I felt acutely uncomfortable. People spoke of so much sadness & misery & talked in what struck me as clichés, repeating phrases like "Take it easy" & "Keep it simple" &—the hardest to hear given my agnostic bent—"Let go & let God." The woman who chaired the meeting began by saying "I'm feeling crazy this afternoon, though not as crazy as I felt yesterday, & not nearly as crazy as last week when I couldn't leave the house." Who were these cripples, & what did any of this have to do with me?

And yet, I reflected on the way home in an unaccustomed calm, there had been something in the meeting that I liked: people talking simply & clearly about important matters to a group of sympathetic listeners. It struck me that what I had felt during the meeting was perhaps akin to a feeling of family, a feeling I'd never known in any hopeful, healthy form. Whatever it was, & despite everything that had sounded superficial & Pollyanna, I liked that feeling. I could use some more of that.

(Relax, dear reader—I understand any discomfort you might be feeling & even share it. You're not going to hear a disquisition on my inner child, & anyway, this part is almost over.)

After two more meetings, I knew I had found something that could help heal me & make my life work. I knew because I had an experience that was completely new & extraordinary.

I was in a department store shopping for a windbreaker. Shopping for clothes always filled me with dread, for my goal was to find something stylish but not fashionable, sturdy, inexpensive, unique, adaptable to different occasions & seasons, & something that showed off my body to advantage but without a trace of vulgarity. I also needed to comb a dozen stores to make sure I was making the best choice while getting the best value for my money. Thus shopping usually meant hours spent in a search that sent me home empty-handed & depressed. On the rare occasions when I found something that fit the bill, I rarely wore it: it had been so hard to find that I certainly didn't want to wear it out & have to go through the same tiresome rigamarole all over again.

That afternoon, I tried on some windbreakers that didn't suit, ended my quest, & then as I made my way out of the store I was filled with a feeling I'd never known. It wasn't alarming, was in fact pleasant, but wholly unfamiliar. It grew as I left the store & walked into the Boston Common. I tried to explore it as gently as possible so I wouldn't damage it or cause it to go away, but it didn't go away; it held & kept growing. It was so strange, so completely foreign, & then it came to me. I was feeling an absence of agitation & anxiety; I was feeling, as best I could guess, what people meant by peace of mind. For the first time in my life, at the age of forty-five, I was at peace with myself & the world.

On my way to Copley Square a few days later, I was reading an Alanon bookmark full of simple resolves for getting through a successful day—"Just for today, I will try to live through this day only. . . . I will take my luck as it comes and fit myself to it. . . . I will exercise my soul in three ways. . . ." Arriving in front of the Hancock Tower as people spilled out of the building on their way to lunch, I turned the card over & read "Just for today, I will be unafraid." The sentence brought me to a standstill as I read it again. "Just for today . . . I will be . . . unafraid." The thought of living a day of my life without fear seemed such an alluring & beautiful idea, but so alien that I could hardly grasp it. And then with the force of revelation it burst upon me—the knowledge that I'd lived my entire life in a continual state of fear. Suddenly I saw how much fear I'd carried with me throughout my life—the years of childhood fearing that I wasn't loved & was the cause of the misery in my home, & the years in school fearing I would never be popular or bright enough, & the years in New York fearing I was a sham & could never live up to my reputation as a golden boyman, & the increasingly desperate years in Boston fearing I was losing my remaining chances at happiness & would end my life a lonely, bitter old man. Rooted to the spot now with hundreds of people rushing past, I began to weep—for the boy & the young man & the older man who had lived for so long with so much fear in their lives. And with those tears came immense relief, for the moment I became aware of my burden, that moment I began to be free.

8

Though little changed in my outward life, life itself soon felt radically different. The trembling fits stopped & the man on the fire escape never returned. I began learning about patience & tolerance, for myself as well as others, & I found that once I stopped complaining about myself, I stopped complaining about my friends & life in general. Teaching became virtually a new career for me when I realized that my responsibility wasn't to criticize my students but to help & encourage them, & then I saw myself as lucky in earning my keep at a career that contributes something to society, while the fact that society doesn't value the contribution became not a goad to resentment but another of the many things I had no control over & therefore shouldn't fret about, not much anyway. Hosanna in the highest for *that* realization of the difference between what I could & couldn't control—for in the dawn of that new light, I knew great freedom & peace of mind.

What *could* I control? How I did my work, treated myself & others, went about the living of my daily life. How I dealt with the burden of the past with its pointless regrets, & how, in the present, I responded to the imperfections & failures that are part of the human condition. I even learned to control the voices to some extent; at least I named them (they slept in my bed, after all, went to the same movies, & took all their meals & vacations with me), hoping that by giving them an identity & placing them outside me, I might stop defining myself in their terms. "Sid Vicious" I called them, & now when they took me by surprise, I told them "Not now, Sid, I'm busy; I'll get back to you later."

In a fundamental sense, the changes I'm speaking of came from taking a systematic, analytical look at my past—not, as it turned out, the discouraging process I feared it would be. Imagine: I become aware of having lived a life fueled by fear & along comes another fear: that if I ever saw myself clearly, I wouldn't like myself. That of course was the root fear all along, the thing that kept getting in between me & my happiness: the abiding sense that I was somehow wrong or insufficient, unworthy, mistaken, a failure of a man. I was finally able to look at the many forms that fear had taken, & for the most part they turned out to be groundless. That's what the man on the fire escape was, the embodiment of all my fears, & thus my sense that if only I could raise myself & look through the window, he would vanish. So he did, & at that point I began seeing the man behind the fears.

It wasn't easy, given the ruses whereby I'd hidden myself from myself for so long—all the deceits & denials, the bald-faced lies, the willful blindness in face of the facts. I'd once stolen three hundred dollars from Luchino, rationalizing that he often spent in a day what I lived on in a year. When it came time to make amends to people whose love & affection I'd abused over the years, I vowed to Luchino that I would never steal again, & amazingly it worked, though not without conscious effort. I made amends to myself too—by returning those stolen books to the Columbia Library, for example. Then when I taught at the University of Paris in the spring of '83, I was so taken with Paris & its people that I bought an apartment there—only 350 square feet of a squalid, seventh-floor walk-up, but it was in an art nouveau building & flooded with light, & once I rehabed it, it was a little jewel, a dream come true, & a sign I was no longer sabotaging myself in the major ways of old. The man so long obscured by fear was finally emerging, & there were no impossible failings or unresolvable shames there: he hadn't ruined his life by a long shot. In fact, he was okay the way he was, & would do just fine between here & the grave.

I'd always known I was a lucky man but it had never made any difference; at long last I came to feel gratitude for my life, partly no doubt because so many people I knew began dying of AIDS. First Howard Collins, then Angelo D'Onghia, then Cal Culver, & when their number grew to ten I began keeping a list—those few names at first, & now the list is over eighty names long & still growing—so many people I've known, with all their hopes & dreams, their odd ways & sayings, their shames & exaltations, their stories of struggle & final reckoning.

I wish I knew more of those stories, but living in Boston I often get news of an old friend's death only after the fact. That's how it happened the first time. I'd known Tim was sick, but he was a hypochondriac who lived an unhealthy life, & anyway this was in 1984 when every fever &

chill didn't portend such dire possibilities. We'd been out of touch for several months when a woman called one night & asked, "Are you the Alan Helms who knew Tim Curley?" A question like that in the past tense?— well, you already know the news. When the AIDS quilt came to Boston, I went to see it, & the feeling in that hall was something I've never known except at the Holocaust Memorial in Paris & the Vietnam Memorial in Washington: a profound sense of sadness, futility, anger, & waste. I was walking around looking at quilt after quilt, & all the photographs & memorabilia, & reading the legends of love & grief & farewell, & I kept searching for Tim's quilt when suddenly there on the wall was a quilt for Norman Kenneson. Oh Norman, my God . . . The quilt seemed instinct with all the years we'd known each other, lived together & gone to bars & the beach & Europe together, shared the trivia of our daily lives & cheered each other through good times & bad. Half a century of life seemed suspended in those few square feet on the wall, & I kept staring at them as if they would yield the secret of Norman's final days. Then a few feet away I saw a quilt for another old friend, & another a few feet away from that. It helped that they'd spread huge sheets of paper in the center of the hall where you could write whatever you wanted. I wrote letters to Norman & the other two friends recalling our times together & saying goodbye, then returned home to a call from Ira saying one of my former lovers had just died of AIDS in Los Angeles.

It's a miracle that I haven't died of AIDS myself, seeing that I was frequenting the baths & having unsafe sex in the early '80s when people first began talking about a "gay cancer." Then, about the time the term changed to "Acquired Immune Deficiency Syndrome," I left the country for six months to teach at the University of Paris. France had only seven known cases of AIDS in 1983, so I felt relatively safe in the Paris baths, especially since I've always been healthy & my sexual habits aren't usually risky ones. When I returned to the States, my sexual activity declined dramatically (through no design of my own) just as we began understanding the disease enough to know what precautions to take against it. It's thus a matter of pure luck that I'm still alive.

I hope it's not ignoble to feel grateful because you're surviving while so many around you are dying, because I did & I do. Yet the new capacity for gratitude that began in me soon after my revelation in front of the Hancock Tower came as much from the knowledge that, though still a somewhat crazy man, I was also one who was finally learning what he needed to work his way toward a modicum of contentment in life. At least most of the time.

5/14/88

Michael offers to drive me to the airport, so great. He's just finished the latest round of AZT & is once again his perky, pre-AIDS self—is even trying to cajole me out of my foreboding.

"It won't be that bad. You'll see your friend in St. Louis, & those Beckmann's too. You say the bars in Indianapolis are fun & you've found a new pool. For heaven's sake, Alan—you'll be swimming where Greg Louganis has dived!"

True, so why am I feeling fraught & fourteen? Why, for that matter, am I letting a man who's dying of AIDS cheer me up about a week's visit to my family?

The flight's rerouted through Chicago so I arrive two hours late, wanting to flush contemporary America down the nearest toilet but vowing as I get off the plane "I will be nicer, I will try harder." My resolution is immediately tested: no one to meet me, which makes two times in a row. After twenty minutes of a busy signal, I get through to Mom who says she forgot the name of the airline, the flight number, & the time of arrival. "I wrote it down but I don't know where I put it. Next time, you'll just have to tell your brother or sister those things"—as if I've done something wrong. By now I'm so furious I toy with the idea of returning on the next flight out, but they'd never understand, & they'd be hurt, & anyway I'm here so let's get this biennial agony over with.

I've regressed some more by the time Mom, sister-in-law Kathy, & my three noisy nieces pick me up, all of them wearing sneakers & earrings. I try to focus on the intention behind the result. Mom's wearing the pearls I bought her in Hong Kong a quarter century ago, her way of marking my visit a special event. "Hello, well hello there, hi, hi," & off we go to Debbie's out in the country for a barbecue with the whole fam-damly: Mom & Dad, Debbie & her husband Darryl, Kent & Kathy & the girls. Counting me, that's ten dysfunctional people. Handshakes & spastic hugs all around (we're still no good at touching) & it occurs to me that this is the first time I've seen them since I sent them my coming-out letter a year ago. Does it cross their minds I'm gay when we hug? I'm asked to admire the new horse barn (immensely aluminum), the horses (they scare me), a new litter of kittens (they trigger my allergy), Debbie's latest stray dog (the sixth or the seventh?), & Dad's neurotic Cocker Spaniel (Debbie's idea for a Christmas present from his devoted children, seeing that he's lived alone ever since he and Mom divorced ten years ago, & she also thought it would "improve his disposition," though clearly it hasn't yet). While the women are inside with the food & the men are outside with the horses & the girls are off somewhere babbling boys, I get a few minutes to myself in the yard to watch the sunset hemorrhage over an Indiana as flat as despair, still daring anyone to make an impression on its empty landscape. In the foreground, columbine flourishes along the driveway. Even my favorite flowers depress me here.

During the course of the evening, Debbie & Kent prepare me for Mom's house. A few months back, five people showed up from the Board of Health, filled two dumpsters with trash from the yard, & threatened to condemn the place unless she got it cleaned up. Rats were nesting among the tires she'd piled against the house. I point out that the same thing happened three years ago. "It's worse this time." "How could it possibly be worse?" Kent says that when he stops by for morning coffee on his way home from the night shift, he sits at the kitchen table in the only empty chair in the house while Mom crawls over a pile of stuff to run water in a pan, crawls over another pile to put the pan on the stove, then sits on a third pile while they talk. "Sometimes she falls in one of the piles, & then she just lays there laughin' till I help her git up." Debbie says that last week when she went for a towel in the linen closet, dried cat turds fell to the floor. "And the neighbors have seen her pickin' things outta the garbage behind the A&P."

"G'bye, g'bye, drive careful, seeya soon," & then the long drive home to Mom's. Debbie & Kent were right, but they neglected to mention that the whole place now reeks of urine. The toilet in the small bathroom doesn't work, the sink is broken in the large bathroom, there's hot water in the kitchen but no cold, & half the food in the refrigerator is rotten. "Mom . . ." I moan, hearing a tone I loathe combined of judgment & whining complaint. "Now don't get me started," she interrupts, her habitual ploy for diverting anything she doesn't want to hear: the threat is that we'll cause her to have a stroke. *Oi veh*—& this visit has only begun.

We sit a few minutes at the kitchen table after I clear a chair of what appears to be a complete set of *National Geographics*. At this same table, in this house that Dad & Henry built where I helped dig the foundation & then went off to Columbia never to return except for these rare & grudging visits, Mom & I have talked & argued, I've yelled at her & hurt her feelings, we've laughed together at family foibles & even cautiously explored her past. We've lived a little lifetime sitting at this table over the past thirty years. But tonight she's distracted & remote, or maybe just tired. Unable to stop myself, I covertly survey the kitchen. The

counters are piled high with dirty dishes, plastic glasses, flashlights &
batteries, empty cans of catfood, paper & plastic bags. There are half-a-
dozen aluminum plates of water & milk on the floor for the cats. The
stove is piled high with pots & pans; the oven door hangs open, broken.
On the breakfront, broken toys & old purses. Mounds of molding
clothes lie in the middle of the floor. Magazines & newspapers & mail-
order catalogs are stacked in precarious piles here & there, & the kitchen
table is littered with packages of cookies & sweet rolls, old photographs,
& pile after pile of coupons, some ten years old. Stains on the walls &
peeling decals, the phone hanging off the wall, three empty garbage cans,
three shopping bags overflowing with garbage & trash . . . Why did I ask
to stay here? To salvage some original sense of family & home? In this
disaster?

Hoping to hide my scrutiny, I tease out an old photograph from the
mess on the table. A girl of seven or eight looks up at me, the fear in her
eyes blended with a longing to please—the expression of a battered child,
as if life were a series of blows always taking her by surprise, always coming from behind. Telephone numbers in Mom's handwriting are scrolled
around the edges; a shopping list spills down the girl's old-fashioned dress.

"Who's that, Mom?"

She ponders, says, "Is that me? I don't rightly remember. Oh well, time
to turn in. It's way past my bedtime."

Down the hall past more piles of old clothes & magazines to the bedroom. The bed sags so much I'd thought of putting the mattress on the
floor, but when I turn on the light, bugs scurry for safety, so a sagging
mattress will have to do. The closet door's hanging off its hinges & the
room's full of stale air, both windows closed. One's stuck shut, the other
won't stay up so I prop it open with a stick.

"G'night, g'night," & so to bed where I lie awake thinking of Dad
with some new understanding that under the best of circumstances life
with Mom couldn't have been easy, given her desperate neediness & the
perpetual jumble of her mind. I studied his face tonight until he caught
me staring at him. He looks like such an unhappy man, & then I recall
those pictures from my childhood in which we're smiling & happy together. If only we could learn to need each other somehow, or just become
real for each other. Sometimes I think I don't love him, but obviously I
once did, & therefore I must have learned from him. But what did I
learn? What Henry taught him & he passed on to me—the care of tools,
respect for a job well done, a kind of Zen of craftsmanship. Solitary pleasures. And the ability to take pleasure from simple things, a great gift. But

also the impatience, the tendency to find fault & nurse grievance, the self-pity that masks rage? Oh well, "Take what you like & leave the rest," if in fact I can teach myself to finally do that.

From outside, I hear the throbbing consolation of crickets, then down a dark, unused corridor of memory, I see Mom putting me to bed as a child, crooning "Good night, sleep tight; Don't let the bedbugs bite." And they don't, but things crawl over me during the night.

Welcome home, Albert Earl.

5/15/88

A pleasant morning in the front yard for "important work," my ruse for daily quiet & a chance to wade through the flotsam & jetsam of my reading life—old *New York Reviews*, old *New Yorkers* (I can't *not* read that piece on Indonesia since it's now the sixth most populous country in the world), publishers' book lists (*Robert Frost, Farm Poultry-Man: Frost's Career as a Breeder and Fancier of Hens*).

Then to the Indianapolis Museum of Art with my nieces—our "quality time" together—where we wander through a collection apparently assembled on the premise that one of almost everybody will do quite nicely. To my surprise, it does. At ages twelve, fourteen, & sixteen, this is the girls' first visit, so I try to shepherd them without being bossy. Are they enjoying themselves? Whether or no, they get a reward for their patience, the treat of their choice, a frozen yogurt. Then I drive them home, where Kent & Kathy are in the den watching television, the treat of their choice. It's a brilliant mid-May Sunday afternoon & we're shut inside in a room where the blinds are perpetually drawn, watching trials for the Indianapolis 500. Around & around & around they go ("Ohboyohboy, he almost got hisself killed, did you see that?"), but I don't care, am even grumpily grateful since there's now no need to muster conversation.

With Mom to an Alanon meeting that evening in her station wagon—the steering faulty, the gas gauge broken, no cap on the gas tank, missing handles on two doors, all the locks broken, the back window stuck open, the back end freighted with hundreds of pounds of newspapers & magazines that she collects from people on her "routes" & sells for ten dollars per hundred pounds, at a cost in gas, time, & wear & tear on her car of triple that amount. But it's her favorite thing to do. "It gets me out of the house"—a praiseworthy ambition considering the house.

"How can you tell when you're running out of gas?"

"I just have it filled up every other day."

"Don't you ever forget?"

"Not often."

Her driving is worse than ever: she guns & coasts, guns & coasts, drifting toward the edge of the road while talking aimlessly. "I'll get some tomatoes. Remember how you love fresh tomatoes? That girl four doors down just had triplets, can you beat that? You should call Emeline before your time gets away from you." About to drive into a cornfield, she snaps to & guns it sharply into the oncoming lane. If we were driving downtown we'd be dead by now.

The Alanon meeting consists of a couple of dozen solid, stolid Hoosiers talking recovery in a hospital conference room where a wall of glass looks onto a parking lot beyond which another sunset bleeds to death. Was the meeting any good? Why am I asking me? I wasn't altogether there, was instead occupied throughout by frets & fumes that erupted on the harrowing ride home.

"Dammit, Mom, watch where you're going!"

"I thought Alanon was supposed to make you nicer."

5/16/88

Another morning in the front yard, & then, in the time freed up by Dad's cancelling our afternoon together (it only took me a week to work up the gumption to ask him, the bastard), a drive down memory lane. My grade school looks the same except they've cut down the tulip tree & added a new gym & another parking lot. Do grade school kids drive to school now? Then past Aunt Ida's where I cut grass & trimmed hedges as a child, and on to 1214 Cruft Street. The trees are larger & they've removed that ugly siding that simulated stone, but otherwise it's not changed much: the same scraggly evergreens flanking the same stubby concrete walk up to the same small front porch; the same front windows looking like sad, downcast eyes.

I park & walk down to Bean Creek. The Second Church of Christ the Redeemer has made way for a parking lot. The creek is polluted & the footbridge has collapsed, but on the farther bank the black locust is still there & just past full bloom. I've only missed it by a week. If I could get to the other side, I could sit beneath its branches the way I did as a child, safe inside its bower of shade & fragrance. A man appears and asks what

I want. "I played down here as a child over forty years ago." Unimpressed, he shuffles off.

A slow drive down the alley behind our house, checking out the Coxes, the Delameters, the Clarkes, all gone now, most of them dead or in nursing homes, their children, my childhood playmates, now grandparents in their turn. In the shade of the garage, Mom's lilies of the valley are fading, but I pick a sprig for her & another to place on the spot where I guess Susie's grave is. How angry & helpless I felt when they called me at Columbia to say they'd had her put to sleep, & without even asking me. Did she understand what was about to happen when Dad drove her to the vet's? At least he would have dug a good grave, level & deep & clean, & would have composed her body. "Thank you, Susie, for helping me through that intolerable childhood." Then further down the alley, half listening for the tinkle/clang of the ragman's cart, past more houses where I used to cut grass, & the grocery store where I was stock boy, & on to Garfield Park where the greenhouses & formal gardens look seedy but the pagoda bandstand is freshly painted & expectant, ready for this summer's crowds of tumescent teenagers.

Emerging from the park, I pass Manual High School where I was Prince Hot Shit in the mid-'5os & learned the most important lesson of all: that school could be my ticket out of here. Then a smooth, clean transit back into the present as I head for the Indiana University pool.

Lap after lap, the tensions disperse in the water as I swim my way back into a different, saner world. Refreshed & restored, I pay an impromptu visit to Emeline, my first-grade teacher almost half a century ago. She shows off the wall in her study filled with awards from various mayors & governors for her teaching & hospital service, then we settle in the kitchen for coffee & talk about her osteoporosis & Mom's eccentricities. "Bless her heart, Albert Earl, she stops by now & then to use the toilet, & she just drops her coat on the floor in a corner somewhere. She won't let me hang it up. She always remarks on how clean & tidy everything is here, says it looks like we have a cleaning lady, can you beat that? I tell her, 'Lillian, everything here has its place, & everything is in its place,' but I don't think she hears. Last week she stopped by, she was wearing a sheer housecoat & no underwear, & you could see right through. I told her, 'Lillian Helms, people can see everything you've got!' She just laughed & said 'It's been so long since anybody wanted anything I've got, Emeline, I don't think I'll let it bother me.'"

And so to Kent & Kathy's for dinner with them & the girls & Mom & Dad. We talk politics, as it were. Mom: "Now that Harry Truman, was he a Democrat or a Republican?" We switch to "Celebrities Alan Has Known" & I'm asked the usual questions about my illustrious past. "I couldn't get over that Rock Hudson dying of AIDS. Did you ever meet him?" I tell an edited version of my Rock Hudson story.

Dad's emphysema is badly advanced & horrible to hear. He wheezes & pants even while eating. He looks permanently furious, like he's wearing a Noh mask of a character called "He Who Is Remorselessly Eaten Inside." Whenever he wants to clinch a point about somebody being a "goddamned fool," he cites their earnings. How does he know all that drek? God, the lives they live: junk food & junk TV & junk conversations about celebrities & the neighbors & sports for Kent & Dad, & deaths & births & weddings for Mom, who gets all worked up about anything unfortunate in the lives of her extended television family, all of whom she calls by first names. Over & over, she asks if I know this one or that one; over & over, I remind her I don't have a television. "Oh no? Well, I just thought I'd die when I heard about Loni's divorce!" Loni WHO, for Chrissakes? And listen to me, carrying on with this lifelong crabfest, as if I'm any saner than the rest of them.

On the short drive home, Mom asks "Doesn't your father seem better?" He's mocked & jeered at her while grousing his way through the entire evening.

"Not a whole helluva lot."

"Well, just look on the bright side."

Up in the middle of the night to rifle for food. I discover three gallons of vanilla ice cream in the freezer, so I settle for two bowls of that with nuts, raisins, & chocolate sauce, first checking the nuts & raisins for mold. There are cobwebs in the kitchen cabinets & moths are flying from room to room. By now I've discovered bowls of catfood everywhere in the house, most of them moldy. When I asked if she was upset when the people showed up from the Board of Health, she said "Not a lot. Oh, they were real nice, & we joked & laughed some. Course, I didn't invite them in." I asked her about picking through the garbage behind the A&P. "Now don't get me started. It's a crying shame what they throw out. You know me—I can't stand seeing things go to waste." How about a life, I wonder. She misplaces things constantly & forgets something every few minutes, which must be another function of the mess—not just to keep people away, but also to provide her with a guaranteed discombobulation that keeps her from dwelling on anything upsetting, like her past. But she's cheerful on the whole, except when others spoil her mood (like me, alas), & she enjoys herself more than anyone else in the family, even more than most outside it. She does what she can, & in some nutty way does well with what she has. And she's clearly not bothered by the mess or the filth or the persistent stink of piss that permeates this house.

Since, however, most of the windows are rusted shut, & there are holes in the screen doors, & tiles are falling off the bathroom walls, & the front yard has gone to weeds, & the roof's beginning to leak, & the paint's peeling throughout, & there are God only knows how many more dried cat turds lying in wait, & since no matter how often a voice says "Don't say it," I'm nevertheless impelled to say it, I try to impress on her that the value of her only asset is declining. "I know, I know. I'm gonna get on this house real soon." Then she looks off into some far, interior distance where I can't follow.

5/17–19/88

I've been clever in planning my visit to Jason in St. Louis. By leaving early on a Tuesday & returning late on a Thursday, I've turned what sounds like a two-day absence into three days. Will any of them realize? Or care? Probably not, & if they do they won't say anything. But I'm feeling sneaky.

Wanting to mend fences & not exactly proud of my behavior so far, I apologize to Mom for my crabbings & criticisms as she drives me down to the Greyhound station, saying it's hard caring for someone & seeing them walk blindly toward a cliff.

"Just don't let it bother you."

"It's hard."

"I know."

The bus is full of toothless yokels, obese women & skinny men in jeans & Disneyland sweatshirts. As we pull out of the station, a great weight lifts. Five hours of cornfields & old *New Yorkers* later, Saarinen's Arch soars above the Mississippi.

An ancient black man drives me to the museum where I wander for a couple of hours among the gorgeous, gut-wrenching Beckmann's, & then the walk to Jason's through a neighborhood out of a Judy Garland musical set in the '40s—big brick & stone houses with generous porches & yards, eclectic in style with here & there an Arts & Crafts design. All built back when there was a solid sense of prosperity in this country, & no inflation to speak of, & a hopeful future, & a lot of things to be proud of.

Jason's in fine fettle, & the two days with him are a godsent reminder of things civil & civilized. Long dinners bring us up to date, & he introduces me to a terrific book, *An Incomplete Education*, that may help some of my students repair the ravages of their miseducations. (Except for Bead, no one in my family has ever recommended a book to me.) Jason has found another paragon masseur, so the accomplished John works the Hoosier tensions out of my body, & my last morning, Jason & I swim at his club before he drops me at the bus station.

Kathy picks me up in Indianapolis & drives me to Mom's. She's on a speedfreak high, whether naturally or chemically induced I don't know, but it's nonstop, frenetic drivel all the way home. Did her two-month drug rehab work last year—the one in which she ripped all the curtains off the windows in the visitors' room? Would anybody in my family know for sure, including Kent?

Mom's still up & waiting. "I couldn't get to sleep till I knew you were back safe & sound." I ask her about Kathy. "Oh, she's a good kid"—not quite the report on Kathy's relation to drugs I was looking for.

Mom's relaxed & unguarded tonight, so I venture onto forbidden territory in the hope of recovering more of my past.

"I was looking at some old photographs I've got in Boston, & I noticed that Bernita & Baldy are almost always holding a can of beer. Were they by any chance alcoholic?"

"I don't know. They held their liquor well. Now & then Daddy'd go off to the hardware store & not come back for a couple days. Is that alcoholic?"

"I wouldn't be surprised. Did I live with them when I was born?"

"Oh yes, & with Ida & George too, & then Bead & Henry took care of you sometimes, & Mary Agnes & Arnold."

"So including you & Dad, I lived in five different homes before I was a year old?" I can hardly control the rage in my voice.

"We did the best we could, Albert Earl. Now don't get me started."

"Did you & Dad come visit me when I was living with those people?"

"Oh sure, we stopped by after work now & then."

"Now & then? Jesus fucking CHRIST, Mom!"

"Do you *have* to talk like that? We visited you a lot, & anyway you didn't spend that much time with those people. Times were hard & work was hard to get. If you're gonna jump on every word I say, we might as well go to bed."

I've ruined it, but what do you do at times like this? Oh, right—you roll with the punches.

Amid the debris on the table, I spy an old photograph of a handsome man with the stubborn, swaybacked stance of the Gakstetters.

"Who's that?"

"You remember Uncle Carl. He was such a nice man, Carl was, always so thoughtful & nicely dressed. He & Louise kept such a nice home. But he & Grandpa fought something awful. Carl used to hold a knife to Grandpa's throat & make him take back what he'd said. I tell you . . . it's a great life, ain't it?"

"Is this Dad?"

"It sure is. That was taken when we were both at Warren High. Ohboyohboy . . ."

"What?"

"Oooooh, I couldn't get enough of that man. Gives me goosebumps just thinking about it."

"You mean Dad was a good lover?"

"My Lord, yes. I woulda done anything for Bud in the beginning."

"Dad, great sex?"

"Your father was a very different man in those days, Albert Earl. It was only after we were married that his drinking got bad."

"Did he ever try AA?"

"We both used to go. And then I went to Alanon but it didn't make any difference, he just kept on drinking."

"You don't go to Alanon to get someone to stop drinking; you go for your own peace of mind."

"Well, anyway, it never worked. He even went into those detox places a couple times, but he got one of his cousins to sneak wine in. Oh, I could've done better too. I should've divorced Bud much sooner than I did. But you can't change the past. Live & learn."

"Who's this?"

"Don't you remember Aunt Bert? She was a sweet thing, but Ed sure gave her a hard time. I'm surprised you don't remember Bert, but she's been dead . . . well, it's almost forty years now. I hope she got some peace & quiet wherever she went."

"Do you ever think about that—where you'll go when you die?"

"Not a lot. I don't much care where I go as long as they got a dance hall there." She winks & laughs, then I remember.

"Hold on a second," I say & run to my room for the sprig of lily of the valley.

"I picked this for you on Cruft Street. It's faded but I thought you'd like to know they're still there & thriving."

She's greatly pleased, so good, I've done something right for a change. On the TV in the living room, a woman begins crooning "It Had To Be You," one of Mom's favorite songs.

"May I have this dance, ma'am?"

"I'd be delighted, sir."

I take her in my arms & we dance through the piles of molding clothes & magazines into the darkened living room where moths flutter about our heads.

>*. . . nobody else gave me a thrill.*

"Have I ever told you how much I love to dance?" Mom asks.

>*With all your faults, I love you still.*

"You have, but I always enjoy hearing it."

>*It had to be you, wonderful you,*
>*Wonnn . . . derrr . . . fulll yooou.*

5/20/88

Lunch with Dad & Debbie, Dad complaining about Kent & the girls.

"He insists on that damned night shift 'cause that pays twenty percent more, & he just keeps seeing that time & a half & double time. Then when he's home there's always things the girls want him to do, but they don't show appreciation. They just nag, nag, nag for more & more, & Kent can't do enough for them, but then he builds up till he explodes. Then, course, the next day he's over it & back to where he started, & the whole thing starts all over again. . . . " Over & over again, because hopelessness repeats itself. Debbie keeps trying but failing to change the subject.

Dinner that night, the farewell bash at Kent & Kathy's, & Mary Agnes & Arnold stop by afterward on their way home from the airport, having returned from a weekend seminar at the Oral Roberts Clinic in Tulsa: physical exams plus some kind of psychological counselling based on the Bible.

"Oh, Albert Earl—I mean Alan—it was wonderful, really wonderful. We went through the church, see, so everything was arranged beforehand. We no sooner got to . . ."

"Tulsa."

"Right, Tulsa—than they met us & took us to the . . ."

"Dormitories."

"Yes, cause the clinic's attached to the university. And those students—they're all so mannerly & well dressed & not at all . . ."

"Rude."

"Oh no, they were all so nice! So we were there for three days as guests of the church. And they gave us a wheelchair so I could get Arnold in & out, & they gave us a room on the first floor, cause Arnold can't manage . . ."

"Stairs."

"That's right. But then that first night the young ones stayed up late & raised Cain, see, so it was kinda bothersome. But, well, I guess that's just . . ."

"Life."

Life is a fountain? No, life is kids raising Cain at Oral Roberts University. Who cares?—I'm almost through the gauntlet.

5/21/88

My last morning, Isabelle Wallace visits, my third-grade teacher. What a nice surprise to find that she & Mom are friends. Then to Kent & Kathy's for a quick goodbye, & back to Mom's where Isabelle has gone home & returned with a jack-in-the-pulpit for me, nicely wrapped in wet paper towels & tinfoil, bless her heart.

Mom drives me to the airport. As always, she cries when we part.

"I hope you had a good time. We get to see you so little."

And so back to Boston, & I survived the trip with a minimum of psychic turmoil. It's a shame, the lives they lead, & a worse shame how it still gets to me, & another shame that the voices won't go away forever. But at least I didn't drown in a riptide of despair, & I could talk a bit with Dad & had some good moments with Mom, & I didn't eat the third gallon of ice cream. Come to think of it, it's the best trip home since I left over thirty years ago. Whadda mouthful, Albert Earl.

One morning a few weeks later I was diddling my way through a daydream when into my mind popped a scene of Dad threatening to kill Mom & me with a gun. He was fully fleshed in my imagination—drunk & waving a gun in the air, shouting that he was going to kill us while we cowered in a corner begging him not to shoot. Where did *that* come from?

I called Mom to check it out.

"Of course not. What's the matter with you?"

But I knew to doublecheck with Debbie that night.

"He sure did, every few weeks or so. Boy, that used to terrify me. He kept the gun down in the basement & Mom & me would go down there to find it & put it in a different place. I remember once we found it in the freezer. Oh, I'll never forget it. He chased us out into the yard one time, Mom was getting in the car to drive away, & he knocked her glasses off & stepped on them so she couldn't see to drive. I was sure he was gonna kill us that time."

So he *had* done it, & I'd repressed the memory for almost forty years. Was I living in a state of chronic shock? Were there other things I'd repressed all that time?

Then another question, one that had cropped up months before & started nagging at me even in my dreams: granted that I'd been someone for whom a dozen helping hands had made the crucial difference in finding my way to a decent life, I'd done the job myself, right? I'd had the wherewithal, the instinct or whatever to ask for help along the way. But what got me going in the first place?

Over that summer, I pondered those questions, but it seemed their answers lay in a past that was daily receding, so the more I searched, the less I had to go on. Yet if I didn't answer the questions, I could spend the rest of my life as an emotional cripple. Help somebody, come quick & help!

Then Mom began to die. It happened very quickly. She'd been complaining of not feeling well, but Mom was no complainer, so something was wrong.

"It hurts when I stand."

"Have you seen a doctor?"

"I keep meaning to."

Debbie called one night, upset & crying. "I went out to the house & she was lying in bed. She couldn't stand & she hadn't eaten or washed herself. I made her some soup & bathed her & put her to bed." Debbie began sobbing.

"What is it, Debbie?"

"She apologized for putting me out."

Two nights later Debbie called to say Mom had been diagnosed with cancer. "She's in the hospital now but she's real bad. You better come quick."

Next morning I spoke to Mom.

"Boy, I never thought I'd see the day I'd be glad to go into the hospital, but I couldn't do for myself anymore. They sure treat you nice in here though."

"You take care & I'll see you tomorrow morning."

"I hate to put you out & have you spend all that money."

"It's not that much, Mom, & I want to come. Just take it easy & I'll see you in the morning."

I was deeply frightened—except for my lifeguarding days when the bodies were anonymous, I'd never seen death face-to-face—but I knew what I had to do.

On my first visit she was cheerful but afraid. When visitors arrived she greeted them, then quickly said, "I don't think I'm gonna make it." Yet a minute later she was cheerful again, joking & making people laugh. She was never happier than when she was making people laugh.

The doctor said her body was riddled with cancer: her lungs, liver, & bones were "saturated" with it, he said.

"Debbie says you don't like that cancer doctor."

"He's no cutup, but I suppose this is no laughing matter."

"Would you like to watch some TV, Mom?"

"Not right now. Maybe later."

"How about some music?"

"I like music but it makes me awful sad."

The last morning of my visit, she was laughing & telling everyone who entered her room, "Do you know what that man did, that sweet thing?" She pointed to Dad who was standing in a far corner, as if studying to see how she was doing it. "Just before he left last night, he came over here & kissed me for the first time in I don't know how long. Liked to take my breath away. I still can't get over it!"

By the time of my second visit, she was close to death. The oncologist had talked her into a chemotherapy treatment—against our express wishes—& it had horribly reduced her. She could speak only in whispers, & the oxygen mask had dried her mouth until her lips were cracked & the ridge of her tongue was covered in sores. But incredibly, she was uncomplaining, calm, cheerful, the fear all gone.

The doctor said maybe four more days, but when we gathered at her bedside the next morning, she said "Bye" to each of us in turn. Then two times in a row: "Want to go, I'm tired." She was composed & even playful, for when the nurses came with a bedpan, she winked & said, "You all better clear outta here."

After the nurses cleaned her, we returned to hover. "Can we get you anything? Is there anything you want?" She shrugged & said, "I don't know what I want," but a minute later she whispered, "Root beer." "I'll get some," Debbie said & was gone. When Debbie returned, Mom managed a sassy "Oh, boy." We gave her the root beer with an eyedropper, three drops at a time. A long, pleasured "Mmmmmmm."

Her last word to me was "Heaven," but by then she was barely audible. "'Heaven,' Mom? Did you say 'Heaven'?"

She nodded yes.

"Somewhere in the sky, they're preparing a big dance in your honor," I said. She smiled. How in the name of everything humanly difficult was she doing it this way? Everything good in her had risen to the surface—her cheerfulness & tolerance, her life-giving vulgarity, her concern for others, her willingness to forgive & accept & let go. Was it because in her dying she'd finally succeeded at the great goal of her life—bringing us together as a family? It had taken half a century, but there we were at last.

I gave her our code phrase, a nonsense joke we shared in my childhood, & she gave me another smile.

Debbie said "It's sure not gonna be as much fun without you."

In the tiniest of whispers: "I know, but we have our memories." Then she closed her eyes & drifted into unconsciousness.

I sat with her through the day & into the night, reading & watching, keeping a hand on her thigh so her body would know she wasn't alone, or so that some consciousness I know nothing of might be reassured by my touch. I mulled over the past, trying to put it together with this present that was happening so differently from my expectations. I'd always assumed she would live into her nineties like most of the Gakstetters, & expected she would become a financial burden on Kent & Debbie & me. I'd always been afraid of her dying, thinking she would become terrified & foolish & more scatterbrained than ever. But her dying was here & now, & she wasn't foolish & frightened.

Then sometime in the early evening it came to me—the answer to the question I'd been struggling with for months about what had made the difference in the beginning to keep me going through all the years of pain & confusion until I found what I needed to begin healing myself. I was touching the answer: it was my mother, her lungs now heaving & her breath coming in rasps. "Oh, Mom, please wake up so I can tell you, please."

Around eleven that night, her body gave a heave, her mouth fell open, & she was still. She lay there dead, but she was warm to my touch. I lifted her chin to close her mouth, & yes, she was my mother; I let it go & the jaw dropped, the mouth gaping open, the life spilling out of an old dead woman, but still my mother.

I told her goodbye & that I loved her, & that despite everything she had been a good mother. I stroked her & tidied her hair & held her in an awkward embrace. I drank her face in, knowing this was the last time I would ever see her. Her skin was smooth as a girl's & less wrinkled than mine. Tiny wrinkles circled her mouth but her lips were full & firm. There was such acceptance on her face, such release & quiet. I thought, "I don't even know whether she liked rain. All the questions I never asked, & now it's too late." Her brow & cheek were still warm as the life kept spilling.

I tidied her bed, pulled her nightshirt down where it had bunched around her thighs, smoothed the blankets over her. I wished her good luck & told her I would miss her, & then the warmth began leaving her body. I repeated myself mindlessly while her spirit hovered in the room, & then the flush on her skin was gone & she was cool to my touch. A doctor came in, then Kent & Kathy were there with shopping bags to pack up & clear away—the flowers & cards & balloons & the few things she'd brought with her—her purse, a telephone book, a little Alanon book I'd given her years before.

Then a nurse pulled the sheet over her head & she was finally dead.

·

·   ·

·

EPILOGUE

Thirty & twenty & even ten years ago I wanted so desperately to be a happy man, but the thrust of my life was toward being popular & sleeping with the humpiest guys so I would be envied & thereby find love. Today I'm a reasonably contented man (still quasi-crazy, of course; this is obviously no story of a saint, no Saul turned Paul), & the thrust of my life is toward my friends & my solitude & learning how to be a better teacher & a better companion to myself. The man in the mirror & I are on good terms at last. I take him unawares sometimes & we talk, renewing our sense that we're lucky to be making the rest of the journey together. What a curse it was all those years banking so much on that other man in the mirror, the one who thought himself so extraordinary, so unique. "What he could not bear," Perez Galdos says of one of his heros, "was that he should be thought an ordinary man, like one of many." What a blessing to learn to think of myself as one of many, an ordinary man to whom some extraordinary things happened. I got beyond the dark pool where Narcissus pines away into the death of the exclusive self, where for years I feared I would drown in despair; I somehow made it to the other side, a flawed man in a new world of healing & hope.

I'll probably always be damaged in some of the ways of the heart, for though the wounds are healing, the scars remain. But who among us isn't damaged goods of one sort or another? Birth itself is pain & loss, & the rest of life, when it goes well, is a recovery. "And we only become as well as we're able to," Ira always used to say before he died two years ago of AIDS. At least I no longer think of myself as despicable & my life as a waste, & I'm not nearly as tormented as I used to be. I know joy some times & often contentment, & I rarely feel deprived any more. Oh sure, I sometimes miss some of the perks of the old life, especially some of the sex & drug highs & some of the rare experiences that came my way—the Great Sphinx beneath a full moon, the Papal Mass in the Palace of the Popes, the good times with Noel & Luchino, the lunches with Ezra Pound & Fellini, those languid nights with Nureyev in Venice, & that afternoon speeding toward Paris when my hero leaned toward me with delight to confide that "Actually, I've written one book that's really quite, quite famous."

But the life I lived, in cahoots with my childhood, nearly did me in, & I've known many who died of it. I learned a few things from it along the way though, about the world's vanities & my own. I learned that being envied is the loneliest pleasure on earth, & that self-absorption guarantees unhappiness, & that the worst motive for action is groundless fear. And I wouldn't cross the street these days to meet someone who's merely celebrated or rich. I've seen so many of those people up close that I know how little such things count for in the effort to make a good life (another thing we're supposed to know but obviously don't).

What counts for me these days? How well Mom died & how well I'm living. Bob Coles's & Freud's "love & work." The fact that in an odd way I've realized my childhood dream of becoming a man I can respect, someone whose life makes a difference for the better, no matter how small the difference. And yes, always now, gratitude for the people who helped me out & taught me how to live, people who saw something worthwhile in me & nurtured it. I was helped so much over the years by so many, & now it's sometimes given to me to help people who are like I was—frightened, erring folks struggling to find a better way. "I take it, and I give it back again."

"It's a great life, ain't it?" Mom still says, looking out of the photograph in my study where I've made a little shrine in her memory. Yes, Mom, the world's a mess but life is great: a mixed bag of blessings & an endless paradox—love out of hatred, strength out of yielding, courage from acceptance. "Accept . . . accept . . . accept . . ."

I hated my life but now I love it. Mom was a silly woman but she became noble in her dying. God keeps on dropping letters in the street but most of us are in a hurry. Yet the geraniums still bloom on the windowsills, & the mail still waits on the hallway tables, & the faces still look out of photos on desks & mantles & bureaus. Out of the silence, memory revolves her massive wheel, & even as I'm writing & you're reading this, there's Bead again under the lamplight in Elkhart sifting through her basket of patches, holding them up to the light to see what can be retrieved & what fits well together as she goes about making another quilt. Not a perfect or important thing, but a comely & a useful one. A gift to keep a friend warm on a winter night.

·

·   ·

·

AFTERWORD

Soon after this book was published & I began doing readings in 1996, I was struck that many people I met simply assumed I was an alcoholic. I wasn't offended but put them down as incompetent readers with their own agendas—just another example of how often the benighted end up on the wrong side of the truth.

Then, oddly enough, my drinking began to increase. For years I'd drunk wine with meals, but suddenly I was drinking more wine, & drinking between meals, & soon drinking hard liquor. Yet I'd gone through bouts of excessive drinking in the past & they'd done no permanent harm. True, I was now drinking alone for the first time in my life, but this was doubtless just another phase that would soon end. Anyway, I held my booze quite well, thank you very much. But people who invited me for drinks on my reading tours offered to walk me back to my hotel, as if I couldn't find my own way. The same thing began happening after dinners out in Boston. Why were people so meddlesome? Why were they so strangely and unnecessarily solicitous?

The following summer I began drinking while gardening on my roof deck, sometimes to the point of blackouts. You might figure that I now had enough evidence to recognize I had a problem, but as any sober alcoholic can tell you, the opportunities for ignoring the truth while in the throes of the addiction are endless. I did have enough sense to know that gardening drunk wasn't normal, so I broached the subject with my therapist. We discussed the problem for almost two years without making headway until one day he suggested I stop drinking for three months & see what happened.

The first two months of abstinence were easy, so of course I was relieved. Then one evening when I was on my deck with two friends, an electrical fire started in my kitchen & I nearly lost my home—& also my life, since I stupidly ventured in & put the fire out by throwing water on it, not knowing people die that way. Firemen arrived seconds later, made impressive holes in my walls & ceiling, & my friends & I went out for dinner. When I asked for water with my meal, my friends protested: "You really should have a drink, Alan, considering what you've been through." Well, yes, I supposed I should, because the experience had indeed been traumatic, & so I did: a glass of wine to go with my food, & then another because I hadn't had any wine in two months, & then a third to celebrate saving my home, & then a fourth as compensation for an awful evening, & maybe a fifth to console me for the prospect of months of mess while repairing the damage, though at that point I lost track. Once again I was off & running, but even though I hadn't been sober the entire three months, not drinking had been so easy for two months that I obviously had no problem. Abstinence had been a breeze, end of discussion.

Fortified by the certainty that I was in control of the situation, I began drinking more than ever, & a month later I had my first fall. One afternoon after a couple of hours of gardening & several vodka & tonics, I fell down half a flight of stairs and crashed into a large window overlooking the street. Fortunately, the window was covered with a sheet of Plexiglas, which kept me from falling through it & plunging four & a half floors to certain death in the street below. At the time, however, I was more concerned with the cost of hiring a carpenter to install new Plexiglas than with the cause of this bizarre "accident." And anyway, I hadn't gone through the window, right? I did, however, set myself the task of figuring out why I was drinking so much.

I've always imagined that when mature people have a problem, they sit in a comfortable chair for an hour or so & ponder it in an organized fashion replete with logic & ingenious syllogisms, whereas when I have a problem, I think about it in bits & pieces on the run while stumbling around in the dark until a happy illumination arrives. But this time I did sit down & think as best I could. It didn't make any sense, really. Alcoholics were unhappy people who drank to drown their sorrows, but I was a happy man, all things considered. I had loving friends, my health, a job I enjoyed that created meaning & value in my life, enough financial security to spare me from worries about money, abundant interests & a lively curiosity, a successful book & what looked like a bright future. That surely wasn't the description of an alcoholic. So I thought & pondered & pondered & thought but I couldn't figure it out, & the more I couldn't, the more I drank. The more I drank, the more I realized that I absolutely had to figure it out because this was becoming serious, but no matter how hard I tried, I failed, whereupon I drank still more. But despite my profound confusion, one thing was clear: I could stop drinking whenever I chose. Two months of abstinence had proved that point. Why not stop then & there? Because I could always stop tomorrow. One last night of solitary carousing—a way of saying farewell to the booze—& then the next day I'd stop.

The events of the next couple of years aren't pretty, so I'll spare you. Besides, although the details differ, all sober alcoholics tell essentially the same story: the failed attempts at reformation, the excuses & rationalizations, the half-truths & lies, the increasing isolation, the growing sense of self-disgust & shame, the horrible awareness of a life veering out of control. By that point I wanted to stop drinking, but no matter how hard or often I tried I couldn't. I even had difficulty looking at myself in the mirror since I was becoming a pathetic version of my father, an alcoholic whose end reminds me of Whitman's "old man who has lived without purpose, & feels it with bitterness worse than gall." But I still didn't think I was an alcoholic.

Then, as if Fate decided to take over my life since I was mucking it up so badly, I became infatuated with a bright, engaging young man who drank even more than I did. I'll always be grateful to him for being the catalyst that finally forced me to face the facts. For four months, we had an intense, complicated, neurotic, & wholly alcoholic relationship. With his example to inspire me, I soon went from a bottle & a half of wine a night to two & even three. I was now drinking so much I could no longer rationalize my way out of the problem. None of my excuses worked anymore, & now when I looked in the mirror I saw a full-fledged, bona fide alcoholic on the verge of destroying his life. That was, you might say, a sobering experience. I soon joined Alcoholics Anonymous & I've now been sober for more than fifteen months. Am I sober for good? Is this whole thing behind me once & for all? It should be clear by now that I'm no good at reading the future.

I've told you this latest chapter of my life for two reasons. First, I simply wanted to set the record straight. In writing this book, I tried to be as honest as possible, but in the Epilogue I present myself as a man who has finally figured out all the important stuff & put the pain & confusion of the past behind him as he heads off into a bright, tranquil future. Guess what. So perhaps this Afterword can serve as a reminder that our lives are always works in progress, & that except in rare & usually tragic cases, it's not given to us to predict the outcome or conclude the story. As Solon cautioned, "Until he is dead, do not yet call a man happy, but only lucky." I've known that quotation for decades; I just keep forgetting it.

In the second place, it's my hope that what I've told you may offer encouragement for others like me—people who keep stumbling forward from one darkness into another, albeit persistently & sometimes luckily. Realizing that I'm an alcoholic has certainly been a stroke of good luck. For years I've prated about the importance of cultivating one's spiritual life but done little about my own. In AA, I now attend to my spiritual life on a daily basis, for as Iris Murdoch said, "We are fed or damaged spiritually by what we attend to." One of the most thrilling things I've ever known is to find myself two or three times a week with folks who are trying their best to become better people. If that sounds corny, it's only because our culture denigrates such things, for where's the profit, the cost-benefit ratio, the bottom line?

Though I'm not sure, I suspect my drinking had something to do with trying to figure out the rest of my life. This book fortunately received good reviews, & at that point it seemed I'd accomplished everything of importance I'd ever wanted. I was thus confronted with a new fear: "What now? What next?" I didn't want to settle into a rut by repeating the same satisfying but predictable routine, but I couldn't figure out what else to do. I thought about the problem in my usual haphazard, catch-as-catch-can fashion, but all I knew for sure was that I didn't want to screw up between here & the end—didn't want to die thinking that I'd somehow botched the final chapter. Yet it turns out that "What next?" is just one more thing I can't figure out. I don't know why I became an alcoholic, or why & how I was able to stop, or how I'm going to live the rest of my life. But it doesn't really matter as long as I can find a way to accept whatever the future has in store for me. Remember "... accept ... accept ... accept ..."?

Boston, April 2003

Alan Helms is professor of English at the University of Massachusetts, Boston, where he has taught composition and American poetry for more than thirty years. He has published widely on contemporary American poetry and was poetry reviewer for *Partisan Review* in the 1970s. He is currently writing about ballet, sex, and aging.